Rolf J. Daxhammer, Andreas Resch, Oliver Schacht

Initial Public Offerings

D1664373

Rolf J. Daxhammer
Andreas Resch
Oliver Schacht

Initial Public Offerings

An inside view

UVK Verlagsgesellschaft mbH • Konstanz
mit UVK/Lucius • München

Bibliografische Information der Deutschen Bibliothek

Die Deutsche Bibliothek verzeichnet diese Publikation in der Deutschen Nationalbibliografie; detaillierte bibliografische Daten sind im Internet über <http://dnb.ddb.de> abrufbar.

ISBN 978-3-86764-739-7 (Print)
ISBN 978-3-7398-0172-8 (EPUB)
ISBN 978-3-7398-0173-5 (EPDF)

© UVK Verlagsgesellschaft mbH, Konstanz und München 2018

Einbandgestaltung: Susanne Fuellhaas, Konstanz
Printed in Germany

UVK Verlagsgesellschaft mbH
Schützenstr. 24 • 78462 Konstanz
Tel. 07531-9053-0 • Fax 07531-9053-98
www.uvk.de

Preface

In a corporation's financial life "going public" by means of an IPO is probably the single most important decision. It turns a private company into a public one. A public company opens itself to the eyes of potential investors in financial markets. Thus, it improves its access to equity capital for funding promising investments, but it pays by providing information for investors' scrutiny and complying with the rules of the capital markets and its regulators.

Our book will provide an inside view of the IPO process. On the one hand, it draws on the insights of an experienced investment banker, who has gone through numerous IPO transactions. On the other hand, it relates the story of an actual IPO through the eyes of a Chief Executive Officer who has taken two of his companies public.

This unique double perspective is our book's defining feature. We do not discuss initial public offerings in a textbook style fashion. What we would like to bring out is a more comprehensive portrayal of a "once-in-a-lifetime" event for most companies and their management, alike. As such, it does require some knowledge of basic financial concepts, which will be introduced in the first part of the book. Readers with a solid corporate finance background and some knowledge about investment banking services may safely skip chapters 2 and 3 heading straight into "where the beef is" in parts 2 and 3 after a short warm up/refresher in chapter 1.

"Initial Public Offerings" should be worth reading for the senior management of a company contemplating an initial public offering. It gives students of corporate finance a real life, flesh and blood perspective on their textbook chapters on IPOs. In addition, it will give the interested public a solid introduction to one of the most fascinating phenomena in today's financial markets.

Such a comprehensive endeavor would not have been possible without the aid of colleagues and friends who have helped us along the way and who we would like to thank cordially:

Barbora Moring and Sarah Steece, experienced capital markets lawyers by profession, investing substantial time and effort in comprehensive reviews and contributions to certain sections of this book.

The teams at epigenomics and Curetis without whom these two IPOs would have been impossible as well as all involved bankers, lawyers, auditors, PR and IR firms, and all other advisors, boards and shareholders, without whose unwavering support such deals would not have been completed successfully.

And, finally yet importantly, we would like to thank André Binanzer and Alexander Schmitz for their support and input into chapters one to three. André was also instrumental in bringing the three parts together into a coherent manuscript.

Rolf Daxhammer

Andreas Resch

Oliver Schacht

About the authors

Prof. Dr. Rolf J. Daxhammer

Prof. Daxhammer joined the full-time faculty of ESB Business School, Reutlingen University in 2000 after almost nine years of work experience in the (investment) banking industry; in which he served in various functions in Capital Markets in Zurich, New York and London. Since 2005 he has been gathering experience as external adviser in numerous IPO-related projects (especially in questions of valuation). His research interests, besides capital markets, include behavioral finance and financial market stability/regulation. He holds a doctorate from the University of Hohenheim in Germany and an MBA from the McCombs School of Business at the University of Texas, Austin.

Andreas Resch

Andreas Resch is an investment banking professional with more than 17 years of experience in corporate finance. To date, he has helped corporate clients raising significant amounts of debt and equity capital (incl. many IPOs). Moreover, he has advised on numerous M&A transactions, primarily in an international context. Andreas is a Managing Director at Commerzbank where he leads the Consumer & Retail sector team within the firm's Corporate Clients business segment. He started his career in finance by joining Citigroup's investment banking division in the year 2000, immediately following his graduation from the German-American exchange program of ESB Business School, Reutlingen University with Northeastern University in Boston.

Oliver Schacht, PhD

Oliver Schacht, PhD, is a serial entrepreneur, CEO and CFO with two successful IPOs and many capital market transactions executed. Following three years with Mercer Management Consulting and then thirteen years with cancer diagnostics company Epigenomics, Oliver has been CEO of Curetis (infectious disease diagnostics) since 2011. He has been a co-founder of several additional start-ups in Germany and the US. Oliver obtained his Diploma in European Business Administration at the ESB Business School, Reutlingen University (GB-link with Middlesex University, London) as well as an MPhil. and PhD at the University of Cambridge (UK).

Contents

.

List of Tables and Figures

Abbreviations

Abbreviation		Meaning
ABS	–	Asset-Backed Securities
AFM	–	Autoriteit Financiële Markten (Dutch Authority for the Financial Markets)
am	–	ante meridiem
approx.	–	approximately
APV	–	Adjusted Present Value
BaFin	–	Bundesanstalt für Finanzdienstleistungsaufsicht (German Federal Financial Supervisory Authority)
BeNeLux	–	Belgium, The Netherlands & Luxembourg (geographic region)
BMWi	–	Bundesministerium für Wirtschaft und Energie (German Federal Ministry for Economic Affairs and Energy)
c.	–	circa
CAPEX	–	Capital Expenditures
CAPM	–	Capital Asset Pricing Model
CEO	–	Chief Executive Officer
CET	–	Central European Time
CE-IVD	–	Certificat Europeen for In Vitro Diagnostics
cf.	–	confer – compared to
CFO	–	Chief Financial Officer
COO	–	Chief Operating Officer
CTO	–	Chief Technology Officer
CURE	–	Curetis NV (stock ticker)
CYA	–	'Cover Your Ass'
DACH	–	Germany, Austria & Switzerland (geographic region)
DCF	–	Discounted Cash Flow
D&O insurance	–	Directors and Officers Liability insurance
DRG	–	Diagnostics Related Groups
DVD	–	Digital Versatile Disc (digital optical disc storage format)
e.g.	–	exemplum gratia – for example
EBIT	–	Earnings Before Interest & Taxes (operating income)
EBITDA	–	Earnings Before Interest, Taxes, Depreciation & Amortization
ECM	–	Equity Capital Markets (department within investment banks)

EMEA	–	Europe, Middle East and Africa
etc.	–	et cetera
EU	–	European Union
EUR	–	Euro (currency)
EURIBOR	–	Euro Interbank Offered Rate
EGC	–	Eligible Growth Company (term defined by JOBS Act)
EV	–	Enterprise Value
FCF	–	Free Cash Flow
FDA	–	Food and Drug Administration (USA)
FSE	–	Frankfurt Stock Exchange
FSMA	–	Financial Services and Markets Authority (Belgium)
GAAP	–	Generally Accepted Accounting Principles
HGB	–	Handelsgesetzbuch (German GAAP)
HP	–	Hewlett Packard Enterprise
HR	–	Human Resources (department / function)
i.a.	–	inter alia – amongst others
i.e.	–	id est – that is
IAS	–	International Accounting Standards
IBD	–	Investment Banking Division (department within investment banks)
IFRS	–	International Financial Reporting Standards
IP	–	Intellectual Property
IPO	–	Initial Public Offering
IR	–	Investor Relations
IRR	–	Internal Rate of Return
ISO	–	International Organization for Standardization
ITF	–	Intention to Float
IVD	–	In Vitro Diagnostics
JOBS Act	–	Jumpstart Our Business Startups Act (US)
KfW	–	Kreditanstalt für Wiederaufbau (German Federal Banking institution)
KISS	–	Keep it Short and Simple
KPI	–	Key Performance Indicator
LIBOR	–	London Interbank Offered Rate
LSE	–	London Stock Exchange

MDx	–	Molecular Diagnostics
M&A	–	Mergers & Acquisitions
MSCI	–	MSCI Inc. (provider of investment decision support tools)
NAV	–	Net Asset Value
NASDAQ	–	National Association of Securities Dealers Automated Quotation (stock exchange in the US)
NPV	–	Net Present Value
NYSE	–	New York Stock Exchange
OTC	–	Over-the-counter
p.a.	–	per annum – per year
PBV	–	Price-to-Book Value (valuation multiple)
P&L	–	Profit and Loss statement
PE	–	Private Equity
PIPE	–	Private Investment in Public Equity
PoA	–	Power of Attorney
PR	–	Public Relations
Q&A	–	Questions & Answers
QIB	–	Qualified Institutional Buyers (term defined by the US Securities Act)
RBC	–	Royal Bank of Canada
R&D	–	Research and Development
ROIC	–	Return on Invested Capital
RONIC	–	Return on New Invested Capital
SEC	–	Securities and Exchange Commission (US)
SEO	–	Seasoned Equity Offering
SME	–	Small and Medium-sized Enterprise
SPO	–	Supplementary Public Offering
telco	–	Telephone conference
TV	–	Television
UK	–	United Kingdom
UKLA	–	United Kingdom Listing Authority
US	–	United States
US$	–	US Dollar (currency)
USA	–	United States of America
USP	–	Unique Selling Proposition

VAT	–	Value-added Tax
VC	–	Venture Capital
vs.	–	versus
WACC	–	Weighted Average Cost of Capital
WYSIWYG	–	What You See Is What You Get
YTM	–	Yield-To-Maturity

Part 1: Initial Public Offering (IPO) – a theoretical perspective

The first part of this book provides a theoretical framework for the IPO-related concepts addressed during an IPO project.

Chapter 1 outlines the basic corporate finance concepts necessary to understand the significance of an IPO for raising equity capital in financial markets. These include the different financing types and sources: equity vs. debt, internal vs. external. Organizational and conceptual differences between investment and commercial banking are addressed, as well. Moreover, past and current developments in IPO markets are described and put into a practical perspective.

Chapter 2 takes a closer look at investment banking's internal processes and explains investment banks' role during an IPO including the individual tasks performed by them. Thus, this chapter addresses the main tasks carried out by investment banks before, during and after an IPO.

Finally, Chapter 3 approaches the difficult task of finding a value for an IPO candidate company from a theoretical perspective. As will be seen, value can differ substantially according to the valuation method used. And there is not one single "correct" valuation method, leaving a lot of room for discussions and arguments in an actual IPO process.

1 Corporate Finance – an overview

1.1 Equity versus debt

This chapter provides a brief outlook on the most common financing means used by companies: equity and debt. It explains the reasons why companies need funding and what financing options companies can choose from. A brief description of the main players in the funding arena will be provided and a brief summary of the current IPO market intends to give a real-life perspective on the theoretical approach.

1.1.1 Why capital is needed

According to widespread economic understanding, only those companies which provide products or services in demand are successful on the long run. Therefore, companies need (innovative) products or services that satisfy customer needs in order to be able to survive in the market. The research and development as well as the production process for these goods and services require resources (also known as "assets"). These assets can either be of tangible (i.e. physical) or intangible nature ranging from machines and buildings to more specific forms like patents. They are acquired through financial activities, commonly referred to as "investments". However, no predetermined financing formula exists as it is common practice to use a trial-and-error process to determine the company and sector specific investment practice. For example, the pharmaceutical industry is known for long testing procedures and approval processes for the national health agencies (e.g. Federal Drug Administration - USA, European Medicines Agency - Europe) whereas other companies' main capital need rests on the establishment of production facilities or (international) distribution channels.

1.1.2 Types of capital

Generally, companies have two major financing options: equity or debt.

Equity in accounting terms presents the residual value (i.e. the difference) between assets and liabilities. From a more company-related approach equity describes its monetary "value" for the owner(s) and their claim on future profits of the company. The different concepts of value and price will be discussed in chapter 3. In this sense, the claim on a prospective profit distribution is sliced into a certain number of pieces that can be traded publicly (called stocks or shares). An IPO is an equity financing method as shares (and therefore equity instruments) are offered for the first time to the investing public. Equity investors are usually compensated for their engagement through dividend payments and/or through an increase in stock value.

Debt capital is based on a contractual relationship between an investor ("creditor"/lender") and a "debtor" or "borrower" which lacks funding. The debtor compensates the lender for not being able to use the capital himself by paying a certain interest rate on the borrowed capital. In economics, this concept is known as "opportunity cost". In the personal realm, debt comes in the form of credit card debt or mortgage loans (special type of loan used to finance real estate). However, corporations also approach financial markets in order to issue corporate debt obligations ("corporate bonds"). The respective interest rate is determined by the pre-determined periodic coupon payments and the face value which will be returned at maturity.

There are also funding instruments in the form of a mixture between debt and equity. They are commonly known as "mezzanine" or "hybrid" capital. Depending on the prevalent characteristics, they are clustered into debt-like and equity-like mezzanine instruments. Mezzanine debt instruments often include options, warrants or other rights. Convertible bonds are a typical example for mezzanine instruments.[1] They pay a fixed coupon and promise the payback of the face value, while giving the investor the choice to exchange the bonds into shares.

1.1.3 Characteristics of debt and equity capital

Debt and equity financing differ substantially. An IPO is considered to be equity financing since it is the first time that a company offers its shares to the public. This paragraph discusses the main differences between debt and equity funding for both, the investors and the issuing company.

With the purchase of equity instruments (e.g. shares of a company) an investor becomes a partial owner of a company. Therefore, depending on the equity form the shareholder is at least liable with the entire capital invested. In case of a non-public (i.e. private) company with unlimited liability an owner commits also all personal wealth in case of filing for bankruptcy.[2] In contrast, debt financing involves no liability and the maximum loss can only amount to the lent capital.

Shareholders, thus partial owners of the company (i.e. equity investors) have also claims on the company's profits (and liabilities in case of losses). Therefore, there is no pre-determined compensation ceiling or floor limiting compensation. Debt is compensated by a fixed interest rate or quasi-fixed interest rate, known as "floating interest rate" (the reference points depend on the specific debt financing instruments e.g.

---

[1] A prominent example for the issuance of convertible bonds is Tesla, an American electric car manufacturer (Financial Times, 2017)

[2] In 2012, Schlecker, a privately-owned and managed German pharmacy chain, filed for bankruptcy holding the founder liable for the integrity of creditors' claims (Deutsche Welle, 2017)

mortgage loans are usually LIBOR or EURIBOR based). Hence, no claims on profits exist for debt instruments. However, in contrast to equity, the pre-determined conditions specified in the contract ("loan agreement") limit the claims on debtors.

In case of a bankruptcy, shareholders can only make a claim on the residual (i.e. remaining) assets after all other third-party liabilities have been compensated. Debtors hold a superior position as their claims are served before those of the shareholders and therefore often retrieve at least part of their invested money. Usually, there is a certain hierarchy when serving debtors according to the issuing date and certain clauses in the issuance contract. Therefore, debt securities are classified as senior and junior-ranked securities.

To a partial owner, equity instruments give (at least theoretically) the right to administrate the company. Therefore, public companies hold annual shareholder meetings, chaired by the company's management board, where each shareholder can exercise his voting rights. As debtors have only a contractual relationship with the company, no direct involvement in corporate matters is sought.

Another differentiating factor relates to time. Equity financing is unlimited as ownership does not terminate at a certain point in time. Clearly, that relationship ends with the sale of the shares or bankruptcy of the company. The debt agreement forms the legal basis of a debt instrument and specifies special features. In its purest form, it spells out a framework with the most basic conditions including the repayment schedule, time horizon, interest rate and calculation form (e.g. annuity, bullet loan, etc.).

The tax treatment of debt and equity differs, as well: Whereas payouts for equity instruments (i.e. dividends) are subject to taxation (the precise rates vary by national jurisdiction), interest payments are tax deductible for the company.

1.2   Where the money comes from

1.2.1   Internal and external financing and sources of capital

In the previous chapter, financial instruments were grouped according to legal differences (equity and debt). Another criterion how funding opportunities can be clustered is the origin of the capital: A company can finance its investment activities internally or it can approach external (third) parties for financing. Therefore, the entirety of financing options open to companies follows a 2x2 matrix which is presented below.

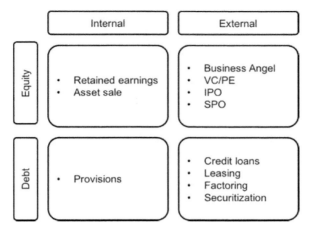

Exhibit 1: Illustration of the main financing options
Source: Own presentation

In "internal" financing, no capital flows from external third parties to the company, and funding is therefore generated by the company's activities itself. The most intuitive form is the sale of assets at a profit (e.g. sale of produced goods, buildings or company cars etc.). Other more sophisticated forms include reserves. Reserves can be hidden (not reflecting the asset's value on the balance sheet) and detectable according to some Generally Accepted Accounting Principles (e.g. German GAAP – HGB and to a lesser extent IFRS). Even though IFRS is based on a "fair value" approach meaning that balance sheet positions are recorded at market values, there exist a myriad of balance sheet positions where hidden reserves are possible.

The most prominent example for observable reserves are retained earnings which result from previous years' profits that have not been distributed to shareholders.

Provisions are another form of self-financing (debt in this case). Provisions are booked when a given periods business activities can be expected to cause a future cash outflow with the exact timing and/or the amount of the outflow unknown.

As noted before, companies generally cannot finance their entire investment activities through internal sources. Therefore, third parties providing capital are needed. External financing refers to the fact that money flows from external parties to the company. Main players in a company's early life include private investors such as family and friends, business angels or high net worth individuals. "Family and friends" financing is often used for start-up companies that have no access to more sophisticated forms of finance or bank loans (due to the high risk associated with the repayment or the lack of collateral). Often, Business Angels are former start-up founders who have turned into wealthy individuals.[3] They acquire stakes of companies and often take on an advising role in a specific sector (usually based on experience and interest). High net worth individuals tend to manage their investments through so-called "family-offices", in which sometimes an entire family-clan is represented.

Another key provider of external financing is the financial intermediary industry. It includes banks, pension funds, investment funds and insurance companies. Banks, for example, provide loans and therefore contribute to a company's financing. Pension funds (e.g. Charles Schwab) administer and accumulate large amounts of private capital in retirement plans and distribute it to different investment opportunities. Investment funds, including hedge funds and private equity funds are also a prime source of equity and debt capital. Insurance providers receive periodically payments by their customers. However, cash inflows and outflows (in case of an insurance claim) do not occur simultaneously. Hence, in order to maximize profits, insurance providers invest the available capital.

Altogether, financial markets provide access to an exchange platform for capital seeking companies. Stock markets (exchanges) and over-the-counter (OTC) markets which comprise less strictly regulated financial markets, represent the main funding means in financial markets on the equity side. Finally worth mentoning is crowd investing, even though it is still in an infant stage. It channels usually small amounts of capital from investors to companies through internet platforms.

1.2.2 Economic functions of financial markets

Financial markets are essential for the entire economic system because of the functions they perform to facilitate the link between savings and real investments in an economy.

Price discovery is the result of market participants' supply of and demand for capital. Demand for capital, thus supply of financial assets stems from companies or other institutions in need of funding. With reference to the subject of this book, companies carrying out an IPO transaction increase the supply of equity instruments. The demand side consists of investors with a funding surplus trying to invest in assets which meet their particular rate of return and/or risk profiles.

In financial markets, liquidity makes sure that investors can trade financial assets at any time they wish to. This type of flexibility allows investors to react to new information on company and environment related issues that may influence their assessment of an investment's value.

Lastly, financial markets can reduce transaction costs for market participants and are, therefore, considered to be an efficient way of capital allocation. Transaction costs

---

[3] The public became familiar with the term Business Angel as the TV format "Shark Tank" was broadcasted in many countries with competing start-ups pitching to local celebrities, including Mark Cuban, Carsten Maschmeyer and others.

include a myriad of different costs the market participants may incur. The search and information costs, for example, are related to the expenses for evaluating the potential investment and/or retrieving relevant information needed for the investment decision.

1.2.3 Transformation task

As an illustration for the transformation tasks one can use commercial banking activities in a "traditional" bank (e.g. J.P. Morgan Chase, Commerzbank, etc.) where a banking clerk checks the references and personal history to accept or reject a loan request. The sole focus of commercial banking lies on the distribution of credit related products, i.e. loans. A commercial banks' customer base is usually well diversified ranging from individuals, SMEs, to major enterprises also including the governmental or municipal sector. Thus, commercial banks carry out the following transformation tasks:

▪ Maturity transformation

Time horizons of investors and borrowers usually differ. Some investors tend to invest only for a certain, often short period of time, whereas debtors need more time to redeem the loan. This process of converting assets into different termed liabilities is called "maturity transformation". Deposits are released at other times than emitted loans are redeemed. Therefore, commercial banks match the time horizon of savers and borrowers. This is possible because many savers and borrowers exist that can compensate for timing differences.

▪ Size transformation

The size transformation is sometimes also referred to as "collection and parceling". Financial markets draw on small amounts of money by a large investor base ("collection") and then redistribute the overall funds into the particular funding amount ("parceling") required by borrowers.

▪ Risk transformation

As investors tend to be risk-averse in different degrees, the invested capital should reflect that risk attitude accordingly and the incurred risk has to be managed. However, borrowers take risk and invest in risky undertakings with no certainty of the outcome. So, risk has to be allocated in different degrees to different investors. In commercial banking, investor's risk can be diversified and therefore be reduced by splitting the overall invested capital and by investing only small amounts of money into specific financial assets.

Investment banking, on the other hand includes various financial services organizing the direct interaction between capital providers (investors) and capital users (companies). Investment banks' customers on the capital supply side are mainly corporate and institutional investors. Their main task is to serve as a financial intermediary and to organize transactions in the corresponding financial market. We will discuss the differences between commercial banking and investment banking in more detail in the next chapter.

1.3 Commercial Banking versus Investment Banking

The previous chapter already explained the theoretical concept and differences between commercial and investment banking. The focus of this chapter lies on providing a more detailed view on processes and organizational structures of both approaches.

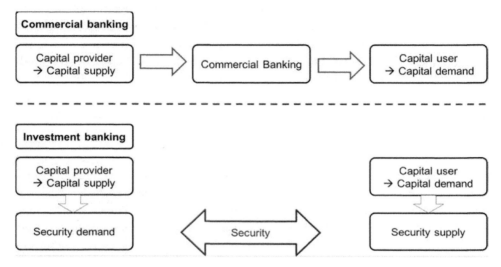

Exhibit 2: Commercial vs. Investment Banking
Source: Own presentation

1.3.1 Institutional set-up of Commercial Banking vs. Investment Banking

Investment banks are usually structured along the services offered. Core investment banking activities include financial markets (sales and trading) and the corporate finance (issuing securities and M&A) realm. Different departments often follow a common logic. The front office plays an essential role as it is closely linked to the revenue generating business. The sales and trading division buys and sells financial products in the market. Sales advises customers (i.e. the issuance) of various financial products according to their financing needs. Structuring includes numerical tasks to originate complex financial products (e.g. derivatives or ABS which have gained a wide media attention during the financial crisis). A third division includes the research by financial analysts often publishing so called research reports (giving a buy, sell or hold recommendation). The recommendations are usually based on primary or fundamental research. The middle office is responsible for the internal procedures and strategy development as well as the efficient treasury handling. Back offices need to make sure that all processes run smoothly and that all transactions are completed correctly. It involves a large portion of computing infrastructure mainly through technological advances or the development of electronic trading schemes.

Commercial banks are also divided into three main areas of business activity. They pool deposits from various individuals who want to save part of their earnings. This task is related to all areas of wealth management even though the main focus lies on saving accounts, especially in Germany. A second task relates to the lending activity to companies or individuals in need of financial resources. A third pillar consists in providing an adequate infrastructure for payment transactions, foreign exchange activity and other capital transfers. These institutions often use a high leverage ratio with little equity. After the financial crisis, regulators required a higher equity base and passed laws to strengthen commercial banks' capital base (the most renowned regulation efforts are Basel II and Basel III).

Many original commercial banks have diversified into investment banking over the last twenty to thirty years and now include also an investment banking division (e.g. Deutsche Bank). Financial institutions that comprise both commercial and investment banking activity are called universal banks. In the past, regulation in some regions (e.g. the US jurisdiction until 1999) restricted universal banking activity, thus, separating investment banks from commercial banks not only functionally but also institutionally. In the wake of the latest financial market crisis, this separation is discussed again to reduce the vulnerability of the financial system.

1.3.2 Services offered in Investment Banking

The financial market related services investment banks provide are various and include advising roles which can be illustrated along the broad spectrum of financial products, covering the entire company life cycle. It begins with a start-up financing including exit options for private equity and venture capital firms by carrying out an IPO. Once a company's shares are publicly traded ("post IPO") secondary equity offerings can also be considered. However, not only equity offerings are undertaken by investment banks but also publicly traded debt offerings can be originated by them. During the IPO process the concept of underwriting is closely linked to investment banking activities which will be discussed in chapter 2. Syndication is another service provided by investment banks. It structures debt obligations into other financial and tradable products (ABS). The sales and trading handles various tasks related to transactions in financial markets. Among these, in brokerage services money is invested on behalf of investors whereas proprietary trading is often related to profit seeking activities by investing the investment banks own capital.[4]

---

[4] M&A is also part of investment banks' IBD departments and sometimes referred to as the original investment banking activity. Since it lies outside the realm of IPO activities, we refrains from a more detailed explanation of this investment banking function.

1.3.3   IPO as part of Investment Banking services

As explained earlier, during the IPO process investment banks bring together investors and companies in need of capital.

In the IPO process, investment banks assist companies with advice which will be explained in greater detail in chapter 2.2. Shares are offered to the public investor base for the first time ("Initial public offering"). Therefore, investment banks can advise prospective IPO companies on questions related to if, when and how an IPO should be performed.

During the IPO, underwriting tasks are carried out by investment banks through which various risk positions are shifted from the issuing company to the investment bank(s). During the process, investment banks offer their capital raising clients business contacts and schedule appointments with financial advisors or directly with investors ("roadshow").

1.3.4   Investment Banking in the US and Europe

The historical development of modern investment banks can be traced back to America in the 1920s when commercial banks acquired stockbroker institutions because after WWI funding was less expensive in the stock market. After some crises and subsequent regulation, globalization after WWII opened the door to new business activities such as currency trading and trading in other financial instruments (e.g. derivatives).

In Europe, universal banks have been the predominant banking model since the early 19th century. The various tasks were mostly carried out on a local (i.e. national) level. England was and still is considered the financial center of Europe being the headquarter of most investment banks. The Brexit referendum and the prospect of Britain leaving the European Union, however, have led many investment banks to reconsider relocation at least in parts to the European Union.

The American origins of modern investment banking can still be observed in today's markets as American investment banks tend to play a dominant role even in European markets. This conclusion can also be reached when regarding the investment banking IPO business environment. More than half of the represented investment banks in the Top 10, ranked by market share, are of Anglo-Saxon origin.

Table 1:   League tables: Global Equity IPO for FY16

Rank	Firm	Market share in %	Volume in US$ bn
1	JP Morgan	6.344	8.540
2	Morgan Stanley	6.023	8.108
3	Goldman Sachs	5.044	6.791
4	Citi	4.677	6.296
5	Deutsche Bank	4.104	5.525
6	Credit Suisse	3.896	5.208
7	Bank of America Merrill Lynch	3.299	5.090
8	UBS	2.459	4.441
9	Nomura	2.459	3.311
10	CITIC Securities Co Ltd	1.980	2.665

Source: Bloomberg, 2017, p. 7

1.4   The global IPO market and its drivers

This chapter gives a short overview of the historic and current global IPO activities and trends. It analyses regional and local peculiarities in IPO markets and provides a brief outlook on the near future.

1.4.1   Overview of international IPO activity

Exhibit 3 points out that the past eight years were quite volatile with regard to the total number of IPOs and the total volume raised thereby. In the wake of the financial market crisis and the related economic uncertainty, global IPO activity remained at a very low level (PwC, 2009, p. 14). In 2010 however, global IPO markets gained momentum and returned to pre-crisis levels. The rising political and economic risks overshadowed 2011 and caused a major drawback in IPO activity. Central Banks' decisions to lower interest rates to historical lows stimulated spending which, in turn, boosted the global economy in 2014 (EY, 2014, p. 1). The following two years again were overshadowed by major political and economic instability. Many recent events including the Brexit referendum, presidential elections and ongoing migrant streams led to a higher uncertainty in capital markets and therefore slowed down IPO activity, again.

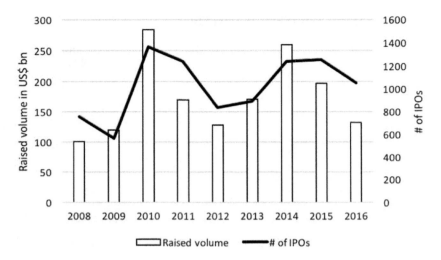

Exhibit 3: Global IPO activity by number & volume raised (2008 – 2016)
Source: Own presentation based on EY, 2016

It is also instructive to look at the regional distribution of IPO candidates. The People's Republic of China has played a dominant role in global activity in recent years (EY, 2016, p. 2). The Asian continent accounted for almost 6 out of 10 IPOs worldwide. The following paragraph examines the regional differences that exist throughout the main world regions.

1.4.2   Asia

As mentioned earlier, in recent years Asia has been the main driver of global IPO activity. Especially China accounts for a large portion of IPOs worldwide (331 in China vs. 1004 overall in 2016). IPO activity is channeled by the CSRC (China Securities Regulatory Commission) as many companies waiting for an IPO acceptance are still in the pipeline (740 as of 2016). Most of the activity comes from Chinas three main stock exchanges Hong Kong, Shenzhen and Shanghai.

During the past couple of years, The Communist Party of China began opening its formerly secluded economic policy. As a consequence, many previously state-owned companies were taken public, leading to a steady rise of China-based IPOs. Since these companies tend to show well-developed and proven business models, state-owned IPOs raised larger volumes when going public compared to their entrepreneurial counterparts.

1.4.3   US

Financial sponsors, i.e. Private Equity or Venture Capital companies have driven American IPOs over the last couple of years. Partly due to the world's Central Banks low interest rate policy, equity markets have risen to high levels. Rising equity markets help financial sponsors due to a more attractive valuation when filing for an IPO. Therefore, many exit strategies of financial sponsors have been delayed in order to make a bet on rising markets. As a consequence, more established and developed companies have gone public.

Popular sectors include technology and health care. Especially the technology sector has drawn a lot of media attention and dominated media coverage. The so-called "unicorns" (Companies whose valuations exceeds US$ 1billion) went or are about to go public. Since American equity analysts have already acquired expertise with technology-based business models, cross listings from European and Asian tech companies in the US are expected for the near future.[5]

For many years, Nasdaq has been the home for the most prestigious technology companies. The companies listed on Nasdaq include both software and manufacturing related companies such as Apple, Alphabet (the parent company of Google), Microsoft, Facebook, and Amazon.

1.4.4   Europe

UK as the financial center of Europe is facing major issues at this point of time. Political risk associated with the UK referendum to leave the EU lowered IPO activity in overall Europe in 2016. In addition, the upcoming presidential elections in some European countries impede IPOs. The before mentioned uncertainties have a great impact on IPO activities. The significant number of withdrawals and IPO cancelations fall into this context. Another indicator pointing towards this development is the decrease in the volume raised in European IPOs (down by 27% in 2016 compared with 2015).

1.4.5   Future Prospects

As mentioned before, capital markets and especially IPO activity are quite sensitive to market volatility. Therefore, forecasts should be taken with more than only a grain of salt.

Europe's stock markets have shown very high volatility but have reached record levels in 2017, nevertheless. The current risks however, are not harming global IPO activity since its main driver is Asia. The Chinese authorities (CSRC) have already approved a large number of IPO candidates, which means that the IPO pipeline is quite full. When it comes to deal volume, companies can be divided up into previously state- owned and entrepreneurial companies. Previously state-owned enterprises account for larger volumes raised than their entrepreneurial counterparts.

---

[5] For more information on the idea of cross listings we refer to chapter 2.1.

As Chinese economic policy moves on to more regulated equity markets by initiating long awaited reforms, overseas investor's confidence might be boosted and more capital inflow and foreign investments are possible.

Potential investors in European equity markets seem to be rather bewildered by current political developments and therefore follow a "Wait-and-see" strategy. Thus, forecasts project a sluggish development with only minor IPO filings for the near future until political issues will have been resolved.

Even though in the short run future prospects are relatively subdued (except for China), projections for the long run are rather optimistic. A study conducted by PwC in 2011 addresses the future development of capital markets by 2025 (PwC, 2011). Whereas past IPO activity was centered on industrial western nations, the authors of the study project a move towards the Asian continent.

The study also suggests that the historical financial centers of the world, London and New York, might be replaced by others. The authors concluded that smaller, regional stock exchanges are continuously challenging them in today's IPO markets.

A different approach to IPO activity can be observed in indirect IPO motivations. In order to get access to developing markets and to assure local liquidity, established companies were seen building regional hubs by listing on local exchanges in the past (e.g. Prada and Samsonite in Hong Kong).

In summary, major changes are on the horizon over the next couple of years. The geographical perspective will change the IPO environment as current forecasts project global IPO markets to shift towards Asia in both volume raised and number of IPOs. This also means that western IPO markets will lose in global significance. Furthermore, the market structure is expected to change as more established equity markets are challenged by new entrants. As a result, global competition will intensify and a more split market structure is possible. In the past, European markets have already acted correspondingly and merged with former competitors to scale up.

2 What Investment Banks do in an IPO

This chapter presents a basic overview of the role investment banks play during the IPO process.[6] We will discuss in more depth the four main functions, investment banks engage in. These, among others, include the advising role for the client on why an IPO (or maybe other equity/debt instruments) is the most fitting (financing) option with respect to the individual circumstances (see 2.1). Once an IPO is planned, a consortium of investment banks assumes one of the key roles in an IPO: the underwriting task (see 2.2). Responsibilities, duties and tasks vary substantially depending on the specific role given to the investment bank. Then, the client and its advising investment bank allocate the shares according to their specific considerations, expectations and plans (see 2.3). Contractual relationships, however, do not end at the moment the company lists its shares on a public stock exchange for the first time (commonly referred to as the "going public" process). Hence, chapter 2.4 examines bank's involvement in post IPO activities ("follow-on transactions").

2.1 Advice

Before a financially motived IPO, a privately-held company first decides on its strategic and operative activities during the periodic planning process. These, among others, can include projects like the development of new products, M&A activity or business expansion. Carrying out these activities requires sufficient financing. As described above investments can be financed by using either equity or debt instruments (or a certain mixture of both, called "mezzanine financing"). For the sake of completeness, it is worth mentioning that there are other types of IPOs in which the financing factor is not dominating. These can be of strategic (e.g. spin-offs, exit options for VCs) and other non-financial nature (e.g. reputation, product marketing or employer attractiveness through offering stock options).

With regard to the prospective size of the IPO, the initial client contact with investment banks tends to differ. If the IPO is expected to raise a large amount of money, many investment banks find it attractive (even though competition can be quite tough) to compete with other rivaling investment banks. Then, those investment banks "apply" to be part of the beauty contest. The following paragraph describes its procedure in more detail. However, if SMEs (e.g. the German "Mittelstand") intend to raise money, the companies often take the initiative and approach an investment bank to ask for advice. Another option is that the investment banks screen the market and, if they find an appropriate company, try to convince it to carry out an IPO (mainly by showing the advantages of an IPO).

---

[6] A more detailed discussion will follow in Part 2, chapters 4 to 7.

Type of Security

One of the most important responsibilities of a company's Chief Financial Officer ("CFO") is the planning of the appropriate capital structure, i.e. the mix between equity and debt. As described in chapter 1.1 both financing options vary in terms of cost and legal consequences. Since this task involves a great deal of risk and requires a wide knowledge and expertise, the financing decision is a challenging task. Since investment banks pool great expertise in financial markets, they offer a wide array of financing related information (e.g. advisory). Those services include, among others, advising the client on what security seems to be the best fit for the company. During its advising activity, the investment bankers get a grasp on the business environment and a more refined view of the company. As investment bankers are constantly screening the market conditions (also known as "investing climate"), they are able to give a sound recommendation on what security may be best suited for the businesses' needs at the given point of time.

Beauty contest

Once an IPO is chosen as the best option to pursue, the investment banks to accompany the project need to be selected. A beauty contest in the context of an envisioned IPO describes the hiring process of an investment bank as a lead advisor and project manager. Starting with a short presentation ("pitch") the invited investment banks propose their IPO concept. The pitch includes detailed marketing strategies, strategic positioning of the issue and a sound demand forecast. In these presentations, the invited investment banks discuss the proposed company value and how many shares can be sold in the market at this point of time. In this context, company executives often run into a real dilemma; the best qualified investment bank may not be the one with the highest proposed valuation. Best qualified investment banks gathered a large expertise in the sector (equity research) and show a strong track record of previously executed transactions (tombstones of comparable transactions). Other criteria incorporated in the decision-making process include fees, international presence (offices or branches), reputation and network. In addition, the firm's main bank is often also invited. Therefore, stable and long-term relationships as well as complementary financial services (e.g. following-on loans) are taken into consideration.

Once all invited investment banks presented their proposals, the issuing company chooses the investment bank it wants to cooperate with for the IPO project. Since resource restrictions apply (time and personnel) and in order to limit risk, the plethora of tasks are distributed among various investment banks. The whole set of tasks include the advising activity (before and during the IPO), marketing and placement activities as well as settlement and risk services (see chapter 2.2). Since many parties collaborate on an IPO the main functions are outlined briefly.

[1] The *Lead manager* is responsible for the successful completion of the IPO process. In large or transnational IPOs, two (but seldom more) investment banks combine their forces to jointly organize the IPO ("Lead manager" & "Co-manager" also referred to as "Joint Lead manager"). In order to relieve management, the lead manager helps the issuing company to coordinate the different tasks and to select the remaining advisors.

[2] The investment bank that collects orders from investors and transcribes them into an orderbook is called the *Bookrunner*. The bookrunner often coincides with the lead manager.

[3] *Regional managers* can facilitate the process of placing the offered shares in certain regions. The regional managers act mostly in foreign or very specific market segments and can contribute especially with their knowledge and expertise to the success of the process.

[4] A special type of regional manager is the *selling agent*. The two differ in that the selling agent does not assume any risk. The investment bank only oversees the placement; it collects and passes incoming orders to the bookrunner.

Hence, the chosen investment bank(s) are responsible for a successful placement. After the evaluation, the company asks for the corresponding "Engagement letter" of the top candidates and signs the best fitting proposal.

Time

Timing can be understood in two different ways: the timing in the company's life cycle and the timing in terms of the projected timeframe.

The advising investment bank intends to organize the process as efficiently as possible. Together with the IPO company, it decides on the timeframe for milestones in order to meet the tight IPO schedule.

As mentioned in chapter 1.4, IPO markets are quite volatile and therefore the so-called "market windows" open and close unexpectedly. Investment banks, therefore try to prepare for a possible IPO opportunity and execute the IPO once the market opens (see Part 3).

Price

Once, the advising investment bank and the company have agreed on the equity financing by issuing shares, pricing of those shares is an important task carried out by the investment bank. The most often applied pricing methods include the open-offer (proposing a fixed price) or the book-building method. Both depend on market demand. As shares represent the partial ownership of a company, the "realistic" stock price reflects the value of a company. Price and value are closely related concepts which will be discussed in chapter 3. During the pricing process, financial analysts prepare complex financial models in order to find the "real value" of a stock ("intrinsic value") and advise the company on the stock valuation. Variables determining the valuation include quantitative factors (largely concerned with past and projected financial performance of the company, its business sector and the overall economy) and qualitative factors (quality of the management team, proven track record or historical achievements in hitting strategic targets). Depending on investors' demand for the issued shares, the proposed share price can be under- or overpriced, both leading to adverse consequences for the involved parties (see chapter 2.2). Hence, pricing shares usually is a very delicate task.

Place

The public company to-be, together with its advising investment bank, also consider the stock market the company wants to list its stock on. The default option would be to list the shares on an exchange in the company's country of origin. However, regulatory requirements may prohibit listing on certain stock exchanges. And many companies decide to sell their shares on a stock market abroad ("foreign exchange listings"). These companies defy the drawbacks such as higher complexity and costs in order to benefit from the advantages. Those benefits might include more liquidity held by foreign investors, the access to more potential investors, higher achieved valuations or specialized markets (e.g. technology-affiliated stock exchanges like Nasdaq in the US.). Other companies also prepare to list on multiple exchanges simultaneously (also known as "dual" or "multiple" listing).

Once the country is chosen, the specific stock exchange needs to be selected as well. An important factor is the reputation of the stock exchange (e.g. NYSE or Börse Frankfurt are globally recognized). As a better reputation is often based on a more transparent and regulated stock exchange, investors' confidence is higher and can be an advantage for the issuing company. Those listing requirements differ from stock exchange to stock exchange and, therefore, are a crucial decision criterion.

Addressees

During the IPO preparation, investment banks also approach possible investors for participating in the IPO. The process can be organized in a private or a public offering. In a private offering, only a pre-selected group of institutional investors participate in the IPO, whereas in a public offering, the offering is presented to a diverse group of investors.

For the execution of an effective marketing strategy in a public offering, investment banks divide possible IPO subscribers into different target groups (called "tranches"). These mainly comprise institutional and private investors (known as "retail") as well as company employees. In some countries (e.g. the US), target groups also include international investors.

As jurisdiction differs significantly between countries, no generalization can be made with respect to the ratio of institutional to private investors. However, it plays a major role when pricing shares and defining purchase clauses for the different tranches. The distribution process is discussed in greater depth in chapter 2.3.

What to expect in the IPO preparation

In the pre-IPO phase, the company needs to be analyzed properly. Depending on the IPO readiness of the company, some formal activities need to be undertaken. So, auditors need to approve financial statements (eventually transfer past financial statements to different accounting standards, e.g. IFRS). Often the company needs to be restructured or to be refinanced to obtain a better capital mix. Important documents need to be drafted and approved by all the involved parties (i.e. public authorities, bankers, lawyers and the management team). In this phase, potential investors and the company itself go through a Due Diligence in which the company may also be benchmarked against competitors in the same sector. Special focus is put on the IPO filing papers to national financial authorities (e.g. SEC or BaFin) and the prospectus.

Once the IPO is approved, the public communication of an IPO and hence the marketing phase begins. The equity growth story provides the most important reason to investors why they should participate in the public offering. Then the roadshow takes place (see chapter 11). Investment banks schedule several appointments per day with financial institutions over a period of approx. 3 weeks in which they try to convince these investors about the investment opportunity. During the roadshow, the company's executives are solely involved in the process and day to day business is managed by other senior management. IPO preparation ends abruptly with the completion of the book building process and pricing of the shares.

What to expect after being public

Even though the IPO preparation is associated with a vast workload for the involved parties, being public is also associated with a lot of additional work. Right after the IPO, investment banks try to stabilize the stock price. Possible levers and means for how investment banks can manage the stock price will be addressed in chapter 2.4.

After the IPO, the company needs to meet many new requirements with respect to financial reporting and disclosure. As being under constant scrutiny by the public, Investor Relations need to develop a consistent and convincing communication strategy of how to inform the public on company issues.

One of the advantages of the IPO is the ongoing access to the capital market. Therefore, the capital market provides further financing options. The detailed mechanisms and possibilities will be explained in chapter 2.4. Also, withdrawals from the financial markets happen sometimes, but are not seen as frequently as offerings.

2.2 Underwriting

As described in the previous chapter, the public company to-be and its lead advisor need to select and assign a plethora of different roles in the IPO process to various investment banks (commonly referred to as "consortium"). This chapter focusses primarily on the role of the underwriting parties.

The general concept of underwriting – a short moment with a lot of risk

Underwriting is not an IPO specific term as it can also be found in a wide array of possible applications throughout the financial realm. Some sources name the shipping insurance business as the origin of this term (Lloyd's, 2017). In the 17th century, insurers placed their names under an insurance contract, possibly the origin of the word "underwriting". In today's world, the underwriting concept is often associated with the following sectors: insurance, real estate (e.g. mortgage) and security origination (i.e. debt and equity). All these market segments share one common trait: they include risk. Here, we will use an IPO related definition.

Risk appears along with the uncertainty about future market conditions. In that way, previously not considered adverse events may occur in the near future. Floating risk is mainly borne by the underwriting investment banks and occurs if investor (or market) windows close. It includes the risk of price adjustments (foremost down-pricing). Investment banks also bear the marketing risk, as these activities are mainly carried out by these institutions, and thus, solely borne by them. However, risks can be limited by waiting for a better market environment until resuming the IPO. Another means of reducing the associated risk is to form a syndicate in which all involved banks assume just a part of the overall risk associated with the IPO ("sub-underwriting").

In an IPO, the underwriting investment bank(s) assist the issuing company in raising capital in the primary market and in deciding on how those securities are distributed among investors (see chapter 2.3). The underwriting investment bank(s) (lead & co-underwriter, also referred to as "consortium") "underwrite" the issued securities.[7]

The underwriting phase starts with the signing of the underwriting agreement (also known as "Sale and Purchase Agreement"), right before the moment of the public issuance (usually the night before). Investment banks intend to limit their risks by having finalized all marketing activities earlier and by having captured investor's confidence during the roadshow (see chapter 2.1). The underwriting agreement includes:

[1] Nature of underwriters' obligation (type of the underwriting commitment)
[2] Statement on the company's situation and warranties

---

[7] In this publication, two closely related terms are used: consortium and syndicate. Whereas the first addresses mainly the cooperation in the tasks carried out, the latter term puts more emphasis on risk and resource sharing.

[3] Clauses on the conditions of the contractual relationship

[4] Listing of the expense structure

[5] Specification of potential lock-up restrictions

[6] Indemnification in case of non-completion

Historical development of underwriting approaches

The involved parties can choose between several forms of how to organize the underwriting process.

The first one is known as a "firm commitment" underwriting. In this "underwriting" process the investment banks assume a great portion of risk as they have already committed to pay a certain, previously agreed amount of money (the raised funds) to the issuing company and now "own" the securities (i.e. the issued shares). Therefore, it is also called "fixed-price method". In this case, risk is shifted from the issuing company to the underwriting investment banks as they carry the risk that no investor is interested in those shares ("floating risk") and additionally they bear the costs of selling those shares. The issuing company, however, assumes no longer any risk related to adverse market conditions (i.e. the share price decreases to a lower price than the banks paid) and can invest its raised proceeds. In this case, the underwriting banks need to wait and hold on to those shares or sell them at lower prices. Both scenarios are unfavorable for the investment banks. The banks aim at selling the issued and now owned shares at the highest achievable price in order to maximize their own profits. The difference between the price per share the investment bank paid to the issuing company and the selling price to investors is also known as the "underwriting spread". Within the firm-commitment approach, commitment can be given at an early state (hard-underwriting), or at later stages, e.g. after pricing occurred (soft-underwriting). Risks assumed by investment banks in both cases can be limited by corresponding restrictive clauses in the underwriting agreement (e.g. Force Majeure).

Even with an extensive market research and a great expertise, many unknown variables influence investors' demand and risks should therefore not be underestimated.[8] As in general, no risk is assumed without compensation, additional fees are paid to the supporting investment banks.[9]

A less risky approach comes in the form of a "standby" underwriting agreement. This

---

[8] The risks associated with an underwriting can be exemplified in IBM's 1979 SEO (seasoned equity offering – meaning that capital is increased by issuing new shares), in which days before going public and after valuation then-Fed president Volcker increased interest rates. Some authors refer to it as "Saturday night massacre". Another famous example is the British Petroleum IPO in 1987. In the twilight of the financial crash, commonly known as the "Black Friday", BP's shares plunged heavily amid adverse market conditions resulting in large losses for the underwriting investment banks (New York Times, 1987).

[9] Please refer to chapter 4.5 for a more detailed discussion of fees.

method implies that the underwriting bank acquires only the remaining shares that could not be sold to investors.

In order to avoid the risks, investment banks can use an alternative option, the "best effort" underwriting when high uncertainty exists about the successful resale ("high risk IPOs"). This process tends to be used when the bargaining power of the issuing company is rather low and it is hard to raise any funds. As the name suggests, the investment banks act on their "best efforts", but do not buy any stocks of the issuing company. All remaining shares will be handed back to the issuing company. In this process, investment banks' task primarily consists in doing the best possible to sell the issued shares and therefore they bear very little risk.

Closely related to the best-effort underwriting is the "All or None" method. In this process, a previously determined number of shares need to be sold in order to realize the IPO. In case that this benchmark is not reached, the IPO is cancelled and the previously collected funds are returned to the investors.

Another, slightly modified underwriting approach is the "Mini-Maxi" technique. It restricts the issuing volume to a certain interval and thereby determines a minimum and a maximum number of shares. Investment banks cancel the issuance if the minimum bar is not reached.

As most of the before mentioned methods include a high level of risk for issuers, investment banks and/or investors, the book building process intends to reduce these frictions. Applied for the first time in the public offering of British Telecom (BT) in 1991, the process was organized by a book runner (if more than one investment banks are assigned with this task then they are called "joint-bookrunners"). It differs from the previously described methods as the price is not set by the investment banks but is explored dynamically. The book runners take orders from investors during the road show and collect the desired number of shares with the offered price in an "order book". When order taking is completed (within a pre-specified period of time), investment banks and the issuing company address the distribution of the shares, as will be discussed in the next chapter. The pricing risk can be reduced by running a "book of interest". During this so-called "indication of interest" period investment banks can adjust prices according to investor's sentiments (if demand is quite low, they lower prices and vice versa). It is also known as "pilot fishing" or "testing the waters". However, those indications are non-binding for investors. Previously full order books may empty within moments if market conditions deteriorate. Hence, investment banks try to limit the time between order taking and closing, turning the offers into binding ones.

Current techniques and future developments

Underwriting methods have been subject to constant change and innovation. Thanks to the rise of the Internet, innovative new underwriting techniques have emerged. One of them is the so-called "self-underwritten offering" (Nasdaq, 2017). This method skips the underwriter parties and intends to place an issuance directly. Since the Internet can easily provide the infrastructure for such processes, transaction costs are reduced dramatically. However, many investors (especially institutional ones) are reluctant to participate in this type of process as they draw a lot of information from the interaction with the investment banks.

In addition, auction-style IPOs has been tried out in the past.[10] In contrast to the widespread underwriting practice in which underwriters determine the price, in an auction process, investors simply quote their offered prices. The highest offered price is the starting price for the auction. In the following, the price decreases until all shares are assigned. However, these new approaches have not always proven to be successful. These innovative techniques are quite efficient at first glance. However, as the saying goes "stock is sold not bought", large institutional investors still base part of their decisions on social interaction with the people standing behind an IPO and therefore do not fully eliminate the personal interaction.

2.3 Distribution

Especially in the book building method, distribution of the issued shares is an essential task for the advising investment banks. In this chapter, the importance of the distribution will be addressed and the reasons why distribution is such a critical task will be explained. At the end, we will take a look at the process itself.

Distribution power as a key element of IPO services

As explained in the last chapter, the bookrunner tries to sell the outstanding shares by filling the order book. However, it is possible, if not even desired, that investors' demand exceeds the number of shares to be issued, a so-called "oversubscription". Hence, a decision needs to be made which investors will get the "scarce" shares.

Different approaches how shares are distributed have been used in the IPO process. For example, a "pro rata" distribution includes a fixed distribution ratio in case of an oversubscription (e.g. 60% institutional vs. 40% retail investors). A "discrete" distribution is closely linked to a firm-commitment approach. Investment banks can independently decide on how to distribute the shares and can therefore select the investors without third party's influence.

Depending on the method, the underwriting investment banks aim at achieving different goals. These include raising the maximum amount of funding for the issuing company or building a long-lasting relationship with a certain shareholder base (e.g. those

---

[10] A very prominent example was the 2004 Google IPO (Forbes, 2004).

planning to be invested in the company for a long time). Therefore, in order to coordinate the distribution of the issued shares not only the highest bid is essential to the distributors. Other factors include the type of investor (retail or institutional, national or international) and the (possible pre-existing) relationship with the investment bank.

As we will see in chapter 2.4, the success of an IPO can only be determined after a couple of weeks, at the earliest. Therefore, in order to avoid share flipping, the investors with a long-term holding perspective are generally favored in the distribution. If the IPO is highly oversubscribed, rejected customers might then approach the secondary market and buy the number of shares they desire in the aftermarket. As mentioned earlier, prices may be heavily influenced by short term profit-seeking speculative investors. Since the reputation of the investment bank depends often on finding the right offering price, they aim at avoiding a mispricing for the IPO. Hence, only a small portion of issued shares is distributed to short term investors.

The total number of issued shares is often divided into different parts, so called "tranches". Investment bankers then decide what portion goes to which type of investors. Often main groups of tranches are domestic vs. foreign investors. Hence, investors may be classified according to geography. This approach is often found in the United States where a solid base of international investor is often considered desirable. However, a certain flexibility is up to the investment banks since demand may vary throughout the book building phase and differ from the bankers' original estimates.

Retail investors are often favored by investment banks even though institutional demand is higher. The latter mainly include investment funds which possess a large amount of capital to be invested. These funds employ many financial analysts who work in specialized research departments trying to identify attractive investment opportunities. Other institutional investors are pension funds or insurance companies. Especially in the US., hedge funds also act as investors, whereas in Europe regional banks are commonly found among IPO investors. Often, regional banks offer "retail investment opportunities" in their asset management branch, thus marketing IPO participation to retail investors.

The retail tranche's major advantage is that it usually follows a more projectable development and it is therefore less sensitive to short term price volatility. However, even if a large retail tranche is desirable, their portion seldom makes up more than half of the issuing volume. Nevertheless, there is no clear rule as to the correct distribution. It needs to be adjusted to the prevalent environment and company specific peculiarities.

Consortia and lead management – the hierarchy of distribution

The lead manager and its co-manager(s) are responsible for placing shares to institutional investors. These, as described in the previous paragraph, represent a large portion of overall shares sold.

For a widespread IPO participation coverage, however, the lead manager cooperates with other institutions. Hence, local underwriting investment banks often emphasize the retail channel. Co-underwriters or external parties sell shares in a second stage to institutional investors as well, but also to sales agents which offer them to private investors.

As mentioned before, various tranches exist. It is common practice that every tranche has an individual group of syndicate banks managing the individual distribution within the assigned tranches. The global coordinator organizes the distribution of the issued shares within the different syndicates.

The volume an investor gets assigned depends on different criteria. These include, investor traits and behavior shown in previous comparable transactions (e.g. late offer placing or speculative intentions). Unfavorable investor characteristics can be penalized by investment banks by assigning them only a portion of the desired number of shares.

Investment banks often face a conflict of interest (especially in the discrete distribution method). Therefore, distribution criteria should be based on a fair judgement (better for the IPO company) and not solely on the commissions paid (better for the investment bank). Since financial regulatory authorities have recognized this drawback, many investment banks only take on an advising role by issuing so called "recommendations to the issuer". These need to be implemented by the issuing company itself.

The importance of widespread coverage

Aftermarket performance and low volatility levels are closely attributed to the investor structure (sometimes referred to as "investor base"). Private and institutional investors should both be included in order to avoid high stock price fluctuations, especially during the period right after the IPO.

As explained above, institutional investors are financial professionals who question a company's strategy and sometimes take an active role. Hence, institutional investors may have a certain degree of influence on company's decisions. It can be a positive signal for other investors if institutional investors put some trust in the company.

Retail investors provide liquidity and hence stabilize the stock price. Also, the individual retail investors hold only minor portions of shares and their intentions to sell do not have a major impact (if any) on the market price.

The geographic origin of investors may round up a well-diversified investor base from a reputational point of view, too. This may inspire confidence in a company's upward trend and trust in its economic success.

2.4   Post-IPO

Being public – listing and the days after

The narrowly defined IPO process ends at the day of the IPO ("first trading day") and the company is called a publicly listed corporation, thereafter. This chapter examines the role of investment banks after the completion of the IPO transaction. It examines various techniques to control share prices on the first trading days. Being a publicly listed company comes with many (financial and legal) restrictions, which will also be addressed in this chapter. One of the advantages of being a public company is the access to the financial market. Therefore, certain follow-on transaction will also be discussed.

Greenshoe option and other instruments of managing the share price

The immediate time after the IPO is often characterized as a phase of instability, as some investors might want to sell their shares to make a short-term profit (speculative motivation). Other explanations focus on the uncertainty regarding the company valuation in the first days of trading. Hence, the adverse situation of a share price trading down is possible. On the other hand, demand can rise swiftly, if investors try to buy the shares "at any price" to be "part of the action". However, it is illegal to intervene in the stock market and set prices (and hence "manipulate" it). There is one exception, though. After an IPO, a "stabilizing" agent can intervene in order to maintain a reasonable stock price within a certain period of time.

If demand for the IPO is high, the investment banks (usually the underwriter) are free to issue more shares (c. 15%) than originally declared. This process is called an over-allotment option.[11] When exercising the option in case the price is up, the investment bank(s) get the shares at the issuing price and sell it at the market price. If the price is down, they buy the shares on the market. Therefore, in both cases the price is influenced indirectly.

Stock prices can also be managed by applying lock up periods. In a set contract, the interested investors commit themselves to hold on to the acquired shares for a certain period (varying between 180 days up to one year). As a consequence, the quick sale of shares is prevented which might make the stock more appealing to other investors. There are two types of lock up periods: Hard lock up (no selling is allowed) and soft lock up (permission needs to be granted by the investment banks). Longer lock up periods are usually applied for the company's management, if it also purchases shares.

New requirements on reporting and investor relations

A listed company is subject to permanent public scrutiny. With respect to financial reporting, there are a lot of different jurisdictions in terms of reporting requirements.

---

[11] It is commonly referred to as a greenshoe option, as this method was first applied in the IPO of Greenshoe Manufacturing in 1963.

However, many reporting duties, especially in the western world coincide. One of the most important factors is the regular reporting (i.e. quarterly and annual reports) under certain standards (IFRS/local GAAP). Other requirements include:

- News affecting the share price need to be made public in a short period of time ("ongoing disclosure").
- Company's executives and non-executive directors need to inform about their shareholdings and trading ("insider trading").
- The company needs to inform the public if a large portion of voting rights are held by individual investors ("major shareholder").
- Salary disclosure of the company's executives and non-executive directors ("compensation").
- In recent years, a corporate governance codex has been established in many jurisdictions in order to facilitate a company's valuation. In addition, after the financial crisis of 2008, some jurisdiction decided to make the company's directors (i.e. CEO & CFO) personally liable for their actions.[12]

The Investor Relations department ("IR") makes sure that company relevant information is spread to the financial audience (i.e. future and/or existing investors). This information may consist of internal news (e.g. product related news) or external developments (e.g. economic situation in a certain market). Main means of distribution is the company's website and special news outlets suggested by domestic financial regulators (e.g. SEC, BaFin). It lies also in their responsibility to organize press conferences and schedule investor meetings. As investors often listen to analysts covering the stock or a certain sector, the main task for the Investor Relation department is getting a sense for their expectations and advising the board in legal as well as economic effects from an Investor Relation point of view. Especially in times of crisis, it is IR's prime task to ensure a transparent communication policy.

Follow-on offering

Some shareholders (mainly large institutional investors or founders) may want to sell a great portion of their shares at some point of time after the IPO (called "non-dilutive secondary offering"). However, if they offered a large number of shares in the stock market, supply would certainly exceed demand leading to an unfavorable decrease in the stock price. Therefore, investment banks assist the seller by selling the shares within a larger period of time or by finding an adequate buyer ("private placement"). The capital raised in this procedure goes to the seller of the shares.

This concept is not to be confused with a follow-on offering (referred to as "dilutive secondary equity offering" or "seasoned equity offering" or commonly known as "capital increase"). In this case, the company intends to raise more capital in the financial market by issuing new shares. As the quota of ownership decreases for "old" share-

---

[12] For more information on this subject please refer to the Sarbanes-Oxley Act

holders since more shares are outstanding, the company grants offering or preemptive rights to them (so that their ownership quota in the company can remain constant). In this case, the raised capital goes to the company.

Taking private

A taking-private transaction describes the withdrawal of a previously listed public company from active stock market trading. To do so, typically one or more investors purchase as many outstanding shares as possible and take it "private" by not trading shares in the stock market any more. This is often the case in the Private Equity industry. One business model of these firms is screening the market for (publicly traded) companies and reorganizing them.[13] Especially struggling companies are often subject of Private Equity taking private transactions. The acquired companies are restructured and often taken public again ("re-IPO") in order to generate profits for the Private Equity firms.

Delisting

Delisting describes the process through which a company ceases to be listed on a stock exchange. Therefore, stocks of the company can no longer be traded on it. Each stock exchange has specific rules (with respect to share prices, financial ratios or volume) that apply for delistings.

Few companies decide voluntarily to delist. In most cases, private equity firms decide, after a taking private transaction, to delist the company since costs associated with listing are quite high and there is no use in being listed for a private company. Also, delisting occurs in M&A transactions of formerly public companies when two companies merge into a new one ("merger") or when a company disappears (by means of an "acquisition").

In other cases, companies are forced to delist. Stock exchanges usually first send warnings for violations of trading rules to the company and in case of repeated violations, cease the company's trading activities. The main reason for a delisting is that companies no longer meet the listing requirements, often caused by inappropriate financial ratios. However, this does not necessarily mean that trading stops altogether, since the stock can still be traded on over-the-counter venues.[14]

---

[13] A recent prominent example is Heinz (famous for its ketchup) which was bought by Berkshire Hathaway and 3G in 2013 (New York Times, 2013).

[14] The American-based mining company Molycorp Inc. delisted from NYSE after previously stating restructuring plans and now trades on OTC venues (Nasdaq Globe Newswire, 2015). A more recent example includes the NYSE delisted Silicon-Valley based computer storage provider Violin Memory whose shares are now also traded on over-the-counter venues (Investopedia, 2016).

3 Value – an elusive concept

3.1 Basic valuation concepts

At the core of any IPO transactions is the pricing of shares. There is not one single right way of determining the value of a company, as there is no way of knowing the future of an enterprise for sure. Therefore, there is a wide variety of different valuation methods. There are two prime reasons for that: first, increased importance of business valuation has led to greater research activity. New findings have been used to develop new valuation methods and to improve existing ones (Ernst et al., 2012, p. 1). Second, different causes for valuation require different valuation methods. In Germany, for example, legal provisions define to some extent the valuation method that must be employed under certain circumstances.

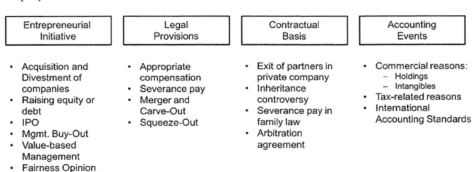

Exhibit 4: Triggering events for financial valuations
Source: Own presentation based on Ernst et al., 2012, p. 1

In contrast to the German literature, valuation methods in the Anglo-Saxon literature are structured based upon its underlying valuation approach, differentiating between market-based, income-based and cost-based valuation approaches (International Valuation Standards Council, 2016, p. 6). Sections 3.1 to 3.3 will briefly point out the different valuation methods in the German literature before turning to the most relevant ones for IPO purposes: the discounted cash-flow valuation and the relative valuation.

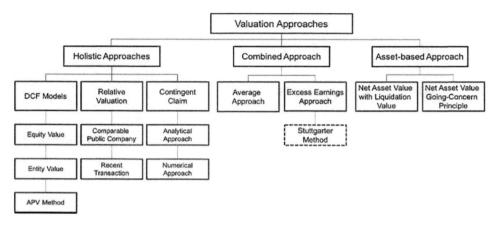

Exhibit 5: Classification of valuation methods in Germany
Source: Own presentation based on Ernst et al., 2012, p. 2

3.1.1 Asset-based Approach

The asset-based approach values the company with its net asset value (NAV) on an effective date. In a first step, all assets are analyzed separately of each other and valued individually. The total of all individually valued assets represents the enterprise value. The NAV is obtained by deducting net debt from the enterprise value.

$$NAV = \text{value of assets} - \text{value of debt} \tag{1}$$

The advantage of asset-based valuation approaches lies in its simplicity since no forecasts are needed. However, as a consequence of its simplicity, the method overlooks profitability, which is commonly regarded as a main value driver. In addition, asset-based approaches are heavily limited in the ability to value intangible assets and do not take account of synergies. Therefore, asset-based approaches are only applied in exceptional circumstances, i.e. companies with poor revenues or in events of insolvency (Ballwieser, 2011, p. 199f).

The German literature distinguishes two variations of asset-based approaches: In the first one, the going-concern principle is assumed for the company. In the second, the NAV is obtained as liquidation value (Ernst et al., 2012, p. 3).

Going-concern is a basic accounting principle that assumes that an entity will remain in business for the foreseeable future (Brealey et al., 2016, p. 79). The idea of NAV based on going-concern principle is to value a company by the costs that it would incur if the company were to be replicated, using a green field approach. The NAV is calculated as follows (Ernst et al., 2012, p. 3):

$$NAV = \text{RV operating assets} + \text{LV non-operating assets} - \text{value of debt} \tag{2}$$

Thereby it is important to note that the reproduction value (RV) of operating assets is based on market values, not on book values. The NAV represents the amount of money that has to be invested to replicate the company as it stands.

In contrast to the NAV based on going-concern principle, the liquidation value assumes the divesture of a business. Liquidation value (LV) describes the value obtained from the break-up of a company where all assets are sold individually (Ballwieser, 2011, p. 199). The NAV is obtained by deducting liquidation costs and debt from the liquidation value (Ernst et al., 2012, p. 5):

$$NAV = LV - \text{liquidation costs} - \text{non-operative assets} - \text{value of debt} \qquad (3)$$

The liquidation value should be applied if it yields higher results than the going-concern approach. Since assets in the liquidation process are often sold at a discount, this is only the case when the business is expected to have ongoing negative results. Quite obviously and based on their static nature, both approaches are not useful for IPO valuation purposes.

3.1.2 Combined valuation methods

One of the main shortcomings of the asset-based valuation approach is the non-consideration of the firm's profitability. To counter that weakness, combined valuation methods were developed, which take into account both NAV and profitability. Ernst et al. distinguish between an average approach and an excess earnings approach. The Stuttgarter method is thereby considered a special case of the excess earnings approach (Ernst et al., 2012, p. 5).

Combined valuation methods are used to get a rough first estimate of an enterprise value. By taking into account the profitability of a business, even though it is only a very crude estimate, they attempt to be more precise than solely asset-based valuation approaches. Nevertheless, combined valuation methods do not yield a reliable, in-depth business valuation and are therefore hardly ever suitable for the more forward looking valuations used in IPO processes (Ernst et al., 2012, p. 5).

The average approach uses the mean of the company's NAV and the capitalized earnings. Capitalized earnings represent the net present value (NPV) of the firm's future profits, discounted at an individually chosen rate of return (Ballwieser, 2011, p. 202):

$$EV = (NAV * x1 + \text{capitalized earnings} * x2) / (x1 + x2) \qquad (4)$$

It must be noted that the weighting of NAV and capitalized earnings are not subject to any rules but personal assessment.

The excess earnings approach is based on the assumption that firms will only achieve a "normal" return on employed capital in the long-term. "Normal" return corresponds to the interest rate paid on, for example, government bonds. Profits that exceed the normal return are considered exceptional and difficult to maintain in the long-term (Ernst et al., 2012, p. 6). Therefore, they are discounted with an additional risk premium. The EV is therefore a combination of NAV and risk adjusted excess earnings:

$$EV = NAV + \text{capitalized excess earnings} \tag{5}$$

The Stuttgarter method is a modified excess earnings approach. Between 1955 and 2008, it was used in Germany to estimate the fair value of shares of non-listed corporations for the purpose of inheritance tax calculations (Ballwieser, 2011, p. 203).

3.1.3   Holistic valuation approaches

In contrast to asset-based and combined valuation methods, holistic valuation approaches focus entirely on future profitability. Therefore, they are more relevant in IPO settings. A business is valued as a unit as opposed to valuing each asset individually. This allows for the recognition of synergies and leads to more realistic valuation results. The most important holistic valuation approaches are the discounted cash flow model, the relative valuation approach, and the contingent claim valuation.

The discounted cash flow (DCF) is the most popular valuation method (Ernst et al., 2012, p. 9). DCF-based methods seek to determine a firm's value by estimating the cash flows it will generate in the future and by discounting them at a discount rate matching the riskiness of these cash flows. The purpose of DCF valuation is to estimate the intrinsic value of an asset (Damodaran, 2006, p. 10). Ernst et al. define three main DCF valuation models: entity valuation, equity valuation, and the adjusted present value approach (2012, p. 9f). The first one discounts free cash flows (FCF) before debt payments and after reinvestment at the cost of capital. The cost of capital considers both debt and equity financing (Damodaran, 2006, p. 11). The purpose of equity valuation is to value the equity stake in a business. Therefore, cash flows to equity, calculated after debt payments, are discounted at the cost of equity. The third variation, adjusted present value (APV), aims to separate the financing effect from the values of the assets. For that reason, in a first step, FCF are discounted at the cost of equity. In a second step, the net financing effect, tax shield benefits minus expected bankruptcy cost, are added. The APV approach allows to see the effect of debt financing (leverage) on the business value (Ernst et al., 2012, p. 10).

In relative valuation based on comparable companies, the value of a firm is derived from the pricing of similar firms. Due to its simplicity, the market-oriented approach is extremely popular in the valuation practice (Damodaran, 2006, p. 16). This approach uses multiples to compare the target's value with market prices of comparable companies. The underlying logic is that similar companies should have a similar value. The result of a relative valuation can be interpreted as potential market price, which could be obtained in a transaction process (Ernst et al., 2012, p. 11).

Contingent claim valuation, also known as real option valuation, is a relatively new valuation approach. Options are securities that are only exercised under certain contingencies. Call options are exercised if the value of the underlying asset outperforms the pre-set value. In contrast, put options are exercised if the value of the underlying asset is lower than the pre-set value (Damodaran, 2006, p. 18). Black and Scholes were the first to establish that an option can be valued as a function of current value, variance in value of the underlying asset, strike price, time to expiration, and riskless interest rate (1972). Real option valuation is increasingly popular as it considers the possibility that firms can learn from real-time developments, as opposed to DCF or relative valuation methods (Damodaran, 2006, p. 18). The approach, however, still awaits a breakthrough in IPO scenarios, probably due to its inherent complexity. Thus, its usefulness in negotiations is still rather limited.

3.2 Discounted cash flow valuation

The underlying logic of the discounted cash flow approach determines the value of an asset as the present value of the expected cash flows it will generate in the future (Damodaran, 2006, p. 25). The difficulty lies in the estimation of discount rates and cash flows. The following sections will cover the estimation of discount rates, the measurement and forecasting techniques for cash flows, and finally different approaches to compute the terminal value.

3.2.1 Estimating discount rates

The discount rates used in DCF valuations should reflect the riskiness of the future cash flows (Damodaran, 2006, p. 27). The more risk an investor accepts with an investment, the higher will be the probability of default. Hence, he will demand higher potential returns for riskier investments (risk-return trade-off) (Campbell & Viceira, 2005, p. 32). Since future cash flows are available to all investors, both equity and debt investors expect compensations for the risks they take. Considering that equity and debt components have different risk profiles and tax ramifications, it must be differentiated between cost of equity and cost of debt (Rosenbaum & Pearl, 2013, p. 127). As shown below, there are two different DCF approaches: Equity method and entity method. It is crucial, to match the discount rate to the DCF approach. In the equity method, only cash flows to equity are taken into account. As a consequence, the discount rate has to reflect the riskiness of these cash flows to equity. In contrast, when the DCF method is applied to determine the enterprise value, free cash flows to both equity and debt investors are discounted by the composed cost of equity and debt. This is called weighted average cost of capital (WACC) (Brealey et al., 2016, p. 492). There is no one single way, which would be better under all circumstances in IPO transactions.

3.2.1.1   Measuring risk

Risk expresses the chance that the actual returns of an investment will differ from the expected returns. Since actual returns can be higher or lower than expected returns, there are two different types of risk. Upside risk describes the chance that actual returns exceed expectations, whereas downside risk depicts the chance of a negative deviation (Damodaran, 2006, p. 27).

Risk is measured as the spread between actual returns, for example in the form of a standard deviation. The greater the deviation, the higher the risk. In practice, it is impossible to estimate the deviation of expected future returns. Hence, the standard deviation is obtained using past returns, assuming that past returns are a reliable indicator for future returns (Damodaran, 2006, p. 29).

The reasons why actual returns may deviate from expected returns can be divided into two categories: diversifiable and non-diversifiable risk (Koller et al., 2010, p. 693ff). Diversifiable risk, also known as specific risk, represents the portion of an asset's risk that is attributable to firm-specific actions. The specific risk can potentially be eliminated by combining several diverse investments in a portfolio, which would reduce the exposure to firm-specific risk (Damodaran, 2012, p. 64). The second category on the other hand, is marked by economy-wide perils that affect all investments (Brealey et al., 2016, p. 174). Non-diversifiable risk, also known as market or systematic risk, are events that cause the entire market to move in the same direction. Therefore, it cannot be mitigated through diversification (Koller et al., 2010, p. 695).

3.2.1.2   Cost of equity based on the Capital Asset Pricing Model

Cost of equity is defined as the rate of return shareholders demand for the risk of investing in a company (Ernst et al., 2012, p. 45). In contrast to the cost of debt, which is directly expressed in the interest rate, the cost of equity is an implicit cost which cannot be observed directly (Damodaran, 2006, p. 28). Therefore, the implicit cost is transformed into an explicit cost using the capital asset pricing model (CAPM). Even though several alternative models to measure market risk have been developed over the last four decades, the CAPM remains the most widely used risk-return model (Graham & Harvey, 2001, p. 232).

The underlying logic of the CAPM is that the cost of equity equals the expected return on an asset ($E[R]$). The expected return is the combination of a risk-free return (R_f) and a risk premium. The risk premium is the product of a market premium ($E[R_m] - R_f$) with a market return of $E[R_m]$ and a company specific risk factor (β) (Sharpe, 1964, p. 442; Fama, 1968):

$$E(R) = R_f + \beta \left[E(R_m) - R_f \right] \tag{6}$$

Beta to capture firm specific risk

The CAPM is built on two key assumptions: markets are frictionless (no taxes or trans-action costs) and reflect perfect information (Fama & French, 2004, p. 25f). Taking these assumptions into account, investors would have no incentive to stop diversifying. Instead, investors would keep diversifying until their portfolio is composed of a small proportion of every asset traded in the economy – the market portfolio (Damodaran, 2012, p. 66). Given that the true market portfolio is unobservable, the DAX, is com-monly used as a proxy for German companies, for example (Ernst et al., 2012, p. 59). In other markets, other indices are used.

The risk of an individual asset is measured in relation to the respective market portfo-lio (Damodaran, 2012, p. 67). If the value of the individual asset and the value of the market portfolio move independently of each other, the asset does not add much risk to the market portfolio since most of the assets risk is firm specific and eliminable through diversification. If, on the other hand, asset and market portfolio move in the same direction, it will add market risk to the portfolio. Therefore, the risk of an asset is determined by the market risk it adds to the portfolio. The covariance describes to which degree the individual asset moves in tandem with the market portfolio (Schira, 2012, p. 93). A positive covariance means that the individual asset and the market portfolio move together, whereas a negative covariance describes an inverse develop-ment. The covariance of the asset with the market portfolio provides information as to whether an asset adds market risk to the portfolio, but in order to compare the riski-ness of different assets, the covariance is divided by the variance of the market portfo-lio. The resulting standardized measure is called beta (Damodaran, 2006, p. 32):

$$Beta\ of\ asset = \frac{covariance\ of\ asset\ with\ market\ portfolio}{variance\ of\ the\ market\ portfolio} \tag{7}$$

Beta can be interpreted as a measure of an asset's systematic risk in comparison to the market portfolio (Mercer & Harms, 2008, p. 166). Since the beta of the market is one, assets with betas greater than one offer little diversification in relation to the market and are therefore riskier than the market. In contrast, assets with betas inferior to one offer protection against market downturns, which is why they are less risky than the average. A beta of zero defines a riskless asset (Mercer & Harms, 2008, p. 166).

In addition to the operating risk, a company's beta is also a function of the financial risk. In good times, the tax shield effect of debt will overweigh the associated interest payments and therefore, increase net income, whereas in bad times the effect is re-versed. Consequently, a higher debt-to-equity ratio increases the variance of earnings per share and subsequently, the risk exposure (Damodaran, 2012, p. 195). In order to compare betas across industries, the leverage effect must be netted out. The equity beta (leveraged beta, β_l) equals a company's operational beta (unleveraged beta, β_u) times a leverage factor, the market value of debt to equity (Koller et al., 2010, p. 255).

$$\beta_1 = \beta_u(1 + \frac{D}{E}) \tag{8}$$

As all investors are assumed to hold the market portfolio, the risk premium demanded by investors is proportional to beta since beta measures each security's contribution to the market portfolio risk (Brealey et al., 2016, p. 201).

The risk-free rate is a theoretical concept

A risk-free rate is the return of an investment where the investor knows the expected return with certainty, leaving no uncertainty that actual returns will match expected returns (Ernst et al., 2012, p. 51). In order to be classified as risk-free investment, there must not be any default risk and no reinvestment risk. This implies that the investment has to be a zero-coupon bond, to eliminate intermediate cash flows. Ideally, the zero-coupon government bond should have the same maturity as the cash flows. However, using matched risk-free rates for cash flows of different periods has shown to have only a marginal effect on the present value (Damodaran, 2012, p. 155). Furthermore, it is important to use government bonds of the same currency as the asset's cash flows, to maintain consistency regarding inflation (Koller et al., 2010, p. 241). Although no investment is ever completely free of risk, even though long-term German or US Government bonds are considered practically risk-free investments because time and amount of repayments are determined and the probability of default approximates zero.

3.2.1.3   Cost of debt

Even though equity is undoubtedly a cornerstone of a company's financing structure, most businesses take on debt to fund some of their projects (Damodaran, 2012, p. 210). Debt is defined as a form of financing, where an external stakeholder provides capital against contractually fixed interest payments and the repayment of the principle (Wöhe et al., 2013, p. 14).

The cost of debt mirrors the cost that would be incurred if a company borrowed new funds (Damodaran, 2006, p. 64). It reflects the company's credit profile at the target capital structure and is composed of two factors: the risk-free rate (R_f) and a risk premium representing the probability of default (R_{Pd}) (Ernst et al., 2012, p. 83):

$$Pre - tax\ cost\ of\ debt = R_f + R_{Pd} \tag{9}$$

As the risk-free rate has already been covered in the course of the CAPM in the previous section, this section will not deal with the derivation of the risk-free rate again.

The second component, the default risk, measures the probability that a firm cannot meet its interest and principal payments. It mirrors the businesses creditworthiness, which itself is a function of two variables: the firm's ability to create cash flows relative to its financial obligations, and the volatility in these cash flows (Damodaran, 2006, p. 64).

For companies with investment grade debt (BBB or better), financial literature unanimously suggests to estimate the cost of debt as the yield to maturity (YTM) on its outstanding long-term, option-free bonds (Damodaran, 2012, p. 211; Koller et al., 2010, p. 261; Ernst et al., 2012, p. 83). These bonds need to be liquid for the market price to be accurate, long-term to match the duration of the company's cash flows, and option-free as options tend to have an impact on bond prices but not the cash flows. With market price, coupon and maturity of the long-term bond being known, the yield to maturity can be obtained by reverse engineering the present value calculation, representing the discount rate required to match the present value of the bond's cash flows and its market price (Koller et al., 2010, p. 261)

$$Market\ price = \frac{coupon}{(1+YTM)} + \frac{coupon}{(1+YTM)^2} + \cdots + \frac{face+coupon}{(1+YTM)^N} \tag{10}$$

For companies with long-term bonds but below-investment-grade ratings (which tends to be the case for most IPO candidates if they issue bonds, at all), opinions on the best approach to estimate cost of debt differ. Damodaran recommends applying the same estimation process for below-investment-grade debt companies as stated for firms with investment grade debt (2006, p. 65). In contrast, Koller et al. argue that the expected cash flows in an enterprise valuation need to be discounted by the promised rate of return. In the case of investment grade firms, the probability of default is low enough that the YTM, actually only a proxy for expected return, converges to a promised yield. For companies with ratings below BBB, the YTM does not approximate the promised return, because the probability of default is too high. Therefore, Koller et al. advise to use the adjusted present value on unlevered cost of equity to value companies with below-investment-grade debt (2010, p. 261). Finally, Ernst et al. suggest deriving the default risk premium for non-investment grade firms as the average YTM of bonds issued by peer group companies. The peer group companies should be equivalent to the target company in terms of business model, financials, and especially, credit rating (2012, p. 83f). For non-investment grade companies, this approach would derive the default risk premium from comparable non-investment grade companies, which is why this method shares resemblances with the one supported by Damodaran.

For rated companies with only short-term bonds or bonds that rarely trade, the default risk premium can be estimated using their credit ratings and the associated default spreads (Damodaran, 2012, p. 211). Financial data provider like Factset offer comprehensive information about the yield spread of corporate bond ratings over government securities. Once the company's credit rating is known, it can be converted into a yield to maturity (Koller et al., 2010, p. 262f).

Table 2:   Yield spread (2009 avg.) in basis points over US Treasuries by bond rating

Rating	Maturity in years			
	2	5	10	30
Aaa /AAA	59	69	58	139
Aa2 /AAA	140	160	139	179
A1 / A+	153	169	139	182
A2 / A	178	193	152	190
A3 / A-	194	210	177	199
Baa1 / BBB+	310	333	288	320
Baa2 / BBB	315	338	292	324
Baa3/ BBB-	408	433	380	416
Ba2 / BB	583	590	545	577
B2 / B	916	925	878	904

Source: Koller et al., 2010, p. 263

Table 2 shows corporate yield spreads over US Treasuries. For a US-based company with a credit rating of A, the total cost of debt would be the sum of the risk-free rate plus the default risk premium over a 10 year US Treasury. Overall, financial literature agrees that the indirect method of calculating the YTM using the company's bond ratings is a good alternative if YTM cannot be determined directly (Damodaran, 2012, p. 211; Koller et al., 2010, p. 263).

Private firms are usually not covered by rating agencies. If no rating is available, there are two alternatives to obtain their default risk (Damodaran, 2006, p. 65): the first one is looking at the most recent cost of borrowing. Despite not having a credit rating, many firms still obtain debt capital from financial institutions. Assuming a company's risk profile remains fairly constant in the short term, the use of the most recently charged default spread on a loan is a reasonable technique to estimate the cost of debt.

The second option is to assign a credit rating to the company based on its financial ratios. For this purpose, financial ratios for the unrated firm are calculated and compared to ratios of rated companies within each rating class. A widely-employed method to compare the default risk of different companies is the Altman Z-score. It is a linear combination of five financial ratios weighted by coefficients (Altman, 1968, p. 609).[15]

---

[15] The five ratios are: working capital/total assets, retained earnings/total assets, EBIT/total assets, market value of equity/book value of total liabilities, sales/total assets (Altman, 1968, p. 594f)

Since each rating class has a defined Z-score interval, it is possible to assign a credit rating to the target company after calculating its score level.

As section 3.2 will show in more detail, cash flows are computed as if the company was completely financed by equity. Consequently, the tax shield effect of debt is not factored into the cash flow calculation. However, since interest payments are tax deductible, the tax shield hast to be acknowledged by deducting the marginal tax rate from the cost of debt (Koller et al., 2010, p. 265):

$$\text{After-tax cost of debt} = \text{tax cost of debt (1-marginal tax rate)} \tag{11}$$

The marginal tax rate is the present value of current and expected future taxes paid on an additional Euro of income (Graham, 1996, p. 190). Knowing that interest expenses are deducted from the last Euro of income, the tax rate should be applied to the last Euro of a company's taxable income as well. Therefore, the marginal tax rate is the preferred rate to apply (Damodaran, 2012, p. 213).

Companies however, need to be profitable in order to benefit from the tax advantages of debt financing. In his research on simulating realizable marginal tax rates, Graham concluded that the marginal tax rate exceeds the future marginal tax rate due to tax-loss carry-forwards, tax-loss carry-backs, and investment tax credits (Graham, 1996, p. 218; Graham & Mills, 2008, p. 386). As a result, he suggests employing the statutory marginal tax rate for investment grade firms, since the probability of operating losses for these companies is relatively low. For other firms, however, which do not always experience the full tax-shield advantage due to operating losses, Graham's research indicates that the actual marginal tax rate is on average five percent lower than the statutory rate (Koller et al., 2010, p. 265).

3.2.1.4 Weighted Average Cost of Capital

The weighted average cost of capital (WACC) represents the required return on the invested capital in a company. It is also referred to as the opportunity cost of capital since it describes the expectations of investors if they were to invest in alternative investments with similar risk profiles (Rosenbaum & Pearl, 2013, p. 141).

With the estimates for after-tax cost of debt (r_D) and cost of equity (r_E) being covered already, the only components missing are the weights of debt (D/V) and equity (E/V) to enterprise value, on market value basis (Brealey et al., 2016, p. 224).

$$WACC = r_D \frac{D}{V} + r_E \frac{E}{V} \tag{12}$$

Due to simplification reasons, the formula only differentiates between equity and interest bearing liabilities. Nevertheless, there is no problem in expanding the formula with additional sources of capital with different risk profiles like mezzanine capital or preferred shares (Ernst et al., 2012, p. 46). The required return for each additional form of capital would be weighted according to its proportion to the enterprise value. If companies have diverse business segments with different cost of capital rates, financial literature suggests performing a sum-of-the-parts analysis (Rosenbaum & Pearl, 2013, p. 141)

Weights for debt and equity should be computed using market values because the cost of capital is a forward-looking approach. It measures the cost that would be incurred if a company decided to raise new funds by issuing securities. As securities are issued at current market prices, the market value is more accurate when assessing the capital structure (Damodaran, 2006, p. 70):

$$\text{Total capital} = \text{equity} + \text{interest-bearing debt}^{16} \tag{13}$$

Instead of using the current capital structure, the cost of capital should be based on a target capital structure. This is because a target capital structure is expected to reflect the capital structure more consistently over the life of the firm (Koller et al., 2010, p. 266). In practice, a combination of three steps has proven to be a suitable estimation for the target capital structure: The first step is to estimate the company's current capital structure based on market values. Second, the current capital structure is compared with the company's peer group. In the last step, the management's financing philosophy is reviewed regarding the possible implications for the target capital structure (Koller et al., 2010, p. 266).[17]

In order to reflect the interest-bearing debt correctly, the outstanding liabilities disclosed on the firm's balance sheet must be adjusted for positions that are not listed as liabilities but still meet the definition of debt capital. The most popular of these off-balance sheet positions are operating lease commitments (Damodaran, 2012, p. 217). In difference to capital leases, operating leases are disclosed in the income statement instead of the balance sheet because the lessee does not assume the risk of ownership of the asset. Instead, the lessee returns the property to the lessor at the end of the lease period (Damodaran, 2006, p. 72). Still, operational lease commitments meet the essential characteristic of debt as they give rise to a tax-deductible obligation. A non-payment of this obligation can lead to bankruptcy or a loss of equity control over the firm (Damodaran, 2006, p. 72). Therefore, all lease payments should be regarded as financial expenses. Additionally, the lease operating commitments in future years should be converted into debt by discounting them to present at the firm's current pre-tax cost of borrowing (Damodaran, 2006, p. 72). The resulting present value describes the debt value of operating leases and should be added to the firm's conventional debt (Damodaran, 2006, p. 86):

---

[16] Even though interest-free liabilities bear also implied costs, these costs are factored in the price of the asset which was paid with the liability (Ernst et al., 2012, p. 46)

[17] This will be discussed in more detail below.

Adjusted debt = debt + present value of lease commitments   (14)

As a consequence of this adjustment, the operating income must be modified as well, adding back the operating lease expenses and deducting the depreciation on the leased assets (Damodaran, 2006, p. 72):

Stated operating income
+ operating lease expenses for current year
− depreciation on leased assets
= Adjusted operating income   (15)

The estimation of a firm's debt at market value is associated with more difficulties than the estimation of equity because very few firms have all their debt in the form of traded securities (Ballwieser, 2011, p. 49). Especially European firms tend to have non-traded debt, with the book value being disclosed in the balance sheet. In this case, Damodaran suggests converting book value into market value (DMV) by treating the total book value of debt (DBV) as a coupon bond, where the coupon is the interest expenses (IE) on the debt. The maturity (t) of the coupon bond is determined by the maturity of all debt, weighted by face value. Last, the coupons and face values are discounted to present using the current cost of debt (r_D) of the company (2006, p. 73):

$$D_{MV} = IE \left[\frac{1 - \frac{1}{(1+r_D)^t}}{r_D} \right] + \frac{D_{BV}}{(1+r_D)^t}$$ (16)

In order to accomplish a more accurate result for the company's debt at market value, the same process can be conducted valuing each debt instrument individually (Damodaran, 2006, p. 73). A third approach allows for the simplifying assumption that book value, in the case of mature companies in developed markets, reasonably approximates the current market value (Koller et al., 2010, p. 267). However, this does not apply if the interest rate has changed since the issuance or if the company has liquidity issues.

In practice, the market value of equity is obtained by mathematical iteration. First, the market value of equity is estimated to get the company's capital structure. On that basis, the provisional WACC is calculated, which in turn, is employed to discount the cash flows and arrive at the provisional equity value to market prices. This process is repeated until the equity value does not change anymore (Ernst et al., 2012, p. 49).

The estimation of market-based equity in private firms can be approached using multiples. Thereby, the equity value of a public peer group company is adopted for the private company (Damodaran, 2006, p. 73).

In the second step for the estimation of a suitable target capital structure, the current capital structure is compared with the capital structure of its peer group companies. Market data reveals that industries with high investments in intangible assets, like healthcare and software, have a very low proportion of debt capital. In contrast, industries with high investments in tangible assets tend to have higher debt-to-value ratios (Koller et al., 2010, p. 269).

Finally, the management's financing philosophy is reviewed. Even though firms are expected to minimize cost of capital in the long-term, individual events can cause the capital structure to diverge from its defined target capital structure (Koller et al., 2010, p. 269), i.e. an acquisition financed by debt is an event that may have a significant impact on a company's capital structure.

3.2.2 Measuring cash flows

The value of an asset derives from its capacity to generate cash flows. In DCF valuations, the expected cash flows are usually divided into two periods: a planning period and the time lapse after the planning period. Therefore, a company's value can be estimated as follows (Koller et al., 2010, p. 213):

$$
\begin{aligned}
& \text{Present value of cash flows during explicit forecast period} \\
+ & \underline{\text{Present value of cash flows after explicit forecasting period}} \\
= & \text{Company Value} \tag{17}
\end{aligned}
$$

This section will cover the process how cash flows are derived from earnings. For that, the first step consists in estimating earnings. The second step entails the analysis of the tax effect on earnings and finally, the reinvestment rate is examined. The next section will deal with the forecasting of cash flows during the explicit planning period, whereas the continuing value, the third part of the equation, will be subject of the final section in this chapter.

3.2.2.1 Measuring earnings

The estimation process of cash flows begins with accounting earnings. In an entity valuation, both debt and capital investors have claims on the company's free cash flows. Thus, the free cash flow to entity is based on the operating income (EBIT). For equity valuations in contrast, cash flows are only available to shareholders, which is why they are based on net income (EY TAS, 2016, p. 158).

When using earnings as a starting point to calculate cash flows it is important to update earnings, to correct the values for accounting misclassifications, and to consider the difference between true earnings and accounting earnings (Damodaran, 2006, p. 80).

The business environment and companies themselves have become increasingly dynamic. Given how much firms can change in the short-term, it is important to use the most recent earnings available to derive cash flows. If companies publish a quarterly report, the data of the most recent quarter can be aggregated to obtain a trailing 12-month financial statement. Using earnings estimated with a trailing 12-month financial statement has shown to provide more accurate results than the last annual report, especially for young firms (Damodaran, 2006, p. 81).

Furthermore, earnings must be adjusted as expenses are sometimes misclassified by accounting standards. Generally, there are three types of expenses that occur in a firm (Damodaran, 2006, p. 81): operating expenses, capital expenses, and financial expenses. The first category to be adjusted is capital expenses which are treated as operating expenses. The most common shortcoming of accounting statements is to classify R&D expenses as operating expenses, reasoning that it is not possible to quantify the results of R&D activities aptly. Consequently, R&D disbursements are expensed in the period in which they occur and the value of the asset created by R&D is not reflected on the balance sheet. Therefore, financial literature unanimously agrees to capitalize capital expenses (Damodaran, 2006, p. 82; Koller et al., 2010, p. 121). For this, the amortizable life (n) of the assets is to be estimated. It is the expected time-period needed to convert the research efforts into commercial products. In a second step, the R&D expenses are obtained for each year of the amortizable life. Assuming linear amortization, the value of the R&D asset can be calculated as follows (Damodaran, 2006, p. 83):

$$Value\ of\ R\&D\ asset = \sum_{t=-(n-1)}^{nt=0} R\&D_t \frac{n+t}{n} \tag{18}$$

To illustrate this process using the R&D expenses for a drug development of a biotech firm, an amortizable life of 15 years seems reasonable since the approval process is long. The cumulated value of the asset would be 1/15 of the R&D expenses 14 years ago, 2/15 of R&D 13 years ago, all the way to the full value of this year's expenses. The value of the R&D asset is then added to the book value of equity and amortized each year using the same amortization process shown in (18) (Damodaran, 2006, p. 83).

The final step consists in adjusting the operating income and the net income. The R&D expenses, which were initially deducted from the operating income, are added back, whilst the amortization of the R&D asset is subtracted from operating income (Damodaran, 2006, p. 83):

Adjusted op. income = op. income + R&D expenses – amortization of asset (19)

R&D expenses are capitalized for companies with a high research activity because they are expected to create benefits over multiple periods.[18] Following the same logic, consumer product firms could argue that advertising costs are a main contributor to brand value and consultancies could capitalize a portion of its training expenses (Damodaran, 2006, p. 85).

---

[18] R&D expenses in pharma & biotech are typically not capitalized due to the very high degree of uncertainty of clinical trial, regulatory environment and market success.

The second category that must be adjusted is financial expenses, counted as operating expenses. The most significant misclassification, lease expenses, has already been covered during the determination of cost of capital in the previous section,

When comparing earnings estimations by analysts with reported earnings, it stands out how often companies beat their estimations. The outperformance can partly be explained by a procedure called earnings management, which describes the use of accounting techniques to avoid reporting earnings decreases (Burgstahler & Dichev, 1997, p. 101). Therefore, knowing that accounting earnings do not always reflect true earnings, a series of adjustments is made to the stated income before using it to predict future cash flows. The first adjustment relates to extraordinary expenses, which are not included in the operating income. Nevertheless, there are two types of extraordinary expenses that must be considered when using EBIT to project cash flows. The first one is "expenses and income that do not occur every year but do seem to recur at regular intervals" (Damodaran, 2012, p. 243). The expense should be distributed over the effective years and the resulting annual average should be subtracted from the EBIT. The second type describes expenses and income "that recur every year but with considerable volatility" (Damodaran, 2012, p. 243). In this case, the value should be normalized by calculating an average over a reasonable period. The normalized expense (income) is then deducted (added) from this year's operating income. The second adjustment refers to the goodwill in acquisitions. If impairments are found during the annual impairment test, the goodwill is amortized (Ballwieser et al., 2005, p. 193). Goodwill amortization will reduce net income but not operating income, which leads to an inconsistency between the two values. Therefore, the safest approach is to use earnings prior to the amortization (Damodaran, 2012, p. 244).

3.2.2.2 Determining cash flows

This section will cover the adjustments that must be made to the adjusted EBIT or net income value to obtain free cash flows.

Free cash flow is the amount of cash that a company can pay out to investors after having met all investments necessary for growth (Brealey et al., 2016, p. 94). Starting point for the calculation of free cash flows is the operating income (EBIT). Thereof, adjusted taxes are deducted to arrive at the net operating profit less adjusted taxes (NOPLAT) (Ernst et al., 2012, p. 32). In the next step, changes in working capital are subtracted from NOPLAT, since they reflect tied-up cash in operating assets. Finally, the free cash flow is obtained by deducting changes in net capital expenditure (Ernst et al., 2012, p. 33):

$$FCF = EBIT(1-t) - \Delta \text{net working capital} - \Delta \text{net capital expenditure} \qquad (20)$$

To obtain the after-tax operating income, a tax rate must be applied to EBIT (Damodaran, 2012, p. 250). Generally, in DCF valuation it is of the utmost importance to preserve consistency between the calculation of cash flows and the calculation of discount rates. Therefore, the tax rate should be applied in the same logic as during the calculation of after-tax cost of debt in the previous chapter. For investment grade companies, the statutory marginal tax rate should be used, whereas for companies with a worse creditworthiness, the statutory marginal tax rate less five percent yields on average more accurate results (Koller et al., 2010, p. 265). This is due to the fact that firms can carry net operating losses forward until their results turn positive, providing the firm with a potential for considerable tax savings. An alternative approach consists in applying the marginal tax rate and adding the amount of the expected tax savings to the firm's value (Damodaran, 2012, p. 254).

The second adjustment that must be made to derive cash flows from adjusted earnings is the net investment in capital. Net capital expenditure is defined as the difference between capital expenditures and depreciation. It makes sense to net out the positions capital expenditures (CAPEX) and depreciation given that depreciation is used to finance (at least a portion of) capital expenditures. Firms' capital expenditure tends to fluctuate significantly throughout the years, moving in the pattern that a period of high CAPEX is generally followed by CAPEX light periods (Damodaran, 2012, p. 259). Therefore, using the CAPEX of the most recent year bears the risk of over- or understating the future CAPEX. Financial literature describes two ways to normalize CAPEX (Damodaran, 2012, p. 259): The first one averages CAPEX over a certain period, commonly the time from one CAPEX intensive year to the next one. However, even the average of a complete CAPEX cycle may not be fully representative, given that there can be considerable discrepancies of capital expenditures between different cycles. The second approach uses industry averages of capital expenditures to project the company's CAPEX. In order to compare figures of differently sized companies, CAPEX is usually expressed in relation to total assets, sales, or depreciation.

The adjustment of capital earnings that are treated as operating earnings has already been subject of the above section. Operating expenses like R&D costs were capitalized and added to CAPEX. Considering that the capitalization of operating expenses creates an asset, the depreciation of that asset has to be factored in as well (Damodaran, 2012, p. 260):

$$\text{Adjusted CAPEX} = \text{CAPEX} + \text{capitalized expenses} - \text{amortization of assets} \quad (21)$$

The change in net capital expenditure is equivalent to the change in after-tax operating income. Therefore, capitalizing operating expenses has no impact on free cash flow but on earnings and reinvestment estimates (Damodaran, 2012, p. 261).

The last adjustment to be made to EBIT is the investment in working capital (WC). Working capital measures the amount of cash tied-up in operating assets. Net working capital for non-financial firms is typically defined as the difference between operating current assets and non-interest-bearing current liabilities (Rosenbaum & Pearl, 2013,

p. 137). Excess cash and marketable securities are specifically excluded, as they are per definition not necessary for core operations. Thus, they do not contribute to the creation of value (Koller et al., 2010, p. 145). Copeland defines excess cash as the amount of cash that exceeds 0.5%-2.0% of revenues (Copeland et al., 2002, p. 187).

Working capital underlies significant seasonal and even yearly fluctuations (Nwankwo & Osho, 2010, p. 8). To counter the fluctuations, working capital should be measures in relation to revenues or cost of goods sold over a reasonable period (Damodaran, 2012, p. 265).

3.2.3   Forecasting cash flows

One of the most important inputs in DCF valuation is the growth rate used to forecast future revenues and earnings (Koller et al., 2010, p. 189). After establishing the length of the detailed forecast in the first place, this chapter will contrast the three basic approaches to estimate growth. It begins with the projection of historical growth rates followed by the second approach to use analysts' estimates for future growth. The third option estimates growth based on the firm's fundamentals such as the amount and quality of its reinvestments (Damodaran, 2012, p. 271).

3.2.3.1   Length and detail of the forecast

The detailed planning period mirrors the phase in which a company's cash flows are explicitly projected for each year (Rosenbaum & Pearl, 2013, p. 131). The present value of the cash flows generated in the explicit forecast period is the first part of the enterprise value, complemented by the discounted terminal value, the continuing value of the firm after the explicit forecasting period. The continuing value must be based on a stable cash flow, as it represents all future cash flows after the explicit forecasting period. Therefore, the explicit forecast period should be long enough for the company to reach a steady state (Koller et al., 2010, p. 188). A company reaches a steady state when it grows at a constant rate and earns a constant rate of return on invested capital (Koller et al., 2010, p. 188).

The time it takes a company to reach the steady state is affected by the size of the firm, the existing growth rate, and the sustainability of competitive advantages (Damodaran, 2006, p. 118). For smaller firms, it is easier to earn and maintain excess returns than for mature firms, as they are less saturated and further away from reaching their maximum potential. Furthermore, research indicates that rapidly growing firms are likely to continue growing above industry average at least in the medium term (Stuart, 2000, p. 803). Finally, a firm's ability to uphold competitive advantages has a strong impact on its capability to maintain high growth.

3.2.3.2   Historical performance

When estimating future growth for a firm, the historical performance is often used as a first indicator even if it tends to be of limited use for a lot of young IPO candidates.

The average growth rate can be computed in two different ways, using the arithmetic average or the geometric average (Damodaran, 2006, p. 121):

$$Arithmetic\ average = \frac{\sum_{t=-n}^{t=-1} growth\ rate\ of\ earnings_t}{n} \tag{22}$$

$$Geometric\ average = \left[\frac{earnings_0}{earnings_{-n}}\right]^{\frac{1}{n}} - 1 \tag{23}$$

The arithmetic mean ignores compounding effects and weights each observation equally. In contrast, the geometric mean compounds observation but ignores any interim trends, as it only considers the first and the last observation (Schira, 2012, p. 246). Both methods can lead to significantly different results, although the geometric mean has proven to yield more reliable results (Little, 1962, p. 391).[19]

3.2.3.3   Analyst estimates of growth

In theory, analyst estimates should be more accurate than historical growth rates, because they can factor in additional information, such as public firm-specific information, macroeconomic information, information disclosed by competitors, or even private information about the firm (Damodaran, 2006, p. 125). Despite numerous studies comparing long-term forecasts of security analysts and time-series models, there is no uniform picture about which method achieves better results.

Nevertheless, analyst estimates should be incorporated into the prediction of expected future growth, especially when there is recent firm-specific information which is not represented in the historical data-based models. However, analyst estimates have to be used with caution because they can contain significant errors, like ignoring the earnings cycle when forecasting earnings for cyclical companies (Koller et al., 2010, p. 758).

3.2.4   Estimation of terminal value

The terminal value represents the company's value after the explicit forecast period. There are three ways to obtain a firm's terminal value. The liquidation approach assumes that the company is shut down at some point and the assets are sold. In the second approach, an exit multiple is applied to the company's estimated earnings or book value. Finally, the stable growth model assumes that the business creates steady cash flows until infinity, which are then discounted to present. For the purpose of assessing IPO candidates only the latter is useful.

---

[19] There are other approaches which measure historical performance better than the arithmetic or geometric average, including ordinary least squares, a method to estimate unknown variables in regression models, or time-series models (Box, 2013, p. 215; Foster, 1977, p. 21). However, they are not analyzed in this paper, as they tend to be of little use in IPO circumstances.

In the going-concern approach, the terminal value represents all future cash flows of a company after the explicit forecasting period, discounted to present (Brealey et al., 2016, p. 498ff). It is important that the cash flow, discount rate, and growth rate used in the TV calculation are sustainable forever. Otherwise, the terminal value will be distorted which would have an immense influence on the valuation as the TV accounts for 60% – 90% of the entity value (EY TAS, 2016, p. 99).

Assuming the company has reached a steady state after the detailed planning period, its cash flows are expected to grow into perpetuity at a constant rate (g). Using the Gordon Model, the terminal value can be computed as follows (Gordon, 1962):

$$Terminal\ value_n = \frac{CF\ to\ firm_{n+1}}{WACC_{n+1}-g} \tag{30}$$

Thereby, the cash flows are either distributed or reinvested in the enterprise discounted at the WACC (Mercer & Harms, 2008, p. 6).

Considering that growth only creates value if the return exceeds the cost of capital, a common approach is to modify the terminal value formula introducing a measure of return (Koller et al., 2010, p. 214):

$$Terminal\ value_n = \frac{NOPLAT_{n-1}(1-\frac{g}{RONIC})}{WACC_{n+1}-g} \tag{31}$$

The expected return on new invested capital (RONIC) expresses the company's ability to maintain competitive advantages, which in turn, result in excessive returns. If the magnitude of competitive advantages cannot be sustained in the competitive industries, the excess returns might eventually draw in new competitors so that the return on new invested capital converges to the WACC and the economic value added equals zero (ROIC – WACC).

The stable growth rate is the input factor that has the biggest repercussion on terminal value. Even small changes can have a significant impact on terminal value (Damodaran, 2012, p. 306). To be sustainable in infinity, the stable growth rate cannot exceed the overall growth rate of the economy for long periods, knowing that overall economy growth is comprised of both younger firms and more mature companies. Thus, the growth rate should be estimated as the expected long-term growth rate for the industry plus inflation (Koller et al., 2010, p. 216).

3.3   Relative valuation

Even though the discounted cash flow analysis is the theoretically most accurate method to value businesses, multiples are widely used to triangulate results. Relative valuation is based on the logic that the value of an asset is comparable to the market value of similar assets (Koller et al., 2010, p. 314).

The first step in a multiple analysis is to identify comparable companies that will constitute the peer group. In a second step, the financial information of the peer group companies is compiled and processed. The third step is to compute the multiple consistently over all comparable companies. Once the multiples are obtained for each peer group company, the fourth step consists in aggregating the median, average, maximum and minimum peer group multiple. Finally, the median peer group multiple is projected to the target company to calculate the firm value (Ernst et al., 2012, p. 190).

3.3.1 Peer group

The prerequisite for a multiple valuation is the availability of peer group multiples. Therefore, the first step consists in selecting a group of comparable companies. Comparable companies are defined as firms with similar cash flows, growth potentials, and risk profiles (Damodaran, 2012, p. 462). In practice, the peer group is commonly constituted using competitors disclosed in the annual report, peers from the same industry, or companies from different industries which still show similar characteristics in terms of financials and size.

While companies from the same industry tend to have similar risk profiles and consequently similar costs of capital, growth and profitability can often vary significantly within an industry (Koller et al., 2010, p. 326). Therefore, it is important to analyze factors that affect growth and profitability such as production methodology, distribution channels, and research and development when selecting peer group companies (Koller et al., 2010, p. 327).

3.3.2 Types of multiples

Since stock prices of different companies cannot be compared directly, the value of companies must be standardized relative to firm specific financials. Multiples standardize a firm's value relating the enterprise or equity value to a certain reference value at a determined point in time (Ernst et al., 2012, p. 190). Analogous to the DCF approach, multiples can be used to estimate the enterprise value or the equity value. The equity value corresponds to the market capitalization whereas the entity value refers to the value of the entire operating business (Brealey et al., 2016, p. 77).

$$Equtiy\ value\ multiple = \frac{equity\ value}{reference\ equity\ value} \tag{32}$$

$$Enterprise\ value\ multiple = \frac{enterprise\ value}{reference\ enterprise\ value} \tag{33}$$

The reference value can be a figure from the balance sheet, the income statement, the cash flow statement, or any other company specific financial information.

3.3.2.1   Income statement multiples

Given that a firm's value depends on its ability to generate future returns, income statement multiples are the most accurate ratios in relative valuation. This section will cover the two most commonly used multiples for equity value and enterprise value, beginning with the price/earnings ratio and moving on to the enterprise value/EBITDA multiple.

The price/earnings multiple is the ratio of the market capitalization (per share) to the earnings (per share) (Ernst et al., 2012, p. 204):

$$P/E = \frac{market\ capitalisation}{net\ income} \tag{34}$$

The P/E ratio can be interpreted as the number of years it takes the investor to regain the invested capital. Given that the reference value, net income, is calculated after interest and tax, the P/E multiple is affected by both the capital structure and the national tax system. Furthermore, net income is calculated after non-operating items such as amortization of intangible assets or non-recurring effects (Koller et al., 2010, p. 317). Therefore, the underlying input variables have to be normalized in order to compare P/E multiples from international companies with different tax systems, varying leverage, and non-operating items.

The EV/ EBITDA multiple relates the enterprise value to earnings before interest, taxes, and amortization (Ernst et al., 2012, p. 203):

$$EV/EBITDA = \frac{enterprise\ value}{EBITDA} \tag{35}$$

This multiple offers several advantages over the P/E multiple. First, there are fewer companies with negative EBITDA than with negative net income. Thus, fewer firms drop out of the peer group analysis. Moreover, EV/EBITDA is not affected by possible differences in the depreciation methods or accounting rules across different companies. Therefore, EV/EBITDA is particularly useful for valuing companies in sectors that are marked by high capital expenditures (Damodaran, 2012, p. 500).

However, using the EV/EBITDA multiple implies that the target firm has the same depreciation rate as the peer group. If the depreciation rates differ, the amortization will be different as well. Adding back amortization to the cash flow, different depreciation rates lead to different cash flows at the same EBITDA level (Ernst et al., 2012, p. 203). Therefore, EV/EBITDA does not constitute a suitable valuation measure for companies with widely different depreciation rates.

3.3.2.2   Balance sheet multiples

As book values are affected by accounting standards, the price-to-book value (PBV) is the only balance sheet multiple that is commonly used in practice (Ernst, et al., 2012, p. 196):

$$PBV = \frac{market\ capitalisation}{book\ value\ of\ equity} \tag{36}$$

The market value of a company's equity reflects the market's expectations regarding its future earning power and cash flows (Damodaran, 2012, p. 511). In contrast, the book value of equity, defined as the difference between a company's total assets and liabilities, reflects the historical development of the company along with its dividend pay-out policy. Therefore, the PBV can be interpreted as the earnings potential of the company's equity.

3.3.3   Principles of relative valuation

The popularity of the multiple approach is mostly due to its lower complexity compared to a discounted cash flow valuation (Rosenbaum & Pearl, 2013, p. 13). However, it can easily result in inconsistent estimates if it is misused. To ensure that the comparable companies reflect the mood of the market correctly, there are three basic principles that must be complied with.

Multiples are financial ratios comprising of a numerator and a denominator. These can be either equity values or firm values. However, it is important to define the multiple in a consistent manner. If the numerator represents an equity value, the denominator must be an equity value as well and vice versa (Damodaran, 2012, p. 456). Otherwise, depending on the individual capital structures, the multiples are not comparable between different companies.

Furthermore, multiples must be defined uniformly across all firms regarding accounting standards and time periods. Only if the same accounting rules are applied to earnings and book values and the values relate to the same period the multiples will be comparable. In addition, the financial information for each company must be adjusted for any non-recurring items and recent events (Rosenbaum & Pearl, 2013, p. 44ff)

Finally, a multiple analysis might yield results that are not meaningful. While the median peer group multiple tends to be less affected by outliners, the average multiple would not be representative. Therefore, outliers must either be ignored when computing the average or substituted by a fixed value (Damodaran, 2012, p. 459).

Part 2: IPO – what does it really mean for a company?

The second part of this IPO book will look at the implications of an IPO on a company from various perspectives. As an experienced investment banking professional, the author draws on his first-hand practical experience from working on numerous IPO projects as a core team member, often leading these IPO projects on a day-to-day basis. During this time, the author has built significant expertise around many IPO-related matters that he discusses in the following section.

Chapter 4 looks at the IPO from a financial perspective and sets out the major financial implications for the IPO company. Key topics covered include the relevance of capital market access, capital structuring considerations, offer structure, use of proceeds and costs of an IPO.

Chapter 5 looks at the IPO from an execution perspective and sets out major aspects of getting an IPO done. Key topics covered include setup of a typical project organization and description of each party's role, project timeline, timing considerations and real-life perspectives from behind the curtain.

Chapter 6 looks at the IPO from a preparation perspective and sets out important considerations around required preparations of a company ahead of a potential IPO. Key topics covered include corporate governance and compliance, management information and reporting systems, business planning and the Equity Story.

To conclude the second part, Chapter 7 looks beyond the actual IPO and elaborates on key considerations of being a public company. Key topics covered include implications of increased media attention and ongoing disclosure obligations.

4 Money, money, money

4.1 Access to public equity capital markets

Private companies have limited equity financing alternatives

Equity capital is a key pillar of every company's capital structure as described in chapter 1.1. As such, the ability to flexibly raise equity capital in the amount and at the time needed can be a decisive factor for a company's success – or sometimes survival – in the market place. Private companies are typically restricted to private equity financing instruments. By far the most relevant instrument in this context is the classic private equity financing, whereby the company raises equity from existing or new investors in a private financing round (not to be confused with transactions where a financial investor acquires the majority or all of a company's equity in a so-called buyout transaction). Issuance of convertible bonds is another instrument that gets talked about a lot in this context; convertible bonds are used in practice but to a much lesser extent than the straight equity financings described previously. In a private convertible transaction, a company issues bonds that are convertible (usually at the bond holders' discretion) into the company's shares at a pre-determined equity valuation in the future. The conversion terms of the bonds can be structured relatively flexibly to accommodate company and investor preferences; conversion timing and conversion price can (but don't necessarily need to) be linked to a successful IPO and the IPO price of the company's shares. There may be other structural features in a convertible bond that incentivize a company to pursue an IPO, such as a periodic coupon payment that increases over time or an obligation under the terms of the bond to conduct an IPO within a certain timeframe.

For both instruments, equity financings and convertible bonds, certain relevant securities laws and regulations must be observed when approaching investors in order for these transactions to be considered "private"; this is necessary to avoid triggering the requirements associated with a public securities offering, including various legal and regulatory obligations and the public disclosure of company information. Exemptions from such requirements are available in most jurisdictions for transactions that qualify as private placements, including in the United States of America, the United Kingdom, Germany and many other countries.

Private transactions provide companies and investors with a high level of structural flexibility, although established market practice (that may vary by jurisdiction and evolve over time) creates certain boundaries to structural innovation. This flexibility is a key advantage of private equity financing instruments. However, there are some disadvantages as well. Most relevant from a practical perspective are limited market depth and available volume, difficulty around pricing and (equity) valuation as well as limited timing windows during which a private transaction can be executed. All these factors can make access to equity financing very difficult for companies, and often times do in reality.

The private equity financing market is most established in the United States (compared to Europe, Asia and elsewhere). There are a large number of investors in the United States whose investment guidelines allow them to invest in unlisted equity securities, which in turn enhances market capacity and possible transaction volumes. Therefore, the largest private equity raising transactions can regularly be observed in the US market. For instance, Palantir Technologies, a US data analytics company, raised US$ 880 million in private financing round closed in December 2015 and Snapchat, a US photo messaging company, raised US$ 1.8 billion in a private financing round closed in May 2016. In jurisdictions outside the US, private equity financings are, at least at times, more difficult to consummate. This is particularly challenging for early stage growth companies requiring equity financing to finance future growth.

IPO is the initial sale of a company's equity to the public market

In order to broaden their equity financing alternatives, raise equity capital and potentially enable their shareholders to sell part of their holdings, companies may decide to undertake an IPO at some point in their life cycle. The first-time sale of equity to public market investors in a public offering hence implies that a privately held company intends to sell part of its equity to public market investors. This represents a major step for such company, as described in more detail in chapters 6 and 7, and entails a number of challenges that have to be overcome on the way to a successful transaction. The target investors in an IPO typically do not follow private companies in detail, not least because of limited public disclosure and lack of immediate investment opportunity. During the IPO, the target investors must be educated on the IPO company to a degree of detail that allows them to make an informed decision regarding an investment in the company's equity. In order to achieve this, a comprehensive yet condensed, multi-step investor education and marketing program is organized by the underwriting investment banks. The equity story, which in essence is a five-minute elevator pitch to potential investors, needs to catch their attention. It needs to trigger investors' willingness to invest time and resources in developing a sound understanding of the company's business model and historical performance, help them develop a view on the IPO company's future prospects and get comfortable with its management team. In recent years, there have been discussions in the financial community, in particular among institutional investors and investment banks, about potential changes to the established IPO process market practice that could better accommodate investors' information needs. In May 2011, BlackRock, a US fund management company, went as far and published an open letter criticizing current IPO practice and calling for changes to the

IPO process in Europe. The letter sparked an intense public debate and impacted IPO deal practice in the investment banks' attempt to address the concerns raised by BlackRock (Euromoney, 2011, p. 1f).

Realistically, the amount of time and resources investors can and want to spend on IPO candidates is influenced by several different factors, such as the general equity market environment, the number of IPO candidates in the pipeline at a given time, the complexity of a company's IPO story and the investor's own level of sophistication. As such, it is critical in an IPO to tailor the process within market practice boundaries so that it best suits the universe of target investors for a specific IPO transaction.

A stock market listing opens up new financing alternatives

Per definition, an IPO entails a stock market listing of the company's shares on at least one stock exchange. Many stock exchanges operate multiple markets within their single exchanges (i.e. the London Stock Exchange offers companies many different options for listing their shares including, among others, the traditional Premium Listed Main Market, for large established companies, and the Alternative Investment Market (AIM), targeted at growing companies); these markets are governed by different rules and regulations and can be broadly categorized into regulated and unregulated markets. The regulated markets are by far most relevant in the context of IPOs in terms of number of transactions and aggregate issuance volume. Therefore, this publication focuses on IPOs with listings on regulated markets.

Stock markets are market places where investors can buy and sell shares of companies listed on that particular stock market. Today, stock market trading is highly automated and electronic trading is the most prevalent form of bringing together buyers and sellers of a particular stock. While rules and regulations and market models (i.e. the fundamental rules of order matching and price determination) vary by exchange, continuous quotations and trading liquidity are common general objectives of stock exchanges across the world. Continuous quotations aim to provide an investor with a price to buy or sell a certain number of a particular share at any point in time (within the opening hours of the stock exchange), whereas trading liquidity refers to the level of ongoing trading activity and allows an investor to buy or sell larger quantities of a particular share.

Thus, a stock market listing is the pre-condition for a more or less liquid market in the IPO company's shares following allocation of the offered shares to investors. As final allocations are typically smaller than investors' orders as explained in chapter 3.3, some investors start building their holding by buying additional shares. Other investors may find themselves with a position they deem too small to hold and/or build and may therefore look to sell their shares. In addition, there are many other reasons that may prompt investors to start trading immediately post-IPO. Trading volumes during the first days following an IPO are typically (substantially) elevated and it takes some days and even weeks for the market to find a sustainable level of trading activity.

Private Companies	Publicly Listed Companies
• Private equity financing: issuance of new shares to investors in a private transaction	• „At-market" capital increase: placement of new shares to institutional investors (usually in an overnight transaction)
• Private convertible bonds: issuance of bonds with the option to convert into equity at certain terms to investors in a private transaction	• (Large) capital increase: issuance of new shares usually at a discount to the prevailing market price in an offer to investors
	• Convertible bonds: issuance of bonds with the option to convert into equity at a pre-determined conversion price to institutional investors
	• Mandatory convertible bonds: issuance of bonds that convert into equity at a pre-determined conversion price to institutional investors

Exhibit 6: Overview of equity financing alternatives
Source: Own presentation

Listed companies have access to a diverse menu of equity financing instruments to flexibly cover their equity financing needs. They can place new shares in a capital increase, either priced "at market" (i.e. with only a small discount to the prevailing stock price) or at a discount (in some jurisdictions involving so-called pre-emptive or subscription rights for existing shareholders to avoid dilution and unwanted value transfer; also called a "discounted rights issue"). "At-market" capital increases are typically limited in size (up to 10% of existing shares)[20] but can be executed overnight and without an offer document. Discounted rights issues can be very large in relative and absolute size, and may take several weeks (at a minimum) to execute. Discounted rights issues also typically require an offer document. Alternatively, companies can issue convertible bonds or mandatory convertible bonds. Both instruments are relatively easy to issue and price off a stock price where there is sufficient trading liquidity in the underlying stock. While a convertible bond is considered debt for balance sheet purposes, the large credit rating agencies such as Standard & Poor's, Moody's and Fitch typically

---

[20] Most recent European prospectus directives now also allow for up to 20% of new shares to be issued without a prospectus (European Commission Bulletin 30 June 2017, effective as of 20 July 2017).

attribute some equity credit for credit rating purposes to it. A mandatory convertible bond, however, represents a forward sale of a company's equity at a premium to the prevailing share price.

4.2 Capital structuring

Finding and implementing a public market suitable capital structure is important

Capital structure, i.e. the mix of equity and debt in a company's balance sheet, is usually an important topic for public market investors in an IPO. Typically, investors prefer a capital structure that is efficient, in line with that of peer companies (i.e. listed companies with a substantially similar business or substantially similar business characteristics) and not overly risky. The latter consideration is based on the notion that a company's financial risk increases with greater use of debt in the capital structure. As a result, public market investors typically dislike companies with high levels of financial indebtedness. It is challenging, however, to come up with specific guidance on financial leverage levels that are deemed appropriate or acceptable in this context. Generally, investors tolerate higher leverage levels for larger businesses with established business models in relatively stable industries and with good predictability of cash flows. Conversely, investors look for low (or even no) leverage in smaller companies, new business models and more volatile or cyclical industries (which typically have less predictable cash flows). Investor preferences regarding leverage and capital structure are subject to change over time. Whereas investors have very much favored conservative capital structures during the financial crisis following the collapse of Lehman Brothers in September 2008, the last two to three years have been marked by increasing investor tolerance for somewhat higher leverage in the last two to three years. A company like Curetis, which will be addressed in Part 3 of this book, would be expected to find itself very much at the extreme end of low to no leverage at IPO.

In preparation for an IPO, it is therefore important to scrutinize the capital structure of the IPO company for any potential necessary changes before its transition from a privately held to a publicly listed company.

Best compromise to balance conflicting views and interests

As described in chapter 2.2, the lead underwriters for an IPO work with the company and its shareholders to define a capital structure that is expected to (i) resonate with the IPO target investors, yet also (ii) supports the company's strategic and financial objectives and (iii) be acceptable for the company's major shareholders. The interests of these three principal parties can and in reality often do diverge, sometimes substantially. In such a situation, it is of critical importance to find a compromise that balances the various views and interests of those involved in an IPO transaction, yet does not result in a mere (and sometimes bad) trade-off.

The starting point of the IPO planning discussion typically focuses on the IPO company's current leverage level, which is often measured by the company's net debt / EBITDA ratio. This is benchmarked against leverage levels of listed peer companies. If the leverage is deemed too high, the company would need to raise sufficient equity capital in the IPO to reduce its leverage. Conversely, if the leverage level is deemed too low, the company may consider raising additional debt and paying a special dividend to its shareholder(s) ahead of the IPO. Companies typically like a strong balance sheet with sufficient cash at hand, whereas shareholders like dividends. Additionally, private companies and their owners may prefer higher leverage levels than public market investors. These differing preferences may impact the discussion on an appropriate leverage level for the company at IPO.

A simple example: A pre-IPO company has relatively predictable cash flows, operates in a non-cyclical industry and is currently owned by a private equity fund. Pre-IPO leverage stands at 5x net debt / EBITDA. The company's management feels comfortable with the leverage and thinks it does not need significant additional liquidity, yet peer leverage levels are in the range of 2 to 3x net debt / EBITDA. The private equity fund intends to sell a significant portion of its shareholding in the IPO. So the company, its owner(s) and the lead underwriters need to figure out how much equity the company should raise to avoid creating concerns with public market investors regarding the company's post-IPO capital structure.

As a rule of thumb, the IPO company should raise sufficient capital so that it will not be required to return to the market for another equity issuance within a period of 12 to 18 months after the IPO.

Dividend capacity and dividend policy are key in many IPOs

In recent years, dividends have become a more important consideration in the context of structuring an IPO. The current low interest environment with central bank rates at or close to all-time lows represents a major challenge for investors. Therefore, the perspective of receiving regular payouts on equity investments in the form of dividends has generally become more attractive and important for equity investors. Dividend payments attach a certain yield to a share and hence are considered a form of down-side protection on the investment. This is particularly important in an IPO, where investors are asked to invest in a company that they know less about than other already listed (public) companies as described above. As such, an attractive dividend story has been a key selling point for investors in many IPOs over the last few years. The IPOs of Talanx, a German insurance company, in 2012, Royal Mail, a UK postal service company, in 2013 and VAT, a Swiss manufacturer of vacuum valves, in 2016 represent good examples in this context. However, in reality there are deviations from this general trend. There have also been very successful IPOs across a broad range of offering sizes of companies that were non-dividend paying and did not make promises on potential future dividend payouts during the IPO. This is particularly true for rapidly growing companies that often times cannot generate sufficient cash flow to finance expansion and pay meaningful dividends at the same time. Curetis, the company serving as reference case in section three of this publication, belongs to this type of IPO companies, with Rocket Internet, a German Internet holding company, Facebook, a US social media company and Alibaba, a Chinese e-commerce company being additional prominent examples.

Therefore, it is important to determine the company's capacity to pay regular dividends post-IPO. This is to be considered in view of the company's plans to raise equity capital as part of the IPO. And while equity raising and dividend payouts represent counter directional cash flows especially if ignoring timing, investors are typically supportive to IPOs that combine a material equity raising and customary regular dividend payments post-IPO.

Once the company, existing shareholders and investment banks have developed a view the amount of dividends the company can and should payout going forward, they typically describe this plan in what is referred to as a dividend policy. The dividend policy often refers to a defined dividend payment per share or to a percentage of net profit ("payout ratio") that the company commits to paying if certain conditions are met.

4.3   Offer structure: who sells how much stock at what price to whom?

Selection of listing venue sets the framework

Selection of the listing venue, i.e. the stock exchange and market segment (see also chapters 2.1 and 4.1), has far reaching implications for the IPO and beyond. IPOs are governed by a comprehensive set of rules and regulations and these vary substantially depending on the jurisdiction of the stock exchange and target investors as well as the various stock markets and market segments.

Equity capital markets are global. Many institutional investors can, in principle but with limitations and restrictions under their investment guidelines, invest in stocks of foreign companies either domiciled or listed outside the home country of such investors. This holds true, in particular, for almost all of the large asset management companies that are often international organizations with established operations in financial centers around the globe. Similarly, most relevant stock exchanges, such as the exchanges in New York, London, Frankfurt, Paris, Amsterdam, Brussels, Hong Kong and Singapore, are open for listings of foreign domiciled companies. In fact, IPOs and listings of foreign companies have become common practice. A number of years ago, for example, the London Stock Exchange emerged as the listing venue of choice for Russian companies. According to an analysis conducted by PwC, 67 out of 117 Russian companies that completed their IPOs between January 2005 and September 2014 listed on the London Stock Exchange, thereof 50 on the Main Market and 17 on the Alternative Investment Market. (PwC, 2014, p. 2) The New York Stock Exchange and NASDAQ continue to attract foreign issuers generally and are regarded particularly attractive listing venues by biotech and medtech companies as well as technology growth companies.

In practice, this implies that companies that are planning for an IPO have various potential listing locations at their disposal. The decision criteria typically applied for selecting a stock exchange are manifold. They include, inter alia, market size and depth, listing of relevant peer companies, general and industry specific trading valuation multiples, research analyst coverage, proximity to company headquarters and management team, corporate governance regime as well as accounting and disclosure requirements. Over and above these factors, there is the notion of a "natural listing location", meaning that one potential listing venue is the main stock exchange within a company's country of domicile.

The choice of listing location also takes into account the target investors. An IPO on a US exchange, such as the NYSE or NASDAQ, entails a US public offer and key target investors are likely to be US institutions located in New York and other regional financial centers in the US. An IPO on a stock exchange within the European Union entails a public offer in one or more countries within the EU and with target investors located in London, the financial centers of the listing jurisdiction and other regional financial centers such as Amsterdam, Brussels, Copenhagen, Frankfurt, Milan, Paris etc. Institutional investors outside the jurisdiction(s) of the public offer(s) can typically be accessed through private placements, although sometimes with certain limitations (especially as to number and type of investors approached in a particular country). Most relevant in practice are private placements to US investors that are regulated by Rule 144A under the US Securities Act of 1933, as amended. This rule in essence requires that only "qualified institutional buyers" (as defined under US law) may be approached and this must be done as part of a private placement (i.e. US investors generally may not be included in the public offerings that take place outside the US and that are not registered with the Securities and Exchange Commission).

Find a balance for offer volume and shares available for sale

The choice of listing venue may also have an impact on the absolute and relative offer size of an IPO. On one hand, an IPO should not be too small in order to ensure a certain level of investor attention and trading liquidity in the stock market trading post-IPO (allowing investors to buy and sell larger quantities of stock without significantly impacting price). On the other hand, an IPO should not be too large, both in terms of volume and in percent of the company's total value. A transaction size exceeding market capacity may not meet with sufficient investor demand to ensure a healthy level of demand overhang in the book building process (see also chapter 3.3).

Depending on the seller, there are two types of shares that can be offered in an IPO. New (also primary) shares are newly issued shares sold by the company to raise equity capital. Old (also secondary) shares are existing shares sold by the company's existing shareholder(s) in order to reduce their shareholding in the company. An IPO may consist entirely of new shares, old shares or any combination thereof.

The outcome of the capital structure discussion as described above is a key driver for the sizing of the primary component of the offering. In addition, shareholders may be willing or even actively seek to sell some or a significant part of their shareholding in an IPO. Especially for financially driven investors and private equity funds, an IPO represents a viable strategy to exit an investment, often as an alternative to a trade sale of the business to another strategic or financial investor. In such a case, the exiting investors may have a preference to maximize the secondary component of an IPO and to minimize the primary component, with the objective of selling as much as possible of their holding in the company during the IPO. As the internal rate of return (IRR) is often a key performance measure for financial investors, the investment period is an important parameter to calculate performance of an investment and hence sets a certain incentive to achieve a swift exit.

It is customary market practice at all major listing venues that the IPO company and its shareholders commit to not selling additional shares in the market for a certain period post IPO (as so-called "lock-up" period). The objective is to ensure an orderly after market for the shares during regular stock market trading and hence these types of agreements are also called "market protection" or "lock-up" clauses. It is a primary objective of companies and the investment banks to avoid a negative share price impact from a speculative or actual supply overhang that may temper investors' appetite to buy shares in an IPO. Lock-up periods typically are six, twelve or even 18 months long. Often, the lock-up periods for the company and even among existing shareholders in an IPO are for different lengths of time. Lock-ups tend to be longer in a more difficult market environment, where investors want more visibility on future supply of additional shares. Most of the time, the lock-up agreements are structured such that the lead managing underwriters of the IPO can waive the lock-up at their discretion, so that either the company or existing shareholders can sell additional shares to the market at appropriate times. Public market investors, however, trust that the lead managing underwriters would only waive lock-up agreements in situations where a waiver is not materially disadvantageous to the IPO investors. Investment banks decide carefully in these situations, as detrimental decisions may harm their reputation with investors (potentially impacting their ability to sell securities to those investors in future transactions).

The fact that only a certain percentage of a company can be sold to public market investors in an IPO and that subsequent placements of secondary shares are most likely subject to lock-up agreements, combined with prevailing market conditions and general future uncertainty, can severely limit the timing of a complete exit of an investor. Therefore, it is rational for exit-oriented investors to seek maximization of the secondary component of an IPO.

However, in reality, these things are often not so simple. There are situations, where even exit-oriented investors do not strive for a maximization of the secondary component of an IPO. These investors may expect share price appreciation post IPO, allowing them to sell their remaining holdings at a (significantly) higher price at a later point in time. The higher exit proceeds may compensate or even outweigh the timing aspect when it comes to IRR. Alternatively, these investors may be focused more on the company's primary equity needs and prefer adequate capitalization over a swift exit.

Investor targeting drives the structure of IPO marketing campaigns

Successful completion of an IPO requires the identification of a sufficient number of public market investors that, in aggregate, create enough demand to successfully place all of the shares offered in the IPO. Given that the term "public market investors" describes a diverse group of institutions and individuals, in reality, this exercise is often a complex process.

Institutional investors have become the key driver of demand in IPOs, as much as in almost all other securities offerings. The umbrella term "institutional investors" comprises a large number and variety of institutions that invest in securities. It includes more traditional asset management companies (e.g. Blackrock, DWS, Gartmore, Union Investment), hedge funds (e.g. Citadel, Marshall Wace, OchZiff), insurance companies (e.g. Allianz, AXA, Prudential), pension funds (public and corporate), sovereign wealth funds (e.g. Abu Dhabi Investment Authority/ADIA, China Investment Corporation/CIC, Government of Singapore Investment Authority/GIC), family offices (multi-family offices such as Pictet, UBS Global Family Office and US Trust as well as single family offices) and others. Over the past few years, many of the larger organizations have developed into multi-asset managers, meaning that they offer a broad variety of investment products and services to different groups of clients. As such, the boundaries between the different categories as described above are becoming increasingly blurred.

There are a very large number of entities within these organizations that can invest in listed shares and IPOs. These entities often feature distinct investment styles (e.g. active vs. passive, value vs. growth, small cap vs. large cap), or focus on certain geographies and/or industries as well as other investment criteria or any mixtures of the aforementioned. There are an even greater number of key decision makers, mainly investment professionals and buy side research analysts, who are the relevant parties to consider for purposes of marketing the IPO shares. Given all this complexity, investment banks provide key value in an IPO by helping to identify the most relevant universe of potential investors and providing access to the key decision makers for the successful marketing of an IPO.

The lead managing investment banks conduct a comprehensive investor targeting exercise during the preparation phase of the IPO in order to identify the most relevant institutions and individuals from the combined pool of market knowledge and investor contacts. As such, it is important to appoint a banking syndicate that brings together banks with complementary distribution capabilities in the form of investor access and contacts (see also chapter 5.1). Given that marketing resources are finite, a focus on the right institutions is of critical importance.

Institutional investor marketing is typically structured as a multi-step process. This process may commence as much as twelve to 18 months ahead of the targeted IPO timing, when the management team, often supported by one or two investment banks, starts meeting with select institutional investors to introduce the candidate company and its management as well as to obtain initial feedback from the investors on their views of the company. Later, during the actual IPO process, there may be an additional round of early investor meetings. In addition, the investor education exercise by the syndicate banks' research analysts and the institutional management roadshow are key elements of the process as described in more detail in chapter 5.2.

Individual investors, often referred to as retail investors, typically are not considered a major source of demand in IPOs. Therefore, dedicated retail marketing campaigns through banks' retail organizations supported by expensive media and advertisement campaigns are relatively rare in practice. They may even be restricted by law in some jurisdictions such as the US. Retail demand may be relevant where the IPO company is already widely known and in jurisdictions where private individuals regularly invest in listed stocks. Also, there may be overriding objectives by the IPO company or its shareholders that warrant a greater focus on retail marketing. A typical example is a privatization, where the public owners may have a political interest in high retail participation. Retail investors are considered less price sensitive than institutional investors and hence incremental retail demand is typically opportunistically captured. Importantly, retail investors can be addressed only through a public offering in line with local rules and regulations, whereas institutional demand can be captured more internationally on the basis of private placement regulation.

Offer price discovery is a step-by-step process

Although the final offer price is determined only at the end of the IPO, the process of identifying the right price starts early on. The price discovery process describes the transition from a corporate finance valuation based concept to estimate potential ranges for offer prices, towards a market and investor feedback based price range and a final price where supply and demand balance. As described in chapter 3.1, value and price represent very different underlying concepts and hence can vary substantially from each other.

IPO lead manager roles are typically awarded to investment banks in a competitive process. In this selection process, banks are asked to provide their views on a fairly standardized set of key topics in connection with the contemplated IPO (see also chapter 2.1), including preliminary views on the IPO company's valuation. It has become common practice for banks to initially reply to a request for a proposal with a written submission and then all banks or a pre-selected group are invited to present in an in-person meeting. Based on the input received, the company and/or shareholders typically select two or more lead managing underwriters (see also chapters 2.2 and 5.1) from the group of banks invited to the selection process. In their position as sellers of shares in an IPO, it is a rational expectation that the company and its shareholders prefer higher valuations. Therefore, investment banks tend to take a relatively aggressive stance on valuation in the selection phase to improve their chances of winning a lead manager mandate, the most prestigious roles in the banking syndicate. These often ambitious valuation views typically represent the starting point for the price discovery process during the IPO.

As the transaction is marketed to institutional investors, investment banks expend substantial effort to solicit feedback from investors on, inter alia, valuation and price. Where early investor meetings take place, the syndicate banks' sales forces solicit initial valuation feedback from those investors that have met with management members of the IPO company. The objective of this exercise is to help the IPO company, its shareholders and the lead managers to improve their understanding of how potential investors look at valuation (and other key aspects of a potential transaction), specifically in relation to the potential IPO. The most relevant feedback in the price discovery process is collected during the investor education period (see also chapter 5.2), when the syndicate banks' research analysts educate potential investors on the IPO company and discuss their views on valuation. This period is also important for the target investors' own independent analysis of the transaction and helps them to firm up their views. The syndicate banks' sales forces solicit explicit and specific input on valuation and price from those investors that have met with the syndicate banks' research analysts. The aggregate input received, which can consist of up to several hundreds of individual data points collected by many different sales persons at all of the syndicate banks, together with other relevant valuation parameters such as peer group trading valuations, is then used by the company, its shareholders and the investment banks to come up with a range of prices within which the shares will be offered to investors. In many jurisdictions, it is either a legal requirement or market practice to include a reasonably narrow (e.g. 15 to 20 percent measured from bottom to top end) price range in the offer document that is published at the launch of the IPO. In some jurisdictions, such as Germany, the price range can be adjusted later in the process, within a specified number of days before the expected pricing date. In this case, it is a major objective to capture as much additional feedback from investors who participated in roadshow meetings with management as possible in order to establish an appropriate price range. The price range is then typically published in a supplement to the offer document.

With the publication of the offer document and the commencement of the public offer, the lead managers typically start the bookbuilding process (see also chapter 3.3). Investors are asked to submit their non-binding orders to the syndicate banks indicating the quantity of shares they would like to purchase at various prices across the price range. The aggregate orderbook hence tracks total investor demand and price sensitivity of the demand within the price range. At pricing, the company and/or existing shareholders and the lead managers decide on a final offer price on the basis of the final orderbook. This decision can be preceded by a heated discussion among the involved parties on what the right offer price is.

Aside from purely quantitative aspects, there are also qualitative factors to be reflected in the pricing decision. As discussed previously, the company and existing shareholders, if acting rationally, should have an interest to maximize price, whereas new investors want to buy at a low price.

There needs to be sufficient excess demand at the chosen final price in order to ensure subsequent healthy demand for the newly listed shares in the immediate aftermarket. This helps to maximize chances that the share price increases in post-IPO trading and to avoid a fall in the share price to below the offer price. Therefore, it is important that the lead managers have a good understanding whether the final orderbook reflects real demand or whether investors have inflated their demand to increase their allocations of stock. Similarly, investors may have understated their real price limit, especially where they show sensitivity within the price range. If this is the case, there may be additional demand at higher prices if the syndicate banks can convince investors at the last minute, to increase their price limit in order to be included in the deal.

Quality of demand is also an important consideration. Investors exhibit very different behaviors in IPO transactions. Some decide to hold their allocation and buy additional shares in the aftermarket, others may want to realize any potential short term gains immediately in the first minutes, hours or days of trading. Still others may act opportunistically and rather unpredictably. As such, the allocation of shares to investors is also a very important element to a successful IPO, together with finding the right offer price.

Given the complexities involved, IPO pricing and allocation are often aptly referred to as an art and not a science.

Flexibility is a key success factor in a volatile world

As described above, the structure of an IPO transaction is defined by a number of key parameters. Many of them are, to various degrees, dependent on external factors that are beyond the control of the company, its shareholders or the syndicate banks. (Geo-) political developments, the macroeconomic environment, monetary policy, sector dynamics, the equity market environment, valuation levels and equity investor sentiment can all have a decisive impact on the IPO environment and the feasibility of IPO transactions generally or in certain markets. Any of these factors may change, quickly and markedly, during the IPO project and have a substantial impact on the structure of an IPO that can be executed successfully. Flexibility throughout the process on key parameters such as listing venue, offer volume, primary / secondary mix and expected price is key to be able to complete a transaction that is satisfactory to all key stakeholders within the anticipated time frame. 'Hope for the best and plan for the worst' therefore describes a sensible and pragmatic approach to plan for the likely scenario that circumstances will change along the way and require an adaptation of plans.

This is not as trivial as it may sound. An IPO is a long and complex project with many parties and stakeholders involved (see also chapter 5). Important decisions to change key structural parameters to get a transaction done often need to be made at (very) late stages of the IPO process, sometimes literally in the last minute, and thus require quick and effective decision making. However, as key structure decisions usually need to be made by organizations (rather than individuals) in order to comply with corporate governance requirements, these issues typically require some preparation time. It is key to plan in advance and anticipate potential changes in order to retain sufficient flexibility and to be in a position to act quickly. This has helped many companies to complete their IPO, even under very challenging circumstances. If a transaction hangs on a thread at the last minute, there is no time for a lengthy decision making processes.

4.4   Use of proceeds (if any...)

Primary secondary mix determines allocation of total IPO proceeds

It is a common misperception that the IPO company receives all of the proceeds raised in an IPO. As described above, an IPO can consist of any mix of primary and secondary shares. Hence, it is the respective seller that is entitled to the corresponding amount of sale proceeds. Proceeds from selling primary shares, often referred to as primary proceeds, flow to the company. Secondary proceeds, i.e. proceeds from selling secondary shares, flow to the selling shareholders. The amount of proceeds also depends on how fees and expenses associated with the IPO process are to be paid (as further discussed below).

In an IPO that consists of primary shares only, the company receives all of the proceeds. Correspondingly, in an IPO that consists of secondary shares only, the selling shareholders receive all of the proceeds and the company does not receive any. Both scenarios can be observed in reality, but it is most common that the offering consists of a mix of primary and secondary shares, with total proceeds split between company and selling shareholders.

It is a specific feature of IPOs that it is possible (and rather common) for multiple sellers to sell securities in one transaction. The company and existing shareholders tend to act independently in further share sales post IPO and once the company is stock market listed (subject to lock-up provisions as described above).

The scenario of an all secondary IPO is somewhat special. While the company does not receive any of the proceeds, it bears most of the burden associated with an IPO project (see also chapter 5.1). This arguably disproportionate allocation of costs and benefits has, inter alia, important legal and governance implications that regularly give rise to concerns. However, it is possible to address these concerns through certain legal and economic arrangements between the company and the selling shareholders.

Investors want to understand what the company will do with all the fresh money

As described in chapter 4.3 sizing the primary component is a key outcome of the capital structuring exercise in combination with the other offer structuring considerations.

The bigger the primary component in an IPO in absolute and relative size, the more investors want to understand the company's plan for using the IPO proceeds. This is due to the fact that the issuance of new shares not only increases the company's balance sheet equity and liquidity but also results in an increased number of outstanding shares. This means that future profits are divided by a greater number of shares and existing shareholders' holdings decline in percentage terms. The effect is referred to as "dilution" and companies and shareholders typically have an interest in keeping the adverse effects of dilution as low as possible. The general qualification of raising funds for "general corporate purposes" is typically not sufficient for most investors and additional reasons must be provided to further specify the purpose of an IPO and the intended use of proceeds.

There are different ways in which the new liquidity can be spent. The IPO company can either repay debt to bring its capital structure in line with peers, in particular if the company does not need substantial fresh liquidity to fund its ongoing operations or future expansion plans. This is often the case for IPO candidates that have a proven business model, have a track record of solid growth in line with gross domestic product or slightly above, operate profitably, generate positive cash flow from operations and, potentially, that employ debt in their capital structure. Many IPO companies with these characteristics are owned by financially driven investors who are seeking an exit to their previous investment.

However, many IPO companies display very different characteristics to those described in the previous paragraph. Over the past few years, the IPO market has become (again) increasingly receptive for IPOs by growth companies, especially from technology, media, internet, health care and biotechnology sectors. These companies often show high or very high growth rates, have not reached profitability (and sometimes even do not expect to do so in the near future), require high investments to support their growth, record negative cash flows and, usually, have little or no debt in their capital structure. In these cases, the investors typically want to understand in a fair amount of detail how the IPO proceeds will be invested and how these investment projects will impact future value creation. They also want to understand if and when the company may need to raise additional equity in the future. All of these considerations can materially impact value and hence are reflected in the investors' own independent analysis of the IPO opportunity.

In reality, there are not only black or white cases, where it is clear if a company can conduct a successful IPO, there are also different shades of grey. Potential IPO companies cannot necessarily be put in a box, with a certain set of characteristics similar to those described above. There is a large variety of potential IPO companies, depending on industry, subsector, size and ownership.

In almost every case, investors want to develop a detailed understanding of the post-IPO capital structure but also understand what the IPO company's liquidity will look like after the transaction and how this liquidity is intended to be used over time. Therefore, the relevant sections in the offer document are very important to investors. They attract a lot of attention during IPO preparation and document drafting and allow the company to craft a sound and convincing use of proceeds story. In addition, investors like to question management during roadshow meetings, particularly on the intended use of proceeds. Some IPO cases are, in fact, unique and unprecedented, hence requiring an extra amount of diligence during preparation to anticipate potential investor scrutiny during marketing.

Selling shareholders' use of proceeds is of low relevance to investors

Depending on the size of the primary component, the selling shareholders may be entitled to receive substantial proceeds from the offering. Nonetheless, investors typically do not show material interest in how the selling shareholders plan to use their, sometimes very substantial, proceeds from an IPO. This should not come as a surprise as secondary shares are outside the sphere of the IPO company and there is no direct effect in the form of dilution or capital inflow. The selling shareholders typically also do not wish to disclose more about their plans for deploying the sale proceeds than they actually are required to.

Disclosure in the offer document in this context is limited. It is typically restricted to transparent disclosure of the quantitative facts rather than any additional qualitative explanation.

From time to time, investors do take a special interest if there is a substantial secondary component in the IPO (rather than the absolute amount of secondary proceeds). This is particularly the case if one or several selling shareholders sell a very large portion or substantially all of their holding in the IPO, resulting in a corresponding reduction of their economic exposures in the company. Investors tend to question the signaling effect associated with these exit plans, especially since the selling shareholders may know the IPO company substantially better than any outside investor. This information asymmetry regularly causes investors to question a significant reduction of a shareholder's stake in an IPO. Therefore, an almost complete exit of a substantial shareholder during an IPO is very rare in reality. Investors generally tolerate a reduction of roughly 40 to 60 percent of a selling shareholder's total holding in an IPO, even though it may be clear that the selling shareholder(s) will seek a full exit over time. A still substantial relative exposure (the remaining 60 to 40 percent of the original shareholding in combination with lock-up provisions) increases comfort in the near and medium term future development post-IPO and typically is an effective means to mitigate potential investors concerns.

4.5   The real cost of capital in an IPO – fees & more

Equity is the most expensive capital – CAPM basics

The capital asset pricing model (CAPM) has become a widely-accepted concept in the financial industry. It is considered the standard approach for explaining the trade-off between risk and return and it forms the basis for estimating the required return on risky assets (Brealey & Myers, 2000, p. 195f).

Equity represents the riskiest type of capital in a company's capital structure. It is subordinate to all other forms of capital including debt (irrespective of whether such debt is secured or unsecured), convertible debt, hybrid or mezzanine capital and preferred equity. Equity holders' claims against assets, cash flows, liquidation proceeds or the insolvency estate (in an insolvency setting) rank below those of all other claim holders. In return, and in accordance with the CAPM, equity is the most expensive form of capital in a company's capital structure. Equity investors expect to achieve the highest returns relative to other layers in the capital structure in return for taking higher risk. It is important to understand, however, that the estimated cost of equity based on CAPM varies greatly among companies. They key driver to this is the estimated level of risk, which depends, inter alia, on non-systematic risk, company size and political risk.

In practice, it is common to estimate a company's cost of equity based on the CAPM. This estimation is becoming more relevant, and arguably more accurate, for a company immediately before an IPO. The estimation of non-systematic risk by looking at comparable publicly listed companies becomes methodologically more adequate. Fungibility and tradability are underlying assumptions of CAPM. Potential adjustments to the risk measure to reflect illiquidity of a private company becomes less relevant.

However, the cost of equity, as indicated by CAPM, is only part of the story in the context of an IPO. Raising equity in an IPO typically comes with significant additional costs and expenses for the IPO company. Some of them are one-off items, directly or indirectly related to the IPO, whereas others are of a recurring nature and have to be continuously borne by the company going forward.

IPO costs are very substantial

The most substantial direct cost components of an IPO are fees to lawyers, auditors and last but not least the investment banks. In addition, there are listing and admission fees payable to the stock exchange, roadshow costs and other travel expenses as well as costs for printing and distribution of any physical offer documents. In some jurisdictions the competent authority, such as the US Securities Exchange Commission (SEC), the UK Listing Authority (UKLA) or the German Federal Financial Supervisory Authority (Bundesanstalt für Finanzdienstleistungsaufsicht – BaFin) may also impose charges in connection with their involvement in the process.

Auditors and lawyers typically charge for their services by the hour, but will sometimes cap their total fees for an IPO transaction at a set amount. It has become common market practice, to pre-agree lump sum fee arrangements based on the typical scope of work in connection with an IPO and the expected complexity of the transaction owing to transaction structure, operational size and organizational complexity of the IPO company as well as other factors. As volume is not a direct driver to these fee arrangements, IPOs with large transaction volumes typically benefit from significant economies of scale with regards to auditor and lawyer fees, compared to smaller transactions. Market rates for those engagements vary by jurisdiction and tend to be most expensive in the United States.

Investment banks typically charge a percentage of the transaction volume for their services, often times split into base and incentive fee components. Incentive fees typically fall due if certain pre-agreed goals are achieved or the IPO company and the shareholders are satisfied with the result of the transaction. Local regulations often set boundaries to the structuring of incentive fee components. The investment banks' IPO fee (in basis points) typically varies for transactions in different size bands. A higher percentage fee is charged for smaller transactions whereas a lower percentage fee is charged for larger transactions. Nevertheless, the absolute amount of investment bank fees is closely related to transaction volume and much more than any of the other material cost elements in an IPO. Composition and complexity of the banking syndicate as described in chapter 5.1 is less relevant in the context of fees. All banks involved in an IPO share the total fee pool with the lead managing underwriters taking the lion's share of typically 70 to 80 percent of the total. Bank fees vary by jurisdiction and tend to be highest for IPOs in the United States. In the US, IPO bank fees typically range from 4 to 7 percent of total offering volume. This implies approximately US$ 7 million of bank fees for a US$ 100 million IPO and can go up to three digit million US$ amounts for very large IPOs. In the case of Facebook in 2012 for example, more than 30 banks split fees in excess of US$ 170 million. The percentage fee was exceptionally low for US standards.

According to analysis conducted by PricewaterhouseCoopers on a sample of more than 600 US IPOs between 5 April 2012 and 31 December 2014, average total costs for an individual IPO range from US$ 3.9 million, for IPOs with gross proceeds of up to US$ 50 million, to US$ 44.0 million, for IPOs with gross proceeds of US$ 301 million and above. The same analysis finds that the average total costs excluding investment bank fees range from US$ 1.9 million to US$ 7.1 million. Investment bank fees therefore account for approximately 54 percent of total costs for small IPOs (up to US$ 50 million gross proceeds) to approximately 84 percent of total costs for large IPOs (gross proceeds of US$ 301 million and above) (PwC, 2015, p. 10).

Investment bank fees, unlike many of the other direct IPO costs, are success based and only fall due in the event of a successful completion of the IPO. If the IPO does not complete for any reason, the company and/or the selling shareholders usually reimburse the banking syndicate for certain costs and expenses incurred in connection with the transaction. This leaves the banking syndicate fully exposed to the non-completion risk of a transaction and often serves, inter alia, as a justification for the above described fee levels.

There may also be additional expenses for public relations advisers, management coaches, an IPO-related image campaign or retail investor marketing activities. Media costs for print, online and TV advertising are also relatively high and may add up to material amounts in case they are extensively used. In reality, however, these additional expenses have become relatively rare.

Beyond the above described expenses, there may be additional costs that may not be directly attributable to the IPO or may be required to prepare the company for its time as a publicly listed entity. This category includes any required tax or legal entity structuring as well as implementation of management information systems and suitable governance and compliance regimes (see also chapter 6.1). These can, individually or in combination, result in significant costs for the IPO company.

The company pays it all!?

Given the magnitude of costs involved in an IPO, the question of who bears which costs in part or in total is important from an economic perspective. The investment bank fees are typically deducted from each recipient's share of the gross proceeds (i.e. company and any selling shareholders). Therefore, each party pays the investment bank fees pro-rata to its share in the total IPO volume.

The banking syndicate usually hires external legal counsel, typically a team of experienced equity capital markets lawyers from a leading international law firm, who advise on all aspects of the IPO. It is common market practice that the IPO company bears the costs for the banks' legal counsel in addition to the costs for its own legal counsel. However, banks may sometimes agree to pay for their own legal counsel. The ultimate structure depends, inter alia, on local market practice, competition on the bank side and cost consciousness on the client side.

Almost all other expenses such as auditor fees, printing costs and travel and roadshow costs for management are borne by the IPO company, at least initially. Depending on the specific commercial agreement, the company also reimburses the banking syndicate and its legal counsel for their travel expenses (which can be significant), either in full or up to a certain amount.

For corporate governance requirements and other legal reasons, the IPO company and any selling shareholders typically enter into a cost sharing agreement in an attempt to share the (directly attributable) financial burden of completing the IPO in proportion to the economic benefits.

Substantial follow-on costs

The completion of the IPO marks the start of the company's life as a stock market listed entity. This has implications on the company's cost base. Typically, there is a need for additional staff to fill new positions (e.g. investor and public relations) and strengthen existing corporate functions (e.g. compliance, reporting, legal, tax, etc.). The majority of companies incur additional costs of more than US$ 1 million per annum as a result of being public, according to a survey conducted by PricewaterhouseCoopers (2015, p. 5). Depending on size of the company, this number can be substantially higher in reality.

5 A big, important project

5.1 Too many cooks?

Big project teams with many parties at the table

The preparation and completion of an IPO involves a number of external parties in addition to the IPO company itself. Important external parties are the shareholders, the investment banks, several law firms, the accounting firm, the financial printer as well as potentially one or several independent IPO advisers and a public relations firm.

Each of these parties deploys a team of professionals, so that the total number of persons contributing to an IPO can easily exceed 50 and, in reality, often is substantially higher. This number does not include others that may work behind the scenes to support the project team members from various parties.

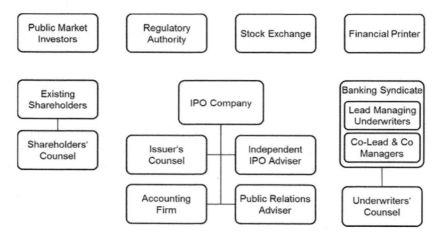

Exhibit 7: Overview of key parties involved in an IPO
Source: Own presentation

In order to organize all the parties and brief them on all key aspects of the envisioned transaction, an organizational meeting takes place prior to commencing actual preparatory work streams. Given the size of the respective project teams, finding a sufficiently large meeting facility often presents a practical challenge. To limit attendance to a reasonable minimum, the company may restrict the number of participants per party.

The IPO project is typically organized around three major work streams, each involving multiple parties and tasks. The corporate finance work stream encompasses, inter alia, comprehensive due diligence of information about the company from a commercial, legal and financial perspective, developing the capital structure and equity story as well as ongoing valuation updates. The documentation work stream comprises preparation of the offer document (including regulatory review and approval) and all legal agreements, including the underwriting agreement and numerous ancillary documents. The marketing work stream deals with all activities around investor marketing, including briefing the syndicate banks' research analysts, participating in investor education, conducting management roadshows as well as all activity in relation to bookbuilding and pricing of the IPO.

The IPO company is at the center stage

Irrespective of the contemplated transaction structure, the IPO company is a key principal involved in almost every aspect of the transaction. The company's IPO team includes senior management including the chief executive officer and the chief financial officer as well as many other managers and employees from across the organization. The company is in the lead or takes an important role in many of the various work streams and labor intensive tasks. The finance department usually bears the biggest share of the burden but other areas including the operating business(es) contribute as required. All in all, the company's level of involvement is very high throughout the IPO process and requires substantial attention of senior management, in particular the chief financial officer. As company meetings with institutional investors are typically conducted by the chief executive officer and the chief financial officer, these two individuals are fully occupied with the IPO during early investor meetings and the management roadshow.

Existing shareholders are key decision makers

As the owners of the IPO company and potential sellers of secondary shares, existing shareholders play an important role in an IPO. They are much less involved in labor intensive tasks on a day to day basis than other key parties; however, the existing shareholders are important decision makers throughout the process. They are involved from the first decision to explore a potential IPO as a strategic alternative for the company until the very end, i.e., pricing and allocation. The existing shareholders typically participate in all key decisions, including (i) selection of investment banks and other advisers, (ii) determining the capital structure and offer structure, (iii) defining key pillars of the equity story and positioning of the company, (iv) confirming decisions to proceed, delay or abort the process at various points in time and (v) finally, participating in the setting of the IPO price and deciding which investors who have placed an order with the investment banks should ultimately be apportioned shares as part of the IPO and in what amount.

Shareholder structures of IPO companies take very different forms. The number of shareholders can range from only one to many. Also, the type of shareholders can be of a diverse nature, including: corporate, financial investor, family holding, private individuals, institutional investors and others. The applicable governance regime and majority thresholds for various decisions drive the decision-making process on the shareholders' side. The facilitation of IPO-related decisions can therefore range from straight forward to relatively complex and cumbersome. Also, the general level of shareholder engagement in the IPO can vary greatly. In some situations, the existing shareholder(s) task management to facilitate the IPO. In other cases, it is the company management that first develops an IPO plan and then needs shareholder support for execution.

Investment banks – advisers and principals

The investment banks are also a critically important party to an IPO. Their role is multi-layered and they contribute on many different levels (see also chapter 2). In practice, an IPO involves a group of investment banks called the banking syndicate. Smaller banking syndicates consist of four to five banks, whereas larger syndicates can easily comprise more than 15 banks.

Not all banks within the syndicate have equal roles, are entitled to the same share of total banking fees or are appointed at the same time. Depending on the number of banks and objectives of the IPO company and its existing shareholders, the banking syndicate is typically organized in two or more groups. The banks in the group of lead managing underwriters have the most comprehensive role among all involved banks. They are often referred to as "bookrunners" or, especially in Europe, "global coordinators". The lead managing underwriters advise the company on key aspects of the preparation and execution of the IPO, including the capital structure, offer structure, transaction timing, development of the equity story and positioning of the company, targeted price range, pricing and allocation. They are responsible for coordinating the activities of the remaining syndicate banks to ensure smooth and seamless cooperation. It is the lead managing underwriters' role to conduct due diligence and develop transaction documentation that is acceptable for all banks in the syndicate. And, like all syndicate banks, they leverage their equity distribution platform to market and ultimately sell the IPO. In their capacity as underwriters, they act as principals in the transaction and manage any permitted stock price stabilization measures in the aftermarket (see also chapter 2.4). The lead managing underwriters are closely involved on a daily basis during all project phases, take the lead on many tasks and provide plenty of resources to advance the project and support the company in labor intensive tasks, such as drafting certain sections of the offer document or marketing materials. Consequently, the role of a lead managing underwriter requires the involvement of a number of different departments across the bank, including: investment banking, equity capital markets, equity research, equity syndicate, institutional sales force, legal & compliance, finance and others. The lead managing underwriters are entitled to the biggest share of the banking fees in an IPO, often in the range of 70 to 80 percent of the total, which reflects their share of the underwriting risk – they are expected to generate the lion's share of total investor demand.

Banks other than the lead managing underwriters have more limited roles in an IPO. They participate in the underwriting, complement the lead managers' distribution footprint with their own capabilities, and provide research coverage post IPO. Their individual shares in underwriting, fees and demand generation are much smaller than those of the lead managing underwriters. In essence, these banks share what is left over from the bookrunners.

Depending on the size of the banking syndicate, the non-lead managers can also be clustered into different sub-groups. Banks in the same cluster are treated equally with respect to their individual share in underwriting and fees. In general, the following principle applies: the lower the position in the syndicate hierarchy, the smaller the expected contribution and share of fees. In a syndicate with eight banks, for example, there could be two or three bookrunners and two or three "co-lead managers" at the level below the bookrunners. The remaining banks, often referred to as "co-managers", would be at the third and lowest level.

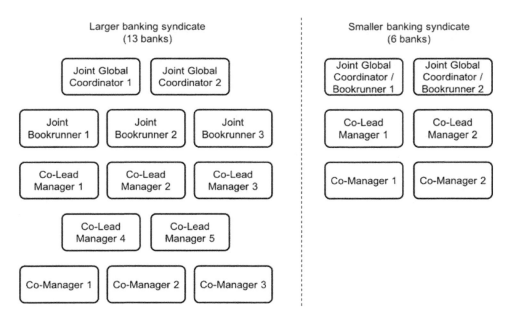

Exhibit 8: Schematic examples for banking syndicates – large vs. small
Source: Own presentation

External lawyers for all key parties

There are many different legal and regulatory angles to an IPO. Therefore, it is common market practice for the key principals to engage external law firms that have required IPO-related expertise and experience. At a minimum, two teams of external lawyers are involved – one law firm advising the IPO company and one law firm advising the banking syndicate. While the IPO company and the investment banks may also have internal legal departments, they draw on external support for an IPO for various reasons.

An IPO company's internal legal team often lacks the capital markets and transaction specific expertise required in the context of an IPO. In addition, the internal legal teams would face capacity shortages in handling other everyday matters given the multitude of tasks in an IPO process requiring legal involvement. As such, there is substantial merit in buying expertise, experience and bandwidth from an external provider. The IPO company's internal legal team is, however, closely involved and often serves a liaison function with external counsel. The IPO company's external legal counsel, also referred to as "issuer's counsel", is involved in all key work streams and many tasks of the IPO process. The issuer's counsel drafts and assists in negotiating engagement letters with other third parties, including the investment banks. The external lawyers also conduct comprehensive legal due diligence on the company and coordinate the drafting of the offer document, which will describe the company and detail the offering of company shares to investors. They often take the lead on drafting large parts of this extensive document, including review and implementation of comments from other involved parties and management of the regulatory approval process. The lawyers also review and provide comments on investor marketing materials that are typically drafted by the lead managing underwriters, based on input from the IPO company, in order to ensure both compliance with all legal requirements for such materials as well as consistency with descriptions in the offer document. Additionally, the issuer's counsel negotiates the underwriting agreement with the lead managing underwriters and their counsel. Beyond these key tasks, the issuer's counsel advises the IPO company on all transaction-related legal and regulatory matters and provides hands-on support.

The lead managing underwriters also appoint an external law firm on behalf of the banking syndicate, often referred to as "underwriters' counsel". Banks typically have sizeable internal legal departments with dedicated resources supporting the banks' equity capital markets business. In particular, banks that regularly act in the capacity of a lead managing underwriter employ lawyers with the know-how and experience required to handle an IPO in-house. Nevertheless, banks draw on external legal support for risk mitigation and capacity management.

Banks are typically very risk conscious. Rather than increasing their individual risk exposure as a principal to the transaction due to in-house lawyers advising the syndicate (i.e., other principals that could later file liability claims), the syndicate obtains outside legal advice in order to mitigate liability in connection with the IPO. Furthermore, as discussed in chapter 1.4, IPO activity is volatile. If all IPO tasks were handled in-house, in a busy IPO market, banks' internal legal departments would quickly face capacity constraints, whereas in less busy times, there would be substantial overcapacities. As banks have become increasingly cost conscious, capacity management has come into focus. It is not uncommon for a major equity capital markets house ranking among the top 5 in a region to employ only two or three full-time lawyers looking after the equity capital markets business in that region. This limited internal capacity restricts the role of the in-house lawyers to being a legal liaison for external lawyers and enforcing the respective bank's policies, procedures and internal views in discussions with other syndicate banks.

Therefore, the underwriters' counsel has a key coordination role, bringing together differing views and positions of the individual lead managing underwriters on various topics and occasions throughout the process. They must develop a common position acceptable to all banks. This role becomes more time consuming and onerous with the increasing number of banks involved in the syndicate. Outside this important procedural aspect, the underwriters' counsel, like the issuer's counsel, is involved in all key aspects and many tasks of the IPO process. The lawyers assist the banks in negotiating key contracts, such as their engagement letter, the underwriting agreement and the agreement among underwriters, which is the contract governing the cooperation of the syndicate banks in the IPO. The underwriters' counsel also conducts extensive legal due diligence on the IPO company, meticulously reviews and provides comments on the offer document and investor marketing materials and provides transaction-related advice and hands-on support. In jurisdictions where it is market practice for banks to publish transaction research as part of their investor education program, the underwriters' counsel leads the process for ensuring the research reports' factual accuracy and consistency with the offer document, prior to publication. Banks are not permitted to handle this process internally in order to ensure the research department's independence.

Both issuer's and underwriters' counsel also provide formal opinions confirming certain legal matters as well as the information in the IPO offer document. These opinions establish certain liability positions of the external law firms in connection with the transaction. As such, they increase the underwriters' and investors' comfort on the accuracy and completeness of the disclosure.

Existing shareholders often retain their own legal advisers, either collectively as a group or at times individually. This is particularly the case where the IPO involves secondary shares. The role of the shareholders' legal counsel is usually limited to negotiations of those provisions of the underwriting agreement and other matters that could expose the shareholders to liability in connection with the IPO.

In particularly large and complex IPO situations, additional law firms may be involved to advise on certain highly specialized legal matters or questions in relation to local jurisdictions not covered by the other lawyers' expertise.

Accounting firm

The IPO company's accounting firm, in its capacity as independent auditor, is often involved significantly earlier than the banks and legal counsel and retains a critical role throughout the IPO process.

The main focus of the accounting firm is around the IPO company's financial statements. It is important for the accounting firm to become involved early, as many pre-IPO companies utilize local GAAP for purposes of their financial reporting and must implement US GAAP or IFRS for presentation of financial information in the IPO offer document. Depending on the desired listing location and offering jurisdictions, IPO companies are required to disclose two to three years of historical financial statements prepared in accordance with US GAAP or IFRS. Adoption of the new reporting standards and conversion of historical financial statements to the new GAAP are complex and labor intensive. This challenge is compounded where the IPO company engaged in internal reorganizations or mergers and acquisitions prior to the IPO. As the converted financial statements must also be audited by the accounting firm, IPO companies and their accountants must commence preparations for these steps early on.

The accounting firm also usually supports the IPO company in the financial due diligence of the banks and in drafting the sections of the offer document that discuss the IPO company's historical financial performance. In addition, the accounting firm provides the underwriters with a "comfort letter", a formal letter confirming the accuracy of the financial figures in the offer document by tracing them back to the IPO company's financial statements or accounting records. The comfort letter also confirms that that there has been no undisclosed deterioration in the IPO company's financial condition or performance since the date of the latest annual or interim financial statements. This letter establishes a certain liability position of the accounting firm in connection with the offering and is intended to increase the underwriters' and investors' comfort in the accuracy and completeness of the disclosure.

Financial printer

The role of the financial printer is process critical. As a specialized service provider, it is the financial printer's responsibility to produce electronic and physical versions of the offer document and arrange logistics for the distribution of any hard copies. While this process may sound trivial, it can be fairly complicated in practice for several reasons. As the offer document constitutes the basis for potential liability claims in connection with the offering, typesetting and printing must be of zero mistake quality. Any typographical errors or omissions of words, sentences or pages could provide a basis for investor claims.

While most distributions of the offer document to investors are done in electronic form via e-mail, organizing logistics for distribution of physical copies is still very important in the overall process. The cut-off time for printing is usually set to as late as possible in the process and changes to the offer document continue until the last minute. This leaves a very short time window (typically overnight or 24 hours) for the printer to print and ship a sufficient number of offer documents to various destinations across the globe. Physical print volumes and the number of shipping addresses have gone down significantly since the introduction of electronic distribution, reducing the complexity of document logistics. However, all banks typically require at least some hard copies of the offer document at various offices and at each location of the management roadshow.

Independent IPO advisers

Many IPOs, especially in Europe, involve independent IPO advisers. They advise the IPO company and its existing shareholders on many different aspects in relation to the planned IPO. Sometimes the shareholders even retain their own independent IPO adviser. The IPO company and shareholders might feel the need for independent advice over and above the advice provided by lead managing underwriters', as described in chapter 2.1.

IPO advisory services are offered by specialized financial advisory firms rather than the large investment banks, which usually prefer more profitable underwriting roles. The advisory approach among IPO advisory firms varies and the scope of services can be customized to the client's particular needs. Often the independent IPO adviser is involved early on and advises on the selection of lawyers and underwriters as well as the negotiation of engagement terms. Throughout the actual IPO process, the independent IPO adviser helps the IPO company and/or existing shareholders navigate the process successfully. This can also involve challenging the lead managing underwriters, especially in situations where a conflict of interest may exist.

Public relations adviser

Especially in European transactions, where external communication in relation to a planned IPO is less restrictive than in the United States (from a legal perspective), the core IPO team often involves a public relations firm. PR firms assist in developing a communication story targeted at a less financially-minded audience as well as a suitable communication strategy. They arrange formal and informal media interviews, ensure consistency of media reporting, draft press releases and provide advice and support as required, e.g., in case of an early information leak.

To the extent the communication strategy also involves a media campaign or dedicated marketing to retail investors, the public relations firm drafts and produces advertisements and spots, develops a media plan in line with the media budget and executes the media campaign.

5.2   Best laid plans

The typical IPO timeline is about 6 months …

An IPO is a strategically important project and takes substantial time to complete. The IPO company's internal preparation phase takes approximately six months or longer, depending on the extent of the work program. During this period, the IPO company prepares itself to commence the formal IPO preparation phase, together with the other external parties described above. Key tasks completed in this period can include: (i) a review of the business plan, (ii) a change of the legal form, (iii) amendments to the company's legal structure and (iv) GAAP conversion of the company's financial statements. Substantial structural measures may be required to form the business that shall be listed in the IPO. These may involve the divestment of certain activities, changes to the organizational structure or the management team and far-reaching legal structuring work. The work program for this phase can vary greatly and in practice looks very different for a small growth company compared to an operationally large, international business or where the IPO business is being carved out of a larger existing enterprise.

The confidential preparation phase with all key external parties on board usually takes at least three months, sometimes significantly longer. Key tasks in this process phase include: (i) comprehensive commercial, financial and legal due diligence of the IPO company, (ii) finalization of the capital structure and offer structure (see also chapter 4.2 and 4.3), (iii) drafting of the offer document and initiation of the regulatory review and approval process, (iv) drafting of all other operative documents, including the underwriting agreement, legal opinions and comfort letters, (v) education of the syndicate banks' research analysts and (vi) drafting of investor marketing materials. In IPOs that involve the publication of research reports by the syndicate banks, a comprehensive presentation on the IPO company needs to be drafted for use by the IPO company's senior management to brief the research analysts in a formal event. The briefing event and the presentation need to provide the analysts with sufficient information to write their research reports.

Exhibit 9: Illustrative high-level IPO timeline
Source: Own presentation

The public marketing phase, which comprises the syndicate banks' investor education program and the management roadshow and ends with price setting and allocation, takes approximately four weeks. During the investor education process, each syndicate bank's research analyst is expected to meet with as many target investors as possible. In six to eight meetings per day, usually over a two-week period, each analyst discusses the IPO company with target investors. It is common for investors to meet with research analysts of more than one bank on the same transaction. Investor education is followed by the management roadshow. Over a scheduled period, which usually lasts about two weeks, senior management of the IPO company meet with target investors in major financial centers, typically in six to eight meetings a day in addition to group meetings over breakfast and lunch.

All in all, an IPO is usually at least a 10-month project. Excluding the IPO company's internal preparation phase, key procedures take at least four months to complete and banks and lawyers typically advise companies to expect a five- to six-month project for successful completion of such procedures.

... but it often takes substantially longer

However, there is no such thing as a standard timetable for an IPO. Every transaction has unique aspects to it that may alter the project timeline, either right from the beginning or at some point during the project. Actual timelines vary substantially in length due to internal and external factors.

The work capacity of the IPO company's organization is a key determining factor given the company's key role in many project work streams. While external parties support the company wherever possible in an effort to make the workload more manageable, many tasks still require substantial involvement of the IPO company. In reality, the IPO company's organization is often pushed to its capacity limit or even beyond and sometimes requires more time than previously planned to work through all of its tasks. The availability of latest financial statements, often interim financial results, can affect the project timeline as well. Private companies typically require more time for preparing financial statements and may not be used to preparing complete interim financial statements at all. As the inclusion of new financial information in the offer document is subject to regulatory review, there are timing limitations on when such information must become available. Hence, the IPO timeline may need to be extended if the preparation of updated financial information requires additional time. In addition, there is always the risk of adverse due diligence findings, where unexpected facts and information emerge during this period of intense scrutiny of the IPO company by lawyers, bankers and accountants. These can cause delays as they often require additional work and attention in order to be resolved. For example, adverse due diligence findings may be of a formal nature, associated with the IPO company's corporate history or in relation to the IPO company's historical or future financial performance, business model or competitive environment. Such findings may need to be addressed before the IPO process can proceed as planned or, depending upon the finding, the IPO plan itself may need to be modified.

In practice, the IPO market environment is one of the most common external factors that regularly extends IPO timelines. As described in chapters 1.4 and 4.3, IPO market conditions can change quickly and at any point of the IPO process. As a result of a significant deterioration, the principal decision makers may decide to extend the timeline for some weeks (or even longer) in anticipation of a market recovery. Other external reasons potentially resulting in an unexpected extension of the IPO timeline are third party attempts to impede the company in the successful completion of the IPO. Such attempts are uncommon in reality, but not at all unheard of. For example, third parties may try to make use of disclosure obligations and timing pressure associated with the IPO. The third party may threaten to or actually file claims or initiate litigation in the hopes that the company will agree to a non-judicial settlement (against cash) in order to avoid jeopardizing its IPO project timeline. This is a risky strategy of such third parties, but it has proven successful in some instances in the past.

The above illustrates that there are numerous internal and external factors affecting the IPO timeline. In reality, it usually takes longer than the four-month minimum as described above. Even after a customized day-by-day timetable is developed and agreed upon by the key project parties, there are many sources of uncertainty that, to the extent they materialize, could give rise to extensions and delays.

Preparation is a critical success factor and takes the most time

Following the rule-of-thumb timeline, as described above, nine out of the ten months of the IPO process are dedicated to tasks and activities of a preparatory nature in relation to the contemplated IPO. The public marketing phase accounts only for approximately one month. To the extent, the overall timetable is longer than 10 months, it is typically the preparatory phase that takes longer to complete. There is not much timing variation to the four-week public marketing phase, except perhaps for a few days deviation depending on the market in which the IPO is taking place and other external factors. This relative allotment of time is a good indicator for the importance and labor-intensive nature of the preparation phase in the overall scope of an IPO project. This does not at all imply that the marketing phase of the transaction is somehow less important. However, thorough and careful preparation is a pre-condition for successful marketing and, ultimately, successfully selling the IPO to target investors.

Based on a large volume of information provided by the company in response to information requests, the external parties familiarize themselves extensively with the legal, commercial and financial details of the IPO company. This exercise, also referred to as "due diligence", provides external advisers with the information base for capital structure and offer structure decisions and helps in the development of a refined and convincing selling story (including for the production of marketing materials) that resonates well with research analysts and target investors. This exercise also helps the advisers to craft high-quality, consistent offer documentation that is water tight from legal perspective.

Across work streams and tasks, this phase is very much about drafting concepts and documents as well as reviewing, discussing and refining them with the objective of optimally preparing for the subsequent marketing phase. The preparatory phase also involves intense discussions among the various parties at the table (within their distinct roles) to ensure the actions taken by the respective parties involved in the IPO process simultaneously promote the objectives of marketability, balanced disclosure, consistency and liability protection.

Orchestration of major work streams and tasks requires rigorous project management

The typical IPO project organization builds on three major work streams, as described above, each comprising a number of individual tasks. Throughout the lifetime of the IPO project, many of these tasks involve different parties and run in parallel on a daily basis, creating a reasonably high degree of complexity. The lead managing underwriters are typically tasked with the overall IPO project management. Together with the other involved parties, they develop a detailed project timetable setting out all key tasks and milestones on a day by day basis. On this basis, they coordinate the tasks of the various working groups for completion of the several work streams and regularly review progress against the timeline to proactively identify and address any looming timing issues.

Several tasks from the various work streams and associated milestones define whether or not achievement of the envisioned IPO timeline will be possible. There is very little room for delays of task completion and milestone achievement without jeopardizing the entire timeline. Therefore, the lead managing underwriters typically behave rather rigorously in their capacity as head of the IPO project management.

The hot phase starts with commencement of formal investor marketing

The entire effort described above targets having all necessary preparatory measures in place on day X, in order for the IPO company to be in a position to proceed to the public marketing phase. The commencement of the marketing phase is also referred to as the "launch" of the offering. There is usually an official announcement by the IPO company of its intention to become publicly listed, also referred to as the "intention to float" announcement. This announcement may still be reasonably unspecific as to offer structure details, transaction volume, timing and other aspects, also in reflection of local regulation of offering-related communication. In practice, however, such announcement indicates that the IPO is fully prepared and investor marketing is to commence imminently. This also implies that, to the extent the syndicate banks publish transaction research reports, these documents will be distributed to target investors and syndicate banks' research analysts will start their investor education activities.

The research analysts' investor education program is followed by the management roadshow, where the IPO company's senior management, usually the CEO and CFO, meet with key target institutional investors in order to convince them to buy shares in the IPO. This is an extremely intense period for the management team, with a tight schedule of six to eight one-on-one meetings with institutional investors per day, sometimes complemented by group presentations over breakfast or lunch, and a very busy travel schedule (see also chapter 11). The typical format of an investor meeting is a concise and convincing presentation by management, followed by a questions and answers session. It is expected that management will deliver a consistent performance throughout all investor meetings and that these company individuals remain fully concentrated and engaged until the last investor meeting ends (there can be up to 80 such meetings in a two-week period).

In parallel to the management roadshow and at least a few days prior to the end of the expected pricing date, the bookrunners start taking orders from investors. The aggregate orders form the "book of demand" (or "orderbook") and the process is referred to as "bookbuilding" (see also chapters 2.2 and 3.3). Investors tend to submit their orders towards the end of the bookbuilding period. Therefore, the orderbook starts to build relatively slowly and develops most momentum, i.e., its highest growth rates, during the last few days of the management roadshow. However, orderbook dynamics may also be very different, depending on the market environment, perceived level of interest in the IPO and other factors. In addition, the bookrunning managers guide investors as to price and demand to support an efficient process.

Pricing, allocation and settlement – the formal end of the project

The bookbuilding ends in the afternoon of the pricing day. Once the orderbook is closed, the bookrunning managers process the information to prepare for the pricing meeting. In this meeting, the principals decide on the final IPO share price. Key criteria that are usually taken into account are, inter alia, demand (respectively, oversubscription) at various prices, investor type, investor quality and track record in other transactions as well as expected stock market direction on the next trading day. Ideally, the final price optimally balances the interests of the IPO company and the selling shareholders (both sellers of shares) with those of the investors buying the shares.

Once the offer price is agreed, the IPO shares need to be allocated to investors, as total demand in a successful IPO will exceed the offer volume. Depending on the extent of the demand overhang, some or many investors may not receive any shares at all. Some others may get a minimum allocation whereas others get an allocation amounting to a certain percentage of their order. Full allocations are rather uncommon.

The lead managers usually come up with a first allocation proposal that then may be more or less controversially discussed by the principals. At this stage, the management team can significantly influence the shareholder structure and may want to reflect their experience from the roadshow meetings in this process. The banks, however, know the investors well, often also from participation in other IPOs, and may have a different perspective on individual investors than the management team.

Allocations are communicated to investors by the syndicate banks either on the evening of the pricing day or prior to stock market opening on the following trading day. On this basis, investors can start trading shares on the stock exchange. Some investors will sell their allocation in part or entirely whereas others may want to increase their holding or build a position. This way, ongoing trading activity develops.

Both pricing and allocation require extensive skill, experience and market knowledge. Both decisions are decisive to the success or failure of the IPO, as measured by after-market performance. It is only apparent with the start of ongoing stock market trading whether the decisions made on price and allocation were right. Ideally, the shares start trading above the IPO price and trade up slightly over the next few days and do not fall below the IPO price, even if equity markets move down a bit. Trading liquidity should be sufficiently high but not excessive on the first trading day and then reach a level that ensures liquid trading on an ongoing basis.

Another important date is settlement, which typically occurs two or three days after pricing, depending on the jurisdiction and clearing system. At settlement, legal title in the shares is transferred from the seller to the buyer and the purchase price is transferred from the buyer to the seller. At settlement, the lead managing underwriter responsible for settlement transfers the IPO proceeds to the IPO company and any selling shareholders.

5.3 Timing is everything

Prediction of the optimal timing for an IPO is a challenge

Given all the required preparation ahead of an IPO, the principal decision by the IPO company and/or its existing shareholders to pursue an IPO needs to be made many months before the earliest possible pricing date. Successfully completing an IPO, however, requires many different internal and external factors to positively play out at the right time. Most of those factors are beyond the control of any of the IPO company, the existing shareholders or the external advisers.

During the fairly extensive preparation process, any changes that happen could materially affect the feasibility or outcome of the IPO. Notably, the potential changes can work both ways and could ultimately help achieve a better or worse outcome, compared to initial expectations. Yet, decisions to pursue an IPO are very much based on status-quo considerations in combination with expectations on future developments. These expectations may not materialize but could have a far-reaching impact on the ultimate outcome of the IPO, including a decision to postpone the transaction or to abandon the IPO plans altogether.

There is a material difference between the objectives of "getting an IPO done" and "hitting the ideal time window for completion of an IPO". The first approach is pragmatic and seeks to complete an IPO on reasonably attractive terms within the anticipated timeline. It can imply that the strategic objective of completing an IPO is more important than achieving the best possible outcome. The second approach focuses on achieving the best possible outcome, although the time windows for actually achieving this may be rare and short and, ultimately, uncertain.

For example, a company operating in an industry with pronounced business cycles such as semiconductors, container shipping or commodities may need to decide to start IPO preparations in anticipation of a cyclical recovery over the next two to three quarters. The cyclical recovery may show less momentum than expected with all other factors being supportive to complete an IPO. In such a scenario, the principals must decide whether to get the IPO done, maybe at less favorable terms than expected, or wait, potentially for an entire business cycle, and hope that the outcome of the IPO when completed at a later date will be superior. Sometimes, companies cannot afford waiting such a potentially long period for financial or strategic reasons.

Market volatility is the greatest enemy of IPO activity

As previously discussed in chapter 4.3, price discovery in an IPO is an important and somewhat extensive process. The involved parties must gather information and data points in order to refine their assessment of appropriate pricing along the way. For the purposes of valuation and ultimately pricing, relative measures and peer group comparisons are very important considerations for all key parties involved. Substantial changes in these parameters are counterproductive to the price discovery process as they spur discussion about the right price in a situation where the buyer and seller ultimately need to find common ground. Such changes become even more disruptive during the public marketing phase when the price discovery process is in full swing.

The degree of variation of stock market index levels or listed company stock prices is often expressed in volatility measures. In prolonged periods of elevated equity market volatility, i.e., where stock market indices and individual stock prices show relatively large daily changes, IPO activity is typically subdued and vice versa. Volatility jeopardizes the predictability of the likely outcome in terms of IPO price and volume. Hence, fewer IPOs are launched in periods of heightened volatility.

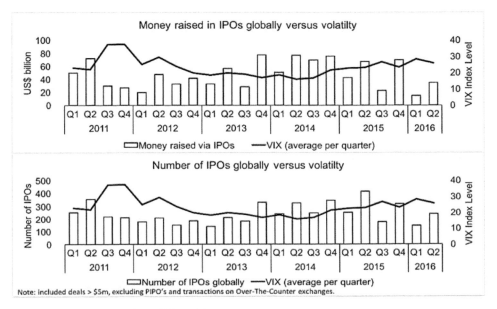

Exhibit 10: Volatility vs. global IPO activity
Source: PricewaterhouseCoopers, 2016

To the extent volatility spikes (unexpectedly) during the public marketing phase of an IPO, the risk of the IPO company and the selling shareholders ultimately not agreeing on a final price with investors increases. This is particularly the case where volatility occurs after the IPO price range is set. In case of pronounced changes in the relevant stock market indices or peer group valuation levels during this period, a final price within the price range may become more challenging to achieve and, in extreme cases, may become impossible to justify, either for the sellers or the buyers of the IPO shares. In such situations, IPOs often cannot be completed. Therefore, parties prefer periods of relatively low volatility for pursuing and completing IPOs.

Get prepared early and act opportunistically – the practitioner's mantra

As it is impossible to reliably predict the environment for a specific IPO many months ahead of marketing and pricing, in particular in a volatile world, parties are forced to deal with external uncertainty in the context of an IPO in a constructive manner. The typical advice to IPO companies and selling shareholders in this context is to be fully prepared as early and quickly as possible to be in a position to launch the IPO on short notice but to also launch the IPO only in a supportive market environment which allows the IPO to be completed with a satisfactory result.

In order to achieve this in practice, "go/no-go" decisions are scheduled at various points along the process during which the principal parties convene to form a decision on whether to proceed with the project to the next phase or not. These decisions can take place at various points during the confidential preparation phase, e.g., before additional parties get involved in the various IPO work streams described above. Typical decision points in this context are immediately prior to: (i) the initial submission of the draft offer document for regulatory review, (ii) the invitation of the banks' research analysts to the briefing event and (iii) the distribution of research reports (if not concurrent with the intention to float announcement).

The most important go/no-go decision point is immediately prior the release of the intention to float announcement. As this point marks the transition from the confidential phase to the public phase in the IPO process, it is also a natural break-point in the IPO process. The key decision makers of the principal parties carefully revisit all relevant available information, including, inter alia, investor feedback received, market sentiment, economic indicators, monetary policy and political decisions and other IPOs currently being conducted. On this basis, the principal parties consciously make a decision about whether to publicly announce the IPO plans and commence marketing or to wait for a few days, weeks or months in the expectation of finding a time window with a more supportive backdrop for the IPO, increasing the odds of successful completion or achievement of a better outcome.

Strategies to get the deal done

With the decision to launch an IPO, the transaction enters the phase during which it is fully exposed to market risk. During these approximately four weeks between launch and pricing, many things can (unexpectedly) happen that result in a deterioration of the backdrop to an individual IPO and which could ultimately jeopardize the chances of a successful completion. Market turbulence affecting the broader market or relevant subsectors may be sparked by unexpected events, such as terroristic attacks, natural disasters, negative surprise information (such as corporate results or economic indicators), a change in investor sentiment or could even develop spontaneously with no specific trigger. Certain structural features are available to reduce the market risk exposure of an IPO, prepare for the unforeseeable and improve chances to complete an IPO even in a challenging environment. These exist in addition to retaining maximum flexibility as late as possible into the process in order to be able to adjust the offer structure, as described in chapter 4.3.

A common feature in this context is the placement of a meaningful portion of the IPO shares to select investors ahead of the formal launch. This is to create a positive signaling effect for the subsequent offering and reduce the portion of the IPO that needs to be placed to investors during the usual bookbuilding process. Typically, the lead managing underwriters seek firm commitments for sizeable orders, sometimes equal to holdings of several percent in the IPO company, at a pre-agreed (absolute or relative) price from few, large and well-known institutional, strategic or financial investors. These so-called "cornerstone" or "anchor" investors need to make their investment decision prior to the publication of the offer document. Therefore, the accommodation of this "pre-placement process" requires additional preparation and marketing efforts outside the IPO process. The cornerstone investors usually benefit from a guaranteed, sizeable allocation of shares. In some jurisdictions, there may also be the possibility to grant a certain (small) discount to the final IPO price.

There are variations to the pre-placement concept across jurisdictions and sometimes even industry sectors, not the least as a result of local laws and regulation, established market practice and the individual IPO company's objectives. In some instances, IPO companies raised a significant amount of capital in a private financing round shortly prior to an IPO, with the primary objective to establish a floor for valuation and price for the subsequent IPO. Rocket Internet, a German Internet holding company, for example, entered into transactions involving the injection of fresh capital with Philippine Long Distance Telephone Company (PLDT), a Philippine telecommunications company, and United Internet, a German technology company, early in August 2014, with the IPO of Rocket Internet expected for autumn of that same year. The transactions valued Rocket Internet at EUR 3.3 billion (PLDT) and EUR 4.3 billion (United Internet) (Rocket Internet, 2014, p. 92), with only one week between the transactions and a rumored IPO valuation expectation of approximately EUR 5 billion. Arguably, private financings similar to those done by Rocket Internet may be considered as independent financing transactions unrelated to an IPO, although their positive spill-over effects on an IPO that shortly follows cannot be denied. In other instances, it is the existing shareholders that provide pre-placement commitments to signal confidence to potential IPO investors.

Another strategy to improve the probability of achieving successful IPO completion in potentially challenging times is to opt for a relatively smaller volume, no secondary component to the extent possible and the objective of attractive pricing from a buyer's perspective. This is in contrast to the often-adopted strategy by the IPO company and its shareholders of maximizing IPO volume and price. By not pushing volume and price to the limit, completing an IPO becomes relatively easier. It also forms the basis for a solid start of the IPO company as a publicly listed company with some share price appreciation in aftermarket trading. Existing shareholders' dilution in a smaller, moderately priced primary-only IPO is slightly higher. However, in the overall scope of things, this effect is usually small if not negligible, especially if there is no secondary component in the IPO, which would imply an actual sale of shares at a lower price. Once listed, and in consideration of any lock-up agreements, the existing shareholders can reduce their holdings in one or several follow-on offerings, potentially at higher share prices compared to the IPO price and potentially even above the price achievable in an aggressively-priced IPO (if such an IPO could have been completed at the time).

Postponing an IPO is (not) an easy thing to do

It happens regularly, though in some periods more often than in others, that the key principals need to decide whether or not to postpone an IPO at some stage of the process. As previously described, there are go/no-go decision points throughout the IPO process, with the most important one immediately prior to the publication of the intention to float announcement.

The intention to float announcement is usually the first public confirmation of the company's IPO plans, even though it occurs at an advanced stage of the IPO process. It may well be, however, that the media or other well-informed sources begin to publicly speculate and create specific expectations prior to the official announcement of a given IPO. Some jurisdictions also require a public filing of the draft offer document with the regulatory authority relatively early, having a clear signaling effect. However, it is market practice for companies not to comment on their IPO plans or any ongoing preparation activity prior to the intention to float announcement, except for unspecific comments on an IPO as a strategic option. In some jurisdictions, such as the United States, pre-IPO communication is even severely limited by law. Given the largely confidential nature of the process prior to the intention to float announcement, the IPO plans can be postponed or abandoned without public scrutiny and the associated potential reputational damage.

After the intention to float announcement, there is full public awareness of the specificity of the company's IPO plans and an estimated timeline to pricing. This leaves very limited leeway to change plans without raising suspicion surrounding the viability of the proposed offering and potentially creating collateral damage from negative publicity around alleged challenges of the company or the transaction. Therefore, the formal launch of the transaction is often considered a point of no return.

Yet, it is possible that investor feedback gathered during the research analysts' investor education program is either weak altogether or weaker than expected, which may suggest an IPO price range below the IPO company's and the existing shareholder's minimum expectation. Both are usually the result of a sudden and pronounced deterioration of the equity and IPO market environment. In such a case, the principal parties may decide not to proceed to the management roadshow phase at all for the time being or to delay it by one or two weeks. A delay makes sense if there is reasonable hope that the market situation will improve and that an acceptable price range for the IPO can be agreed. A delay of more than two weeks at this stage is usually difficult as the IPO loses momentum with potential investors. It then requires renewed marketing by the research analysts to reignite investor interest prior to the start of the management roadshow. Timing flexibility for longer delays at this late stage may also be limited by new company information, such as interim financial information, becoming available. This information would need to be communicated to research analysts and potential investors and would require formal incorporation in the offer document.

It is very rare that the IPO process is terminated during the management roadshow and once the IPO price range has been published. After the start of the management roadshow, an IPO usually runs until the end of the envisioned timeline and either prices or cannot be successfully priced. The latter is regarded as a "failed IPO".

5.4   Once in a lifetime experience (except for some ...)

There is only one IPO in the life of a company

An IPO marks the transition of a company from being privately held to becoming publicly listed. This transition can happen only once in a company's lifetime. However, this is not the only aspect defining the uniqueness of the IPO project for a company.

The IPO represents the first time that shares of a company are offered in a public offering. This implies that many aspects of the process are of a first-time nature to the company in some shape or form. The internal team of the IPO company brings together people and functions that may never before have worked on a common project of such an intense nature. Many of the tasks to be completed as part of the IPO process have only little (or no) similarity with what employees usually do within the IPO company. Conversely, all external parties have substantial experience in IPOs and some external team members may do nothing except work on IPO projects.

A follow-on equity offering by the company represents at least the second time that shares are offered in a public offering. Then, the company can usually draw on the work product, knowledge and experience gathered during the IPO project. Many aspects of a follow-on offering repeat processes initiated as part of the IPO, even if some of the internal company team members have changed and several years have passed since the IPO. All in all, the IPO is often a "learning by doing" experience for the company and helps to build the internal structures for subsequent equity offerings.

Substantial management attention implies a risk of distraction and business disruption

The labor-intensive nature of an IPO project, especially for the IPO company, represents a significant burden for large parts of the organization, not least for senior management, who are periodically fully tied up with the IPO project. Hence, an IPO has the potential to cause meaningful disruption to the operating business of the IPO company. However, it is of critical importance to ensure that the IPO and any associated disruption do not have an adverse short-term impact on the operating and financial performance of the business. The company needs to perform in line with research analyst and investor expectations when starting to report as a public company. These expectations reflect guidance given by the management team during the IPO process in accordance with the IPO company's business plan. Financial results that fall short of market expectations in the initial reporting as a public company seriously undermine investor trust in the senior management's ability to run the business. Investors usually act rather rigorously in such situations and may start selling shares of the IPO company. This usually prompts significant selling pressure for the IPO company's shares and may result in material share price declines.

At this early point in time, investor trust in management is still of a very sensitive nature and without a long history. As such, a prolonged disruption or even destruction of the trust relationship can occur relatively easily. Restoring investor confidence in such a situation may take a lot of time and extra effort by management. This underscores the importance of delivering a strong performance from day one as a publicly listed company (see also chapters 6.2 and 6.3).

Moments of mental and physical exhaustion for some along the way

An IPO is a once in a lifetime event for a company, often of strategic importance. The project timelines often turn out to be too ambitious along the way, as individual tasks may be more labor-intensive than initially expected. Under mounting time pressure, parties usually step up their efforts, deploy additional resources and, if required, add night shifts to deliver on time. It is rather normal for the working level IPO company employees and bankers and lawyers involved in the transaction to work 24 or even 36 hours without substantial sleep ahead of important deadlines.

These night shifts are not the exception to the rule but rather normal during particularly active phases of the IPO project. As a result, IPO projects are always very intense periods for the key working team members of all involved parties and have a tendency to become physically exhausting. Senior management of the IPO company in particular may be pushed to their capacity limits. During investor marketing, senior management, especially CEO and CFO, is practically unavailable for the daily business or any other IPO-related matters outside of marketing the IPO to investors. Everything else must then be taken care of outside of normal working hours. This can be a very stressful period for the management team, both physically and mentally, not least because the marketing days consist of many meetings, intense travel and the pressure to perform (see also chapter 11). When asked, many CEOs and CFOs would honestly admit that they could easily renounce doing a second IPO because of all the pressure and exhaustion it can cause. Company employees are usually happy that an IPO is a one-off event and even the professional service providers generally show signs of relief once an IPO comes to an end.

The re-IPO as exception to the rule

But some executives participate in more than one IPO in their lifetime and, as the exception to the general rule, even some companies undergo more than one IPO. This is the case where a publicly listed company is acquired by investors in a transaction which also encompasses a withdrawal of the listing, also called a "take private" transaction (see also chapters 2.4 and 7.4). Such take private transactions are often done by financial investors. After a holding period of a few years, these investors seek an exit and an IPO is often a viable option (next to a sale or merger transaction). A successful IPO in such a scenario is referred to as a "re-IPO". And a few years after the re-IPO, there may be another take private, and so on. Consequently, there are companies out there that have completed more than one IPO in their lifespans.

6 Public market readiness essentials

6.1 Corporate governance and compliance

Basic concepts and key principles

From an IPO company's perspective, going public entails substantially more than purely executing a securities transaction. As a public company, the post-IPO company must comply with a broad variety of new obligations and requirements imposed by stock market rules and regulations, applicable laws as well as the company's shareholders and, more broadly, the capital markets participants in general. The IPO company must be prepared to comply with these various requirements and standard market practices upon the successful completion of an IPO.

Transparency is one of the key concepts in this context. The importance of transparency has grown substantially over time, and so has the requirement for a newly publicly listed company to meet transparency requirements from day one. Corporate governance, risk management and compliance are key considerations in this context.

Corporate governance is an often-used term with many different economic, legal and practical definitions and can mean different things in different contexts. In the context of this book, corporate governance refers to the framework governing the relationships among a company's key decision makers (such as members of executive management, of the board of directors and key shareholders) and other stakeholders, such as employees, customers, suppliers and regulators.

Corporate governance is closely related to the concept of compliance, which describes the observance of all applicable laws and regulations as well as internal policies by a company, including by its executive management, board of directors and employees. Consequently, compliance also covers all corporate governance related aspects. It represents an important aspect of the overall corporate governance framework.

Risk management in this context refers to identifying, assessing, monitoring and managing potential significant risks associated with a company's business activities. These risks may result from strategic decisions, operational activity or external factors and can be of a legal, commercial, financial or reputational nature.

For an IPO company to be able to deliver transparency and comply with all listed company obligations, it is essential to have in place appropriate corporate governance, a working compliance function and a robust risk management system. Unlike for a private company, where governance, compliance and risk management may be less stringent (with the agreement of the existing shareholders), shareholders, in particular institutional investors, expect public companies to adhere to certain (high) standards. Therefore, it is of critical importance for an IPO company to start developing appropriate structures ahead of time in order to prepare for its life as a publicly listed company. Usually, this is not directly part of the IPO preparations. Nonetheless, it is of critical importance and may pose additional strain on the IPO company prior and during the actual IPO preparation phase.

Governance structures vary by jurisdiction and legal form

In most jurisdictions, only a limited number of legal forms of a company qualify for a stock market listing. These are usually forms of stock corporations where the company's equity is securitized in the form of equity shares (in contrast to individual companies) such as "corporation" in the US, a "public limited company" or "plc" in the UK, an "Aktiengesellschaft" or "AG" in Germany and a "societas europeae" or "SE" within the European Union.

The respective board structure of these legal forms is an important feature of a company's overall corporate governance framework. The legal forms, usually governed by a set of laws in the jurisdiction in which a company is incorporated, provide more or less specific guidelines for required board structures but often leave significant freedom for adaptation to individual circumstances. Broadly speaking, there are two principal types of board structures: a one-tier board, primarily found in Anglo-Saxon countries, and a two-tier board structure found in many European countries and, notably, China.

Irrespective of the number of tiers in the board of a company, it is important that there is an executive management team in charge of the company's day-to-day operations and a board that is tasked with supervising the executive management team and making principal strategic decisions. In a one-tier board of directors, at least some members of the executive management team also serve on the board (as executive directors), together with non-executive directors who are not involved in the company's daily business. In a two-tier board, there is an executive management board and a supervisory board. The two boards have no overlap, i.e., no individual can be simultaneously a member of both the executive board and the supervisory board.

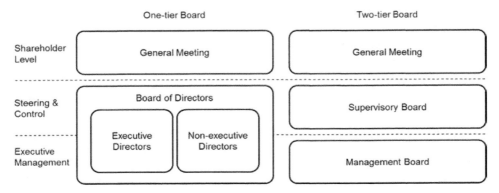

Exhibit 11: Illustration of one-tier board vs. two-tier board structure
Source: Own presentation

The segregation of duties between the two boards is important, in addition to clearly defined responsibilities and binding rules of procedure for each of them. The key objective is to provide for transparency of corporate decision making and ensure adequate supervision and control. Usually, the members of the board of directors or the supervisory board are elected by shareholders, whereas the executive management is appointed by the board of directors or the supervisory board.[21]

As a result, the ultimate power in a stock corporation resides with the shareholders. It is formally exercised in the annual general shareholder meeting when votes are cast on certain resolutions that are submitted for shareholder approval, either because this is required by law or the company's constitutional documents or because deemed appropriate by the board(s). From time to time, there may be need to hold an extraordinary shareholder meeting to vote on important, time critical matters prior to the next regular meeting. While the detailed formalities around convocation and holding of shareholder meetings vary by jurisdiction and requirements of the company's by-laws, the principle of the shareholders as ultimate decision makers of a company is universal.

"One share, one vote" please!

IPO investors attribute significant importance to an appropriate governance framework that forms a solid basis for adequate safeguarding and representation of their interests. This is particularly important as the IPO not only represents the transition from private to public ownership but also entails a significant change to the IPO company's shareholder structure. Privately owned companies often have concentrated shareholder structures with one or few shareholders substantially controlling the company. Upon completion of an IPO, the IPO investors in the aggregate usually own some 15 to 30 percent of the share capital, with the existing shareholders still exercising significant influence over, if not control of, the company. This implies that one or few existing shareholders with a large stake in the company jointly own(s) the IPO company together with a fairly large number of IPO investors who individually hold relatively small equity stakes. Interests of the various groups of shareholders are not necessarily fully aligned.

Therefore, IPO investors generally look for shares that have voting rights attached, so-called "voting shares". Moreover, there is a preference for share structures with only one share class, i.e., where all shares of the IPO company are identical in terms of economic interest and voting power. This ensures that each party's voting power is in proportion to its economic interest in the IPO company and vice versa.

---

[21] As an exception, for example, in the Netherlands the supervisory board proposes management board candidates but it is indeed the General Shareholder Meeting that elects/appoints the management board members.

Many jurisdictions allow several classes of shares. One variation to the "one share, one vote" concept described above is so-called non-voting shares that do not have a voting right (but may be entitled to a slightly higher dividend as compensation). Another variation is so-called super-voting shares that are equipped with multiple voting rights. By combining two or more share classes, it is possible to implement voting power and shareholder control that is disproportionate to the distribution of the economic interests.

In particular, family-owned companies pursuing an IPO frequently consider employing these structural features in order to secure long-term control over the IPO company. These structures are often carefully scrutinized by IPO investors. However, in certain situations such as where there is a very compelling investment opportunity, IPO investors may be willing to accept (sometimes even substantial) deviations from the concept of proportionate voting power and economic interest and to give up (part of) their voting power. A very prominent example in this context is the IPO of Facebook, a social media company, which took place in 2013. At IPO, the company had a dual share class structure. Class A shares, which were offered to investors and traded under the ticker "FB" on the public market, were entitled to one vote per share. Class B shares, which were owned by company insiders, including Mark Zuckerberg, the CEO, president and founder, were entitled to 10 votes per share and were convertible into an equal number of Class A shares at any time. The Class B shares were not initially publicly traded. Following the IPO, the holders of Class B shares held approximately 96 percent of the voting power of Facebook's outstanding capital stock. Mark Zuckerberg had the ability to control approximately 56 percent of the outstanding capital stock (Facebook, 2012, p. 1). While this matter and the broader governance structure of Facebook were subject of discussion ahead of the IPO, the attractions of Facebook's investment proposition ultimately outweighed investors' concerns and the IPO was heavily oversubscribed. However, investors typically make less concessions in IPOs of companies that are not considered "must own" stocks.

Adequate board representation by independent directors

Composition of the controlling committee, i.e., the board of directors or supervisory board, is also an important consideration in the context of an IPO. As a private company, the controlling committee is comprised of representatives of the existing shareholders (and, depending on company size and jurisdiction, employee representatives).

Depending on the pre-IPO shareholder structure, the committee may be relatively large in order to allow for adequate representation of each significant existing shareholder. With a view to becoming a publicly listed company, the overall size of the board may need to be reduced to bring it in line with market practice for board size of comparable companies. At the same time, it is important to complement the board with additional members representing the interests of the IPO investors. These new members are referred to as "independent directors" as they do not represent any of the large existing shareholders but speak for the IPO investors who collectively (together with any small existing shareholders) form the initial "free float" of the company. Free float refers to the shares held by investors who individually hold relatively small shareholdings (in percentage terms) and are considered more or less freely tradable.

IPO investors usually require meaningful independent representation. A share of independent directors in proportion to the targeted level of free float is often considered adequate in this context. IPO investors look for independent directors that are experienced executives or industry experts with credibility in the investment community, potentially already holding similar directorships with other companies. Ultimately, investors want to be comfortable that their interests are properly represented at the board level and vis à vis the directors representing the existing shareholders.

Separation of company and shareholder spheres is imperative

A privately held company's relationship with its shareholders can be multi-layered and is not always entirely clear cut. This holds true for many pre-IPO situations, including family businesses, private equity exits or the IPO business is being carved out of a larger existing enterprise. There may be so-called related party transactions such as loans to or from shareholders, employment or service contracts with shareholders and intercompany transactions. While many related party transactions are legal, the terms and conditions of such transactions are often different than those that would be available to unrelated parties. In addition, there may be allocation of private costs and expenses to the company, private use of company resources as well as informal influence on operational and strategic decisions.

An unrelated investor may (with good reason) not be willing to indirectly "subsidize" other shareholders or accept influence outside the formal governance framework. Hence, it is important that there is a clear separation between the spheres of the shareholders and the company, with the objective of reducing related party transactions and ensuring any related party transactions that occur are on market terms. This goes beyond identification of any potential conflicts and providing transparent disclosure of potential issues and may include terminating practices that blur clear shareholder-company relationships.

6.2   Management information & reporting systems

Management needs relevant, up-to-date information more often

Another topic that is often discussed in the context of public market readiness is the availability of adequate management information systems. Almost irrespective of management style, managers usually take relevant business information into account when making management decisions. Therefore, it is important to have systems in place that provide decision makers on all management levels with appropriate and correct information in a timely manner.

In practice, however, the implementation of management information systems that provide sufficient and adequate information on a timely basis is often not a primary focus for privately owned companies. This holds especially true for rapidly growing companies that can be overwhelmed by the challenges of managing their growth. The development of management information systems that keep pace with the increasing size and complexity of the business is often of lower priority than growing operations, revenues and profits. Even in the absence of rapid growth, management information systems can be overlooked, either because of the costs of implementation, perceived lack of need by management or focus on other topics. This is usually acceptable to the existing shareholders as long as they are pleased with the results delivered by management.

However, with the commencement of IPO preparations and certainly as a publicly listed company, the IPO company's senior management team regularly needs up-to-date management information. During the IPO preparatory phase, management need, inter alia, such information as a basis for the investment bankers' business due diligence and for many of the corporate finance related work streams (see also chapter 5.1). Timely availability and regular updates of important information and relevant key performance indicators (or "KPIs") are crucial to understand the current performance of the business and outlook. The availability of current performance measures on a weekly and monthly basis is often useful to help external parties better understand business dynamics and any seasonality or cyclicality. As a publicly listed company, the information need of senior management also continues to be of high importance on an ongoing basis. Research analysts and investors expect management to be well-informed on all aspects of their business at all times. As part of ongoing investor relations practices, almost real-time availability of key information, both aggregated and in a fair amount of detail, is needed to respond to external inquiries in a manner that signals that senior management is in full control of the business. As the management's focus following an IPO shifts more towards the company's short-term performance, the company's reporting systems need to be capable of capturing and analyzing information to allow for timely decision making.

In order to be able to meet these information needs in terms of breadth, depth and integrity, as well as timeliness of availability, many IPO companies need to upgrade, often substantially, their existing management information systems. And while it is advantageous to have sufficient management information available already during IPO preparation, it is imperative to have adequate management information systems in place as a publicly listed company. Even if an IPO company initiates the upgrade of its management information systems well ahead of the IPO and commits significant resources, such efforts could still prove insufficient or ineffective and require further attention during or immediately following the IPO process. As this could have a material adverse impact on the business and financial performance of the IPO company, lawyers and bankers often advise the company to include appropriate language in the risk factor section of the offer document to provide a defense against investor claims in case such shortcomings occur.

No negative surprises for research analysts and investors, please!

An IPO company's senior management is expected to be well-informed on the business of the company and industry trends that could affect it at all times and to a considerable level of detail and granularity. Regular timely updates on business performance therefore are essential to bring senior management into a position to benchmark current and future business performance against external expectations, in particular from research analysts and investors. To the extent, the management information indicates that there may be noteworthy deviations from expected performance, the management team can react quickly by taking appropriate action to bring business performance back on track to meet or slightly exceed expectations. Alternatively, if corrective action is not possible, senior management can start actively managing research analysts' and investors' expectations (downwards) to avoid negative surprises upon official publication of financial results.

Public market investors prefer visibility and predictability of company performance and financial results, especially earnings. Their preference also extends to IPO companies that are newly listed. The concept of "visibility" in this context refers to the existence of parameters that serve as a good proxy for future earnings, i.e., that can be regarded as lead indicators. A good example of a lead indicator is a company's order book or project pipeline. The concept of "predictability" refers to the probability that an expected earnings level can be achieved and that earnings develop in accordance with a specific pattern.

Therefore, it is important for the IPO company's management team to have management information systems in place that provide optimal support in delivering the highest possible degree of visibility and predictability for earnings and company performance to analysts and investors during marketing of the IPO and as a publicly listed entity. This may necessitate a more or less substantial change to the existing management reporting that may have been implemented with a focus on different objectives and at a time when an IPO was not on the company's strategic agenda.

Publication of financial results: more often and more detail

Regular financial reporting, including the publication of interim results, is a further key feature of publicly listed companies for which an IPO company needs to be adequately prepared. It is common market practice (as well as to a large degree a requirement) for companies listed on a regulated stock exchange to publish interim financial results on a quarterly basis, i.e., for each of the first three quarters of each fiscal year, in addition to an annual financial report. A few stock exchanges, such as the London Stock Exchange, require only an interim financial report for the first six months of each fiscal year.

The interim and annual financial reports must comply with the requirements set forth in the respective accounting standards of the applicable GAAP, i.e., such as US GAAP or IFRS. Under IFRS, for example, it is accounting standard IAS 34 that sets out the minimum content of an interim financial report and the principles for recognition and measurement in financial statements presented for an interim period (IAS Plus).

While most pre-IPO companies have interim reporting in some shape or form to satisfy the information needs of their existing shareholders or creditors, the established reporting format often does not comply with the applicable GAAP in terms of principal components and the level of detail of the disclosure. The established underlying business processes may be unsuitable to support GAAP compliant interim reporting. Therefore, IPO companies must often implement reporting systems and processes that support the regular, timely production of complete interim financial reports that comply with applicable GAAP standards and satisfy ancillary information needs of research analysts and investors. This new form of disclosure is usually substantially more comprehensive and many IPO companies find it challenging, at least initially, to produce complete interim financial reports every three months.

As first time production of GAAP compliant interim financial reports often forms part of the IPO preparations, any initial challenges around this task may impact the IPO project timeline as described in chapter 5.2.

While private companies are used to preparing annual reports, a conversion to GAAP as described above may give rise to additional challenges at the time of the preparation of the first annual report as a publicly listed company.

Cycle time – investors and analysts want financials quickly

In addition to the effort of producing suitable interim (or annual) financial reports, it is also important that this information is produced and published within an appropriate time period after the end of the respective accounting period, i.e., the end of the quarter (or financial year).

IAS 34, for example, does not prescribe how soon after the end of an interim period an interim report should be published, but leaves this for decision by other parties such as stock exchanges and securities regulators. The timing for the latest possible publication of interim financial reports varies by stock exchange and ranges from within 45 days (NYSE) to within two months (LSE, FSE) after the reporting period end.

Some other stock exchanges may allow a bit more time for interim reporting and the time window is generally longer for annual reports.

In practice, the IPO company has approximately six to eight weeks for preparing its interim financial report (usually including a review by its auditors) before it needs to be published. Investors and research analysts generally have a preference to receive this information rather sooner than later and often benchmark timing to publication against that of listed peer companies. These externally imposed cycle times are, sometimes even substantially, shorter than what many IPO companies are used to from their interim reporting as a private company when deadlines are more generous and less binding.

As a result, IPO companies are confronted with the need to substantially speed up the preparation of interim financial reports, representing a challenge for many organizations. Together with the enlarged scope and increased frequency of disclosure, IPO companies need an appropriate level of preparedness to avoid being overwhelmed by the public market requirements around financial reporting.

Information technology infrastructure: spreadsheets and beyond

Management information and financial reporting largely depend on the availability of data and information in systems that support efficient handling, correct analysis and flexible outputs. Given the large amounts of data and information available within IPO companies today, the availability of appropriate, integrated technology infrastructure and software tools has never been more important.

However, in reality things are often far from perfect and IPO companies tend to be underinvested in this respect. It is not uncommon, especially for smaller and medium-sized IPO companies, for spreadsheets and a suite of spreadsheet-based tools to form a very important part of these companies' IT backbone. A lack of systems integration across functions and legal entities as well as the need for manual manipulation can often be observed as well.

With a view to the above-described requirements in terms of public market readiness, it is important that an IPO company operates an IT infrastructure that is able to adequately support the company during the IPO preparation phase as well as in meeting its obligations as a publicly listed entity. This has become an important focus area in the context of IPO readiness assessment and operational risk management.

6.3 Planning and ability to deliver on promises

Future performance – a key focus at IPO and beyond

While a company's actual historical operating and financial performance is important in the context of an IPO, analysts, investors and other capital markets participants focus more broadly on the future. They are "forward-looking" and place great importance on expected future operational and financial performance in their assessment of investment opportunities and, ultimately, investment decisions. The expected future development of a company is much more relevant to valuation and value appreciation than its historical performance (see also chapter 3.2). And while historical developments and trends in performance represent important information, past performance is not necessarily a good indicator or a guarantee of future results.

The forward-looking focus of analysts and investors is highly relevant in the context of an IPO and subsequently when the company becomes publicly listed. Research analysts and investors want to develop a robust understanding of the IPO company's expected future metrics such as earnings growth, profitability and select key performance indicators. They also want to benchmark the IPO company against relevant peers by comparing key future metrics in order to develop a detailed understanding of the expected relative performance of the IPO company within the peer group. Both the absolute and relative assessment of the expected future performance of the IPO company form important parts of the overall investment analysis.

In order to bring the research analysts and investors into a position to conduct their financial analysis in the context of an IPO, the IPO company needs to provide adequate guidance as to its expected future performance. Guidance is usually given to the syndicate banks' research analysts during the analyst briefing phase. The IPO company's guidance usually extends two or three years into the future and includes information on the development of key income statement line items such as revenue, EBITDA and taxes, as well as development of working capital, other important cash flow relevant items and indebtedness. It may also include select operating metrics. The guidance, together with their own assumptions, should allow the research analysts to develop a reasonably detailed financial model of the IPO company, comprising an income statement, a cash flow statement and a balance sheet. Research analysts discuss and share their projections with investors as part of the investor education process. These projections represent an integral part of the IPO process and are highly relevant for valuation and price discovery in the IPO as well as for setting market expectations for operating and financial performance during the initial months following the successful completion of IPO. Therefore, it is critically important that the IPO company is comfortable with the research analysts' projections.

The concept of the company providing guidance to the research analysts is established market practice in an IPO process. All key information that is given to research analysts in this context must also be included in the offer document, but not necessarily in the same level of detail and granularity. As companies generally avoid including formal projections in the offer document, primarily for liability or other regulatory reasons, there is a limit as to what information can be shared with research analysts as part of the guidance process.

Robust business planning – a major effort

In order to provide the research analysts with guidance information and in the light of the importance of research analysts' projections in the IPO, the company must have a good understanding of its expected future performance. The guidance information is usually sourced from the IPO company's business plan. While most companies have a business plan in some shape or form, the underlying planning effort and the robustness of the business plan vary substantially in practice. Similar to management information systems as described above, the implementation of a robust business planning routine with adequate processes and regular updates is often not a primary focus for privately owned companies.

As a result, the IPO company's business plan draws much attention during IPO preparation, especially in the early phase. The business plan undergoes comprehensive due diligence by the investment bankers who seek to understand the underlying robustness of the planning process, question developments and trends in the financial figures and check their plausibility. The objective is to ensure the business plan is sufficiently sound for the purposes of the IPO and supports an appropriate valuation and price. This effort must be completed before any guidance information is confidentially shared with the syndicate banks' research analysts.

Post-IPO, research analysts and investors continue to expect senior management to regularly provide reliable, reasonably specific information on expected business developments. Such "outlooks" are usually provided at the beginning of the financial year and updated regularly when publishing interim financial results or, if required, on an ad-hoc basis. During the IPO process, companies often encounter the necessity to upgrade their business planning to be in a position to effectively meet market expectations by delivering forecast information that is up to date and reflects the latest information on actual performance and external developments (e.g., regarding the market and competitive environment and input costs).

The importance of being able to deliver

The IPO company's business plan is closely interlinked with its strategic plan which sets out the longer-term strategic objectives of the company. Guidance and strategic goals communicated to research analysts and investors in the IPO establish the expectation level against which the IPO company and its management team will be measured. Communicated guidance and strategic goals are usually regarded as "promises" by the IPO company's senior management team. In the absence of a track record of successfully operating a publicly listed company, it is important that senior management quickly gains the trust of research analysts and investors regarding its management capabilities. In order to achieve this, it is imperative that in the initial financial reporting post IPO and at each reporting date thereafter the company's actual results meet or, better yet, slightly exceed the established expectation level.

This also has a meaningful impact on the job profiles of the IPO company's senior management team. They need to be the right team to successfully manage the company and internally establish ambitious yet achievable operating and financial goals as well as a convincing strategic roadmap for the future. In addition, they must adequately communicate externally to establish appropriate expectations with research analysts and investors and, if necessary, manage these expectations on an ongoing basis. Last but not least, they must ensure that actual company performance is in line with market expectations. This often represents a significant expansion of the job profile of existing management. Therefore, it is not unusual to see personnel changes in senior management positions in the lead up to an IPO to better align the management team's capabilities with public market requirements. Having a suitable management team in place is mission critical for a successful IPO and life as a publicly listed company.

Trust is a delicate plant …

During the IPO process, the senior management team starts building relationships with research analysts and investors. However, this is only the beginning of a long-term effort, and research analysts and investors usually take a substantial leap of faith.

Therefore, it is crucial that senior management quickly builds credibility and trust with research analysts and investors, ideally by showing a spotless track record of fully delivering against market expectations. Supported by a professional investor relations effort, this should show results quickly. However, in the early stages, the trust of research analysts and investors in the management team is somewhat delicate. It can take relatively little, e.g., a surprise earnings miss or unexpected profit warning, to cause serious damage to the relationship (and consequently share price). Restoring trust takes substantial time and extra effort.

6.4   The Equity Story – giving a share a life of its own

The five-minute elevator pitch

A convincing investment proposition that appeals to public market investors is a key prerequisite for any company considering an IPO. It forms the basis for the IPO company's ability to attract investor interest and compete against investment alternatives in the form of already listed companies. The investment proposition is a vital consideration if not the single highest hurdle in the context of public market readiness. There is merit in considering an IPO only if the company's investment proposition is strong enough, which involves a subjective judgment by experienced professionals rather than meeting a set of clearly defined criteria. In some instances, individual views on a specific company may vary. In addition, research analyst and investor preferences evolve over time and may change relatively quickly, which may complicate a reliable judgment even more.

The "equity story" represents a high-level summary of an IPO company's investment proposition in a condensed format and tailored to the use of research analysts and professional public market equity investors. It is the five-minute elevator pitch summarizing they key arguments as to why an investor should invest in the IPO company's shares. The equity story aims at communicating the company's core competencies, competitive strengths and future strategy. It often draws on the successful historical development of the IPO company to invoke future upside potential. Key arguments of the equity story are typically based on attractiveness of the markets in which the company operates, the company's proprietary know-how or technology, its revenue and earnings growth potential, profitability or cash-flow generation, capital returns, financial strength, quality of the management team, etc.

Owing to the great importance the equity story has on the success of an IPO, the IPO company and investment bankers spend substantial time formulating, refining and fine-tuning the equity story. There needs to be detailed information that effectively underpins each of the arguments and makes them more powerful. This often represents a challenge, as the most compelling information may not be available or cannot be substantiated for inclusion in the offer document. In this case, investment bankers' creativity kicks in, resulting in the use of proxies and other props to craft a convincing equity story.

There is, in some instances, substantial leeway for spinning the equity story in different directions, much to the like and dislike of the involved individuals. This also extends to the IPO company's positioning against publicly listed peers and peer groups, and often prompts heated debates among investment bankers, the company and the existing shareholders. Each party may have a distinct view on the equity story outline, its key building blocks and detailed formulation.

"KISS" – not always easy to achieve

The characteristics of companies considering an IPO are very diverse. Business models can be anything from relatively simple to understand to highly complex. This also holds true for other aspects such as geographic footprint, number of business segments and degree of diversification, technological edge, specificity of and focus on niche markets, client exposure and other areas. Generally, the overall complexity increases with the operational size of a business, but there are exceptions to this observation in practice.

Simplification is a key concept when it comes to developing the equity story for an IPO. The KISS principle, interpreted as "keep it short and simple" in this context, describes what often works best. But in practice, this is easier said than done. While the five to ten main building blocks of the equity story, the "key investment highlights", are mostly obvious and uncontroversial to identify, at least in principle, there is usually a good deal of discussion in the working group when it comes to fleshing each of them out. There is often a tendency to pack many different arguments and facts together, which ultimately can lead to a dilution of the key message to be conveyed. Cutting through complexity and distilling the right messages that resonate well with research analysts and investors requires discussion, practical experience and deep understanding of the target audience.

Tailoring the equity story to the target audience can be less straightforward than it sounds. Research analysts are usually familiar with the IPO company's industry and its key peers as most investment banks assign research analysts to IPOs on the basis of the individual's geographic and sector coverage focus. The universe of target investors tends to be relatively diverse, ranging from sector specialists to generalists. The equity story needs to appeal to the broadest possible set of different investor types within the target investor universe. In some instances, this may resemble the squaring of the circle and is a key reason why IPOs in some sectors, such as biotech, medtech and semiconductors, put a heavy focus on targeting specialist investors.

Buy on hope?

The equity story often strongly emphasizes the future upside potential of the IPO company rather than actual earnings and cash flow. This is particularly the case for younger companies and businesses that experience accelerated growth. These companies raise fresh equity in the IPO to finance future growth and the focus is less on profitability. In this context, judgment is necessary on how mature the company needs to be for a successful IPO. This requires an assessment of how much credit research analysts and investors are willing to give the IPO company and its management as to their ability to achieve future milestones and which of those milestones actually need to be delivered at the time of the IPO. For example, this may refer to the question of whether a biotechnology company can (or should) do an IPO based on the results of late phase clinical studies but prior to obtaining formal regulatory approvals for its planned products. IPO investors may not be willing to bear the risk of not obtaining these approvals, which would have a material impact on the value of the IPO company and its share price and could result in significant investment losses. If the biotechnology company requires additional funds to achieve the approval milestones, it may be better advised to conduct another private financing round prior to conducting an IPO. Investors participating in such financings usually have a greater tolerance to accept risks, but expect higher returns in exchange.

Generally, such key milestones for IPO readiness from an equity story perspective may be of an internal and external nature. They can relate, inter alia, to levels of commercial traction, length of track record, regulatory approvals and sometimes even political decisions. They are highly case specific and are often characterized by an element of subjectivity and discretion.

The equity stories of recovery situations, i.e., where the IPO company projects strong improvement of the revenue and earnings growth post IPO, can also be somewhat delicate. Investors may or may not take the required leap of faith. They usually want to see an improvement in the actual financial results for two or three quarters rather than making a bet without any evidence that those improvements are coming through.

It's the fashion, darling ...

The IPO market is subject to fashion trends. Certain industries, business models or other key characteristics are especially popular with IPO investors while the particular trend lasts, similar to the dynamics of a true fashion trend. This may reflect the exceptionally favorable development or attractive outlook of a certain industry, new business models reaching a certain maturity stage and demonstrating their attractiveness as well as many other different factors. With respect to IPOs, this means that certain equity stories work better at certain times than they probably would at a different time. Conversely, there are times when waves of IPOs, i.e., IPOs of companies that share common key features, simultaneously flood the market. These time windows may last anywhere from a few months to several years. It is usually easy to identify IPO trends relatively quickly, but difficult to predict how long the trend will last. Therefore, IPO candidates may try to rush to the market in order to "ride the wave" and not miss the window of opportunity. With hindsight, it is often evident that even weaker companies managed to successfully complete an IPO as part of a wave. Such waves are typically followed by shake-outs and after a few years a number of the IPO companies may even cease to be listed.

From 2005 to 2008, for example, IPOs of solar companies were very much en vogue. There were numerous successful IPOs in Europe, the United States and Asia of companies such as Solarworld, Q.Cells, centrotherm photovoltaics, First Solar, Sunpower, GT Solar, Yingli Solar, Solarfun, Suntech Power and many others. Today, only a few of these companies continue to be publicly listed. The others either went insolvent or were acquired during a prolonged industry shake-out caused by changes to the regulatory framework for promoting solar power in many jurisdictions and a fierce competitive environment.

The IPO wave of 3D printing companies in 2013 to 2015 and the post-dotcom renaissance of biotechnology IPOs from 2013 onwards represent further examples in this context. IPO activity in the biotechnology sector in particular reflects renewed risk appetite by investors for the all-or-nothing bets that biotechnology IPOs often present.

IPO heritage for the company

The equity story also forms the basis of the IPO investor marketing. It can also have significant after effects as it defines the investment proposition of the IPO company, at least in its initial phase as a publicly listed company. The initial equity story developed by the company during an IPO process will continue to frame external communication and the investor relations dialogue. Only as the IPO company develops further, will the equity story evolve, although this is usually a gradual process. It is fairly rare to see significant changes to the key building blocks of the equity story soon after an IPO, not least for reasons of continuity and avoidance of surprises to research analysts and investors. Owing to the intensity of the IPO marketing, the equity story is usually deeply rooted in research analysts' and investors' minds.

The company will be measured against expectations raised by the equity story in terms of reaching operating and financial goals as well as strategic milestones. Investment bankers and other IPO advisors have great interest, not least for reputational reasons, to see an IPO company deliver against the targets it sets and this becomes a daily focus of the company's management following the IPO. In situations where it turns out that the IPO-related goal-setting, for reasons of achieving favorable terms in the IPO or otherwise, was too ambitious, the company and its management feel the effects most significantly. There are rarely direct negative repercussions for parties involved in the IPO project other than the company and its management and shareholders. This is a key reason why development of a favorable yet realistic equity story is of great importance during the IPO process.

7 Public company status implications – forever!?

7.1 Media attention...there is no off the record

Public ownership drives public interest and media attention

Initial public offerings of almost all transaction sizes tend to attract media attention, in particular from newspapers, magazines and TV channels focusing on business and economic affairs. The media usually becomes fully engaged with an IPO upon publication of the intention to float announcement, when the transaction is in an advanced stage and reasonably likely to be completed. Media coverage of the IPO company and the transaction moves both into the spotlight of public interest.

While media attention may peak in the final weeks and days of the IPO timeline, interest in the IPO company, especially from a corporate and financial communication perspective, continues once the IPO is completed and the company operates as a publicly listed entity. As such, the IPO often marks the point in time when a company's corporate and financial affairs move onto the public radar screen and become subject to regular, more or less intense media coverage. This can represent a marked change for many newly listed companies that did not attract substantial media interest prior to their IPO, due to smaller size, an intentional effort to stay out of the spotlight or other reasons. The stock market listing, research analyst coverage as well as a broader and more diversified shareholder structure drive general visibility of the IPO company and subsequent media interest to serve the public's information needs.

Privately held companies, especially family-owned companies, often adopt rather secretive behavior when it comes to external communication. Disclosure of financial and corporate matters is frequently limited to the bare minimum that is required by law. Those companies also tend to handle other external communication very restrictively, with the objective of deterring public interest as well as media attention and preserving the company's privacy to the maximum extent possible. While this general attitude towards external communication may not change with the IPO, companies have to accept that the media will take a greater interest in their affairs post IPO.

Media attention – a double-edged sword?

Some IPO companies, however, decide to change their attitude towards external communication and interaction with the media as part of going public. This often reflects the fact that a public company status will impose some required changes regarding more open communication, regardless of company wishes, and that an increased level of media and public interest can also be beneficial to the company; as they say, if you can't beat them, join them.

In reality, increased media attention and public interest usually work in two ways. Good and bad news flow from the company is picked up quickly and spread widely almost in real time. This can be either helpful or detrimental for the company.

Apart from dissemination of information to the financial community, increased media focus can help boost the general awareness of the company and build its profile with the public. This in turn can have positive spill-over effects in other areas, such as recruiting and retaining talent or acquiring new customers for the company's products or services. However, the media pick up on positive and negative news with equal intensity, meaning that media attention is not a one-way road but can also work against the company's interests. And while companies clearly prefer good news over not-so-good news, the media tend to be neutral at best.

There is no choice – communicate carefully!

As there is no alternative to dealing constructively with higher level of interest and attention in an IPO, an appropriate line-up within the internal organization is of critical importance. Clear policies and procedures help ensure clarity for all employees as to who should communicate what to whom and when.

This sounds rather trivial in theory but is greatly important in practice. Mishaps in external communication are an all-too-frequent occurrence. Naturally, there is more potential for errors when there is a greater need or demand for external communication. In addition, the consequences of poor external communication are likely to be more severe for publicly listed companies than for private companies, not least because of litigation risk from shareholders or other claimants and greater perceived financial strength as a target of court proceedings.

Even simple statements, believed to be rather unimportant, have the potential to prompt share price movements, trigger regulatory or judicial consequences or give rise to public outrage. A prominent yet extreme example in this context is the statement of Rolf Breuer, then-CEO of Deutsche Bank, a bank, in an interview with Bloomberg TV, a news channel, about the doubtful creditworthiness of Kirch Group, a German media group. Kirch Group filed for insolvency two months after the interview and its owner Leo Kirch sued Deutsche Bank for damages. The bank settled the claim and agreed to pay Kirch's heirs EUR 928 million following a lengthy legal battle. Subsequently, the bank claimed damages from Breuer and under their directors' and officers' liability insurance policy which also resulted in a settlement, this time in favor of the bank. (Spiegel Online, 2016)

Of friends and enemies

The media can be very influential. Therefore, it is advisable to actively maintain professionally managed relationships with a broad range of relevant media outlets and journalists. Individual journalists and entire organizations who serve as opinion leaders are of particular importance in this context and deserve special focus and attention. Being on constructive and friendly terms is helpful as media outlets often have substantial leeway in spinning stories around company news flow. Conversely, poor relationships with journalists or other individuals in various media outlets can be very harmful. Journalists tend to dislike restrictive communication styles, which can damage a company's various media-driven relationships.

Management of a company's media relations can require a substantial effort by a sizeable internal organization. A constructive, transparent approach to dealing with the media is usually favorably recognized. Some journalists may still ask for off-the-record conversations and other special favors with the objective of building proprietary knowledge. However, not least for legal reasons and to uphold equal treatment, there should be clearly defined lines. Off-the-record content is beyond the company's control and has the potential to become on-the-record at any point in time. Companies should beware of information asymmetry or communication of material non-public information, as these and other disclosure issues can lead to serious consequences.

Digital communication – social media et al.

The internet has facilitated pronounced changes to the media landscape. Today, information can flow in real time around the globe. New forms of media have emerged, such as social networks and instant messaging platforms, featuring different dynamics than established media platforms such as newspapers, magazines and television. The patterns of media consumption keep changing.

These developments also significantly affect companies' external communications. Many publicly listed companies have developed their own apps as an additional means to distribute company news and investor relations content, such as financial reports, trading statements, etc. It is common for companies to maintain a presence on social networks, such as Facebook, or on instant messaging and other platforms, such as Twitter, for consumer marketing and news distribution.

This diversification of media in combination with the expectation of delivering to public company standards in terms of corporate and financial communication has set the bar higher for public companies, requiring more resources and a broader skill set.

7.2   Disclosure obligations

Mandatory disclosure is comprehensive

Publicly listed companies must comply with a broad set of rules and regulations such as the applicable corporate law, stock exchange rules and financial markets regulation. In aggregate, these rules and regulations result in comprehensive disclosure obligations going substantially beyond the regular financial reporting requirements. These obligations vary in detail by jurisdiction and stock exchange, but the resulting level of transparency is largely comparable for many of the larger established local capital markets.

The various elements of mandatory disclosure beyond financial reporting vary in nature and cover different areas. Some key items are (i) the ongoing disclosure of share price sensitive facts and developments ("ongoing disclosure"), (ii) disclosure of any trading activities in the company's shares or related financial instruments by members of the company's boards ("insider trading activities"), (iii) disclosure of information on holders of shares and other related financial instruments exceeding certain thresholds in ownership or voting rights ("major shareholder reporting") and (iv) detailed disclosure of board member compensation ("compensation reporting"). There may be additional items required for mandatory disclosure. Keeping track of and ensuring compliance with all obligations requires significant resources. Associated costs can be substantial and often represent an important consideration in the context of an IPO, especially for smaller companies (see also chapter 4.5).

With the completion of an IPO, these disclosure obligations apply to newly listed companies. In some markets, certain relief or exceptions may be available to companies meeting certain criteria in order to facilitate capital markets access for these (mostly smaller) companies. In 2012, for example, the Obama administration enacted the Jumpstart Our Business Startups Act (the "JOBS Act") in the United States. Among other things, this act established a new category of issuers, so-called emerging growth companies ("EGCs") and provides EGCs with easier access to US capital markets for their IPOs. EGCs benefit from more relaxed disclosure and other requirements that are phased in over a period of up to five years following an IPO. For purposes of the JOBS Act, an EGC is generally any domestic or foreign company with total gross revenues of less than US$ 1 billion during its most recently completed financial year. (Practical Law, 2016)

Source of information for owners and stakeholders

Disclosure obligations for publicly listed companies aim at ensuring a certain level of transparency vis-a-vis the companies' owners and other stakeholders. Most public companies can identify only a part of their shareholder base, which may consist of hundreds or even thousands of different parties. Consequently, direct communication with all shareholders is neither practicable nor would it be efficient. Therefore, formal disclosure of company information to the public via appropriate distribution means represents the key source of company information for its shareholders and the broader financial community. This implies that, at least at times, even sensitive company information must be publicly disclosed in order to comply with disclosure obligations. This is, of course, not always to the liking of the disclosing company (although its clients, suppliers or competitors may find it very interesting).

Disclosure obligations define the minimum level of information to be published. In order to cater to shareholders' and other stakeholders' additional information needs, publicly listed companies often decide to disclose more information than the required minimum. This can refer to a greater level of detail in the ongoing financial reporting, both in terms of quantitative and qualitative information, or shareholder education on company strategy and future outlook in the form of more or less regular updates on these subjects.

While not all information is of interest to every addressee, all material information needs to be made accessible to all shareholders through publication. This reflects the principle of equal treatment of all shareholders, whether codified in applicable law and regulation or just reasonably expected by shareholders, and also extends to the provision of information.

This does not contradict the established investor relations practice of publicly listed companies providing special services, such as one-on-one meetings with senior management to large and important institutional shareholders or conference calls with senior management at the release of financial results to research analysts and investors. The company, however, must always ensure that all material information is available to all shareholders.

Why bother?

Full compliance with disclosure obligations is very important for several reasons. First and most obvious, non-compliance, intentional or unintentional, implies breaching rules and regulations that are of a statutory nature in most jurisdictions. Violations trigger consequences in the form of fines, administrative action or other sanctions. For example, regulators such as the US Securities and Exchange Commission, UK Listing Authority or German Bundesanstalt für Finanzdienstleistungsaufsicht monitor disclosure practices and, from time to time, identify publicly listed delinquents that are in violation of certain filing and disclosure obligations, and impose punitive measures. In addition, violations may form the basis for shareholder claims against the company.

Second and of at least equal importance, obvious non-compliance and failure to disclose important information on a timely basis is very much disliked by the financial community. If intentional, it creates a notion of the company being shareholder unfriendly and if unintentional, it sheds negative light on the company and its ability to keep its house in order. Both scenarios are unlikely to positively influence investor interest in the company and hence share price development.

Fine lines and fine balance

There are not only black and white issues when it comes to fulfilling publicly listed company disclosure obligations. A substantial part of the required disclosure is relatively clearly defined, such as financial reporting, insider trading activity and others. Ongoing disclosure, however, can involve a substantial degree of judgment, which makes it challenging to handle in reality. This kind of disclosure usually requires publication of share price sensitive facts and developments without undue delay and making such information accessible to all market participants at the same time in order to avoid share trading on the basis of inside information.

The company has to judge, often in uncertain situations, whether a new fact or development is of a price sensitive nature and must therefore be disclosed. The company must ultimately form a view and act accordingly. Another important aspect of ongoing disclosure requirements is timely publication, without undue delay. This requires the company to have efficient policies and procedures in place to ensure that potentially price sensitive information is brought quickly to the attention of senior management, who can then assess its disclosure relevance.

There are some exemptions available that allow companies to postpone the publication of price sensitive information under certain circumstances. In such instances, the company often has to weigh its interest in confidentiality against the interest of the capital markets in obtaining the information.

With sometimes substantial judgment involved, there is a risk that especially when the circumstances are scrutinized in hindsight, a decision to delay publication or not to publish at all can appear questionable or outright wrong. The company can then be held liable and must deal with the consequences. The same holds true if the disclosure is misleading or incomplete.

A well-known example in this context is a class action suit filed against Citigroup, a US bank, by some of its shareholders in 2008. The investors claimed that they were deceived by Citigroup as it hid the extent of its dealings in toxic subprime debt during the financial crisis. In 2012, Citigroup, denying all allegations, settled to pay US$ 590 million to investors who purchased its stock in 2007 and 2008 (Wall Street Journal, 2012).

The Citigroup example illustrates that the consequences of improper disclosure can be very substantial. It is therefore important that publicly listed companies find the right balance between an appropriate level of disclosure, protection of their own interests and risk management.

7.3   Investor cheer & scrutiny & headaches

It's all about share price development!?

Investors buy shares of publicly listed companies in the expectation of achieving an appropriate return on their investment. In general, the total shareholder return consists of two principal elements. These are (i) capital appreciation, i.e., the increase in value of the company's equity and (ii) dividend payments, i.e., distribution of profits to the company's shareholders.

Investments in publicly listed companies in the US and Europe returned 7.9% p.a. in real terms over the 30-year period from 1985 to 2014, according to a recent study by McKinsey Global Institute, the business and economics research arm of McKinsey & Company, a consulting firm. Going forward, McKinsey Global Institute expects these returns to be substantially lower, ranging between 4.0% to 6.5% p.a. over the 20-year period from 2016 to 2035 for a number of reasons (McKinsey & Company, 2016, p. 20ff). According to MSCI, an information services provider, the dividend yield of the MSCI All Country World Investible Market Index, a broad stock market index covering approximately 99% of the global equity investment opportunity set and used as a proxy in this context, stood at 2.60% as of 30 June 2016. (MSCI, 2016, p. 1) On the basis of the forward return expectation of McKinsey and assuming a similar level of dividend yield as indicated by the index proxy, the capital appreciation element is expected to deliver 35% to 60% of expected total shareholder return.

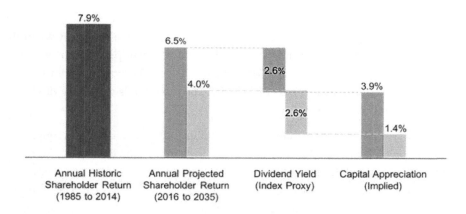

Exhibit 12: Shareholder returns – capital appreciation vs. dividend yield
Source: McKinsey & Company, MSCI, own analysis

While the above analysis is simplistic and general, it illustrates that both elements of shareholder return are very important to meeting return expectations. To the extent companies only pay small or no dividends at all, which is often the case for IPO companies, the capital appreciation element has to contribute up to 100% of total expected shareholder return. This in turn explains why investors put very much emphasis on positive share price performance, the principle driver of capital appreciation.

Research analysts & investors can (and do) change their views

As long as the share price of the company increases, investors tend to be happy. This is particularly the case if the increasing share price is the result of continuously improving performance, i.e., growing revenue and profit, increasing profitability margins and the achievement of strategic milestones and objectives. This also holds true for IPO companies that deliver on promises made to investors during IPO marketing. IPO companies often start their corporate lives as publicly listed companies with substantial tailwind from research analysts and investors. The very intensive IPO marketing campaign results in the creation of meaningful camps of supporters with a positive view of the newly listed company (particularly for those that have invested in the IPO). Continued or increased positive sentiment for a company by investors often corresponds with the length of positive performance by the company following its IPO. Research analysts demonstrate very similar behavior to investors in this context.

As long as an overall rosy picture is intact, research analysts and investors are relatively easy to deal with from a company and senior management perspective. There is usually strong support for the existing management team and their strategy. Investor meetings, research analyst events and other investor relations activities tend to run smoothly in the absence of critical questioning. Sometimes, however, driven by a continuous upgrade of research analyst and investor expectations, the share price of a company can get ahead of itself. This is the point in time when the company enters dangerous territory, as it becomes ever harder to fulfill external expectations.

Receiving tailwinds from the financial community is not a one-way street. The situation can change quickly in the event that initial cracks appear following an IPO and begin to destroy the formerly rosy picture painted during IPO marketing. Issues can originate from a weaker operating and financial performance, slower than expected or lack of progress towards achieving strategic milestones, general industry weakness and many other reasons that are sometimes completely beyond senior management's control. Even former star performers can lose their sparkle relatively quickly in the eyes of the financial community. Where this happens, the share price usually enters into a, potentially prolonged, period of decline. There are many publicly listed companies that share the fate of former stars moving out of favor, including well-known ones such as Microsoft, a software company; Nokia, a telecommunications company and Apple, a technology company. IPO companies that started strong but subsequently experienced fading backing in the financial community include prominent examples, such as Rocket Internet, a German start-up holding company, or Alibaba, a Chinese online retailer.

For these reasons, senior management teams of publicly listed companies face substantial performance pressure on an ongoing basis, both to meet expectations and remain in the favor of the investment community – quarter by quarter, year over year.

The hot seat is much less comfortable

To the extent a publicly listed company's performance is softening or even turning weak, research analysts and investors can quickly become uncomfortable with senior management and the company and may begin to scrutinize the company in much greater detail. They often begin challenging senior management with more critical and detailed questions in investor meetings and conference calls and asking for specific plans to remedy the situation and return the company on track to a positive performance. The more or less subtle increase of pressure on the management team is often an attempt to cause management to take effective action as quickly as possible and make the company a profitable investment for investors.

Management, in turn, usually dedicates more time for addressing issues with research analysts and investors in an effort to retain investor comfort with the company and not cause them to abandon their investment.

During prolonged periods of weak share price performance, investors' pressure on management usually increases and calls for action become louder. Sometimes, investors may also demand management changes to address certain issues or call for strategic action such as a sale or merger. In conclusion, the negative repercussions on management from non-performance and weak share price performance represent a powerful incentive and omnipresent latent pressure to deliver successful company performance on an ongoing basis.

The rising importance of activist investors

In recent years, so-called activist investors have gained importance, initially in the United States but more recently also in Europe. These investors adopt a much more active approach to asserting power as owners of the companies in which they are invested. Activism in this context covers a broad range of activities and includes, inter alia, private discussions or public communication with boards and management, press campaigns, putting forward shareholder resolutions, calling shareholder meetings and facilitating change in senior management teams and company boards.

Activist investors may invest in companies with the objective of increasing shareholder value by creating trouble. Typically, these investors screen the market for companies that they deem undervalued or undermanaged. They specifically look for shareholder value creation opportunities with the objective of extracting short-term gains from their investments. Activist investors usually take a sizeable stake of up to several percent in the target company's equity. They may attempt to obtain the support from other large shareholders to increase the weight of support behind their initiatives.

Assets under management by activist investors have grown substantially in recent years, not least due to strong investment returns outperforming relevant benchmarks and investment alternatives (J.P. Morgan, 2014, p. 3). With more capital behind them, these investors can make bolder moves and target more and bigger companies.

According to a study by McKinsey, shareholders generally benefit from activist campaigns. This study found that the median activist campaign reverses a downward performance trend by a target company. It generates excess shareholder returns for at least three years following the campaign. This analysis is based on a sample of 400 activist campaigns, out of 1,400 launched against US companies over the last decade (McKinsey & Company, 2014, p. 1).

In principle, any publicly listed company with a high free-float and institutional ownership can become the target of an activist campaign. Well-managed, efficiently valued companies that do not offer short-term value creation opportunities are usually the least susceptible. Conversely, activists represent a real threat to publicly listed companies and management teams that show weakness in their performance.

Investors such as Cevian Capital, Elliott Management, Icahn Enterprises, Knight Vinke, Trian Partners and Third Point are very active players in this field. Prominent campaigns launched by these investors targeted companies such as Apple, a US technology company (Icahn, 2013), ThyssenKrupp, a German industrial conglomerate (Cevian, 2013), UBS, a Swiss bank (Knight Vinke, 2013), Dow Chemical, as US chemicals company (Third Point, 2014) and many others.

7.4   Exit route "take private"

There is no "easy escape" from being a public company

Being publicly listed has far-reaching implications for a company. These are of a financial, operational and strategic nature and comprise both benefits and disadvantages from the perspective of the company and its shareholders. The decision to pursue an IPO and become a publicly listed company is usually based on the expectation of benefits outweighing disadvantages. Publicly listed companies, however, can conduct a similar analysis of benefits and disadvantages of being a public company on an ongoing basis and may arrive at the conclusion that a revocation of their stock exchange listing and a return to being privately owned would be, on balance, the superior alternative. Significant additional costs, as described in chapter 4.5, and operational burden imposed on public companies usually represent important considerations in this context.

Many jurisdictions and stock exchanges, however, discourage the voluntary revocation of an existing stock market listing by the company under ordinary circumstances. There are often high legal and regulatory hurdles in place that make it extremely difficult or effectively impossible to discontinue the listing in the absence of a major event such as a takeover offer for or insolvency of the company. This is to protect shareholders, who require on the fungibility and tradability of shares as well as adequate disclosure as key features of their investments.

A "take private" transaction explained

One way to effect a de-listing, i.e., abandon the stock market listing and become privately owned, that is permitted in most jurisdictions, is a "take private" transaction. In such a transaction, an investor or a group of investors ("offeror") launch a formal offer to all shareholders of the listed company with the objective of acquiring substantially all of the company's equity for cash. If a sufficient number of shareholders accept the offer the applicable acceptance thresholds in the formal offer are exceeded, the offeror usually obtains the right to acquire the shares owned by shareholders that did not accept the formal offer subsequent to the formal offer. This procedure is referred to as a "squeeze-out", with acceptance thresholds varying by jurisdiction and typically ranging from 90 to 95 percent. Once the offeror owns all of the company's equity following a successful squeeze-out, the offeror can usually effect a revocation of the target company's stock market listing relatively easily and quickly.

Formal offers, often referred to as 'public tender offers' or 'takeover offers', are subject to comprehensive legal regulation that may vary substantially by jurisdiction. In many jurisdictions, other forms or variations of formal offers and other transaction structures to effect the acquisition of a publicly listed company for cash or share consideration are feasible (e.g., a one-step merger in the US).

Offers may be launched with ('friendly') or without ('unsolicited' or 'hostile') the support of the target company's boards. The initiative for a take private transaction can originate from the company's board(s) or the investor(s). In situations where the board of a company is seeking to revoke its stock market listing, the board can confidentially engage in conversations with suitable investors with the objective coordinating on steps to take the company private.

Repeat performers – the "re-IPO"

The negatives of being publicly listed often have more weight for smaller companies, while for larger companies there may be no alternative to being publicly listed. In addition, smaller listed companies may not enjoy the same level of attention by the financial community as large companies. Valuation inefficiencies and the desire to become privately owned have the potential to form the basis of an attractive investment case for a take private transaction, in addition to several other considerations.

Take private transactions are commonly pursued by private equity investors. In addition to their own equity, they usually employ debt, often to a significant extent, to finance the acquisition of a public company. Post-acquisition, the cash-flow generated by the company is used to service such debt. The company's capacity to sustain debt and the availability of debt financing in the capital markets are key considerations in this context. Both private equity and debt capital are and have been abundantly available in recent years, impacting the number of and amount of capital deployed in take private transactions, especially in the US. According to Bain & Company, a US consulting firm, take private transactions accounted for nearly 60 percent of the value of US buyout transactions in 2015 but only for two percent in Europe (Bain & Company, 2016, p. 16). With prevailing capital abundance across asset classes and markets, the upper end of the size spectrum for take private transactions has reached very substantial levels. For example, Silverlake Partners, a US private equity investor, and Michael Dell, CEO, took Dell Computer, a PC company, private in 2013 for US$ 22.4 billion in one of the largest take private transactions to date. According to Weil, Gotshal & Manges, a US law firm, however, the average transaction size for take private transactions by private equity investors stood at US$ 2.1 billion in 2014, based on a global sample of 34 transactions with a transaction value of at least US$ 100 million (Weil, 2015, p. 2).

The investment horizon of private equity investors is usually three to five years, after which they seek to exit from the investment and realize any gains. As described in chapter 4.3, an IPO often represents a viable exit channel from private equity investments, in particular if the portfolio company used to be publicly listed prior to its acquisition by the private equity investor. According to Bain & Company, private equity exits accounted for 186 IPOs globally in 2015, a similar number to 2013 and down from approximately 250 in 2014. The IPO of a private equity portfolio company that was acquired in a take private transaction is commonly referred to as a "re-IPO".

While the IPO is considered a once-in-a-life-time event for a company, some companies (choose to/have to) do more than one IPO. For example, RePower Systems, a German wind turbine manufacturer, went public for the first time in 2002. Subsequently, Suzlon Energy, an Indian wind turbine manufacturer, acquired RePower Systems in a take private transaction in 2007. Centerbridge Partners, a US private equity investor, acquired RePower, which had by then been renamed to Senvion, from Suzlon Energy in 2015. Senvion completed its second IPO on the Frankfurt Stock Exchange early in 2016.

Part 3: The Curetis IPO – a European success story

The third part of this IPO book will look at a real-world case study of a European IPO in the biotechnology industry. As a serial entrepreneur, the author draws on his first-hand experience from two IPO transactions more than a decade apart. Chapter 8 examines how the first-time IPO and its aftermath have had significant impact on decision making many years later as to the preferred choices for capital raising and exit routes for investors in another company.

Chapter 9 maps the various pre-IPO preparatory steps and projects that were a necessary prerequisite to even beginning the IPO project proper. These include various aspects of accounting, investor education and selection of banks and advisors, respectively.

Chapters 10 and 11 form the core of the case study with a step by step depiction from kick-off meeting, via prospectus drafting, due diligence all the way to planning and executing various roadshows across Europe and the US. Key aspects in decision making on allocating shares and pricing an IPO are dissected from various perspectives such as management, the board of directors, VC shareholders, new investors and banks advising on the IPO. Chapter 11 offers an insider's view to the practical, analytical but also emotional and subjective aspects of being on an IPO roadshow and needing to succeed in bringing the deal across the finish line.

Chapter 12 highlights the need for looking well beyond the actual IPO transaction and focusing on the part of 'being public' once the IPO transaction is done. Drawing upon many years of experience as CFO in running a publicly traded company, the author reflects upon key lessons learned and critically examines how these learnings informed the post IPO choices and activities in the Curetis context.

8 From "Never again" to "Yes we can"

In this chapter 8 the author examines how a virtual non-possibility and non-option of doing an IPO with Curetis AG, a small Germany-based biotechnology start-up based in Swabian Holzgerlingen near Stuttgart ultimately became the one and only route the company could and would chose.

8.1 The epigenomics IPO and its aftermath

Epigenomics AG was my first start-up company. As a co-founder and its CFO between 1998 and 2011 I was part of the New Economy and the dot.com bubble in Germany. Berlin was one of the most exciting places to be in the late 1990s and when we started the company in a Berlin Prenzlauer Berg backyard the very first investment round had cemented the preferred exit route. All shareholders had agreed that "an IPO is the preferred exit scenario" in a private shareholder agreement.

Following a series A financing round closed in 1999, a strategic M&A deal with a US based competitor, ORCA Biosciences (PR Newswire, 2000), and a EUR 28.3 million series B led by Boston based MPM in the year 2000, epigenomics was on track for an IPO in the following year. Founder and CEO Dr. Alexander Olek was named "Entrepreneur of the Year in 2001" (Epigenomics, 2001), the company was one of Europe's 50 hottest tech firms (Die Welt, 2004) and one of Germany's 50 best employers (Spiegel Online, 2004a). For those who were there at the Alte Oper in Frankfurt on 11th September 2001 for the celebration and award ceremony by Ernst & Young for the "2001 Entrepreneur of the Year" Award it will be one of the most memorable days of our lives. Black tie event, Henry Kissinger on stage, delivering a speech on "Leadership challenges in the 21st century" to a backdrop of the huge screens behind him coming alive in the early afternoon hours CET to the biggest attack on US soil in recent history... little did we know how profound the impact on the capital markets in the tech industry would be(come).

A week later once air travel resumed, we held a series of meetings in makeshift bank offices at Lehman Brothers who had lost their buildings near the Twin Towers and had relocated to a hotel in Midtown Manhattan across the street from Times Square. The spirit in those days and weeks was one of defiance, resilience and a common perception that things would quickly turn around and capital market activity would resume after the dip created by the bust of the dot.com bubble. In fact, so much so that on Thanksgiving Day in 2001 a senior investment banking team from New York's and London's UBS offices pitched to the board of epigenomics in Berlin for an IPO to take place sooner rather than later. A Concorde flight back from London to New York made sure that day that the senior banker would enjoy his family Turkey dinner at home. One of the junior bankers at the table was a fellow by the name of Paul Tomasic who would 11 years later be the lead banker for the Curetis IPO.

The reality, however, turned out to be much worse than anyone would have anticipated in the 9/11 aftermath. There were virtually no IPOs and certainly no tech IPOs in Europe – let alone in Germany – in the 2001 to 2003/04 period (Going Public, 2004a, Going Public, 2004b). Nonetheless the various followers of IPO activity continued to publish regular updates of so-called "IPO Watch-Lists" (e.g. Going Public) over the years that followed. A shortlist of biotech companies was repeatedly mentioned in one order or another in such lists. Suffice it to say that epigenomics continued to somehow find its way onto these lists. One reason may have been the signing of one of the largest diagnostics partnering deals of its time with Roche Diagnostics. When Roche Diagnostics executives made some public bullish forward looking statements with regards to expected 2010 cancer screening test sales by Roche to an interested investor audience at the Bank of America conference in 2002, it was simple maths for most industry observers to calculate the NPV of future royalties on such billions of Swiss Francs in sales. And this was in simple terms the IPO story for epigenomics.

When in early 2004 the analysts and bankers from Morgan Stanley that had previously been the only ones in 2000/2001 to decline the opportunity to pitch came back with their assessment that we were now "ready for an IPO", it did not take us and the board very long to quickly put together a syndicate led by Morgan Stanley, with Lehman Brothers and DZ Bank in the mix. The IPO was on shaky grounds to say the least. Following the IPOs of Mifa, Wincor-Nixdorf and Postbank, the epigenomics IPO was the first tech start-up that IPO'ed in 2004 since the bubble had burst and 9/11 had shut things down for years. As much as analysts, bankers and the press had cajoled and coaxed anyone willing and daring enough to try an IPO and despite all the rhetoric of "home field advantage" and "national heroes" it was the opposite. The press was all over the IPO and did not spare us any flak (Manager Magazin, 2004). Rather than pulling back we ended up cutting the book building span and eventually priced the deal at the very low end of the price range. On the finish line, it was an order from existing VC funds that put the IPO over the finish line and helped raise EUR 41.6 million in fresh growth equity capital. Morgan Stanley ended up winning the 2004 "IPO lemon" award for the epigenomics IPO (Going Public, 2004c) and our CEO felt compelled to tell the Spiegel news magazine that doing an IPO for a loss making and cash burning biotech company in Germany had felt like running a brothel (Der Spiegel, 2004b).

Suffice it to say that a former colleague and friend of mine should be right in his assessment that the company would never again see its original EUR 9.00 per share IPO price. The analyst covering the IPO from Morgan Stanley's side, had put out an EUR

18.00 price target – not even years later after a 1:5 reverse split would the stock ever get to that level. Don't get me wrong – a lot of issues were home-made and the years that followed were not exactly a case study in stellar corporate governance. A founder and CEO asked to leave overnight in August 2006 (Epigenomics, 2006), a strategic partner Roche walking out despite good clinical data in December 2006 (genomeweb, 2006), hiring a new CEO in February of 2007 and multiple PIPE transactions and rights offerings later made for a rocky ride in the public eye. The stock price chart can only begin to show some of the highs and lows along the way.

Exhibit 13: Epigenomics Stock Price Chart 2004-2017
Source: Finanznachrichten, 2017

The fact that even in the darkest days of the global financial crisis and banking melt-down in 2008 we somehow managed to pull off a EUR 13.5 million rights offering (Epigenomics, 2008) and in 2010 convinced the public Abingworth fund of one of our long-term VC shareholders to back another major financing (Epigenomics, 2010), goes to show that there were always fundamentals strong enough to weather any capital market storm. And when asked by a Deutsche Börse executive whether I had regrets for having gone public with epigenomics, I told him my honest assessment: "Without the IPO in 2004 epigenomics would no longer exist as a company since the IPO had allowed it to go back to the capital markets time and time again" (Statement made at Eigenkapitalforum 2010 in an interview with Deutsche Börse).

There had been several potential merger opportunities along the way and I had come to the conclusion that it was not sufficient to talk about the strategic focus on the US market for epi proColon® our first in class blood based colorectal cancer screening test. When rubber had to meet the road the board collectively shied away from making the tough decisions necessary to move the headquarters and company squarely to the USA I made up my own mind and decided that the fate of the company needed to be put into other managers' hands (APA-OTS, 2011).

If as an executive you have spent close to seven years explaining to the public and the capital markets why things took longer, cost more, why FDA approvals needed additional trials to be run, that trial data was neither black nor white, why corporate partners ended strategic alliances despite solid clinical data and why the next financing had to take place no matter what at deep discount valuations then your appetite for running a public company or let alone do another IPO might be understandably satiated for a while. It was against this backdrop that I had originally decided to join the Curetis AG supervisory board as a non-executive director in early 2010. I had just signed a new 3-year CFO contract with epigenomics and the company was once again evaluating "all strategic and tactical financing options". Part of the appeal quite frankly was that in a privately held company backed by top tier venture capital funds you can have a real discussion and debate at the board level with the founders and management. All behind closed doors rather than weighing your every word based on advice from corporate PR & IR advisors, lawyers, auditors and banks in the limelight of a small cap publicly traded company.

8.2 Considerations for Curetis when joining

M&A or trade sale vs. IPO considerations – a shareholder and stakeholder value perspective

When I received a call from Dr. Jörg Neermann in late 2009, by now partner at venture firm LSP Life Sciences Partners in the Netherlands and Germany, formerly chairman of the supervisory board of epigenomics and the original venture backer of the company, I knew it was a credible story. Honestly, I had never heard of the small obscure and as far as PR and visibility was concerned notably absent company in Holzgerlingen… where on earth was this ?? Despite the fact that I had spent two years studying in Swabia at ESB Reutlingen and had lived in Tübingen between 1990 and 1992, it had to be a google maps search first. Located smack in the middle of a big forest, next to many of Germany's automotive industry's heartland – 10 minutes from Mercedes and literally next door to a family owned Mittelständler making doors for the E-class at the Sindelfingen plant was a 10-person small start-up. Unlike the new economy "boy groups" in the hippest locations in Berlin, Munich and other cool places, this was a down to earth outfit of 40 to 50 year olds with 15 to 20 years of industry experience – mind you not in start-up companies but with some of the world's leading makers of medical equipment such as Hewlett Packard, Agilent and Philips. The VCs had just agreed to fund Curetis AG with what happened to be the largest single round of venture capital financing in 2009 in the biotech industry in Germany midst of the global financial crisis (BioSpace, 2009). The board was to be made up of three VCs representing the three main investors, aeris CAPITAL, LSP and BioMed Invest. Also, the team had already secured the support from two non-executive directors, Hans-Günter Hohmann the former Head of R&D in Europe of HP and Agilent as well as Detlef Sasse the former head of commercial operations EMEA at Beckman Coulter, one of the world's leading diagnostics industry players (Bionity, 2010). The VCs, however, also wanted someone from within the diagnostics industry, someone who had not yet retired and who was still very much active in the IVD (in vitro diagnostics) space and who might know a thing or two about life in a start-up company. So apparently, I fit that bill in general terms and as non-executive would have no conflict of interest given that Curetis' sole focus was in severe hospital infections whereas my own company epigenomics was cancer diagnostics player.

Walking into my first board meeting in February 2010, little did I know that the VCs were secretly looking for someone to join the rather R&D heavy and engineering-focused founders' team in due course. Following the first closing of a EUR 20 million Series A financing round in November 2009, with about a third of the capital having been paid into the company as first tranche with the other two thirds being dependent on certain product development milestones in 2010 and 2011, respectively, it came as a bit of a surprise that the management team tabled a decision proposal in early 2010 to begin investing about a third of these funds raised in the years ahead into a highly automated, state-of-the-art clean room manufacturing facility… for a disposable cartridge that did not yet exist, to be run on a hardware system that had not been fully developed (they had an alpha prototype at that time) to have content on it that still needed to be defined and developed.

Shortly after having taken the decision to indeed make this major industrial scale up manufacturing investment, the board was invited for a "strategy discussion" held at the LSP offices in Munich in spring of 2010. Driven by the common understanding of all stake-holders, that the only viable or at least the most reasonable exit route for Curetis would be a trade sale immediately following a technical and product development proof of concept, the sole purpose of this meeting appeared to be generating a list of likely acquirers and figuring out who might be best positioned to approach them and when. Valuation ranges were discussed solely from the perspective of the VC investors' need for a 3x to 5x multiple on their cash invested within a time frame conducive to an IRR (internal rate of return) that would please their limited partners. The underlying assumption ran something like this: Curetis needed to develop the Unyvero system, put a single cartridge for severe hospital pneumonia patients onto the system, make some of those cartridges, get to clinical validation sufficient for a CE-IVD marking in Europe and show some commercial proof of concept by selling a few of these cartridges in Germany, Austria and Switzerland (DACH region). And for the truly adventurous around the table maybe a distribution partnership with a Spanish firm that happened to be well known to some of the board members.

Interestingly the notion of a trade sale being the only viable exit route for the company was consensus around the board room, including founders, management and supervisory board directors, and there was not even a hint of a discussion of any other scenario at this time. So when over a lunch that same day some of the investors took me aside and asked whether I would consider joining the team at Curetis as the company's CEO – a position to be newly created since the team so far was entire operations and R&D driven – the role was portrayed as one of ensuring the company moved through the motions in product development and then prepare and execute on a strategic sell-side process with a trade-sale being the desired outcome – and all that from the relatively comfortable position as a privately held company. Gone would be the quarterly reporting to a public capital market, no need for broad IR campaigns and roadshows, no worrying about short term stock price development and trading patterns etc. Quite an attractive proposition for a small cap publicly traded biotech CFO who just came out of yet another round of prospectus based public rights offering in spring of 2010 at record setting low stock prices driven down by the market forces who can read balance sheets all too well and play the illiquid stock for what it would be worth to ensure a deep discount entry price.

Looking at a trade sale exit from a company's founders' team perspective it is also not too difficult to understand the economic rationale and appealing financial logic. Typical VC termsheets and shareholder agreements will have what is called a liquidation preference clause (Wilmerding, 2003). In an exit event such as a trade sale the amount of cash invested by the VCs and holders of preferred Series A stock would be returned first – often with a multiplier above 1x such as 1.5x or even 2x and in distress situations 3x before any remaining exit proceeds would be shared on a pro rata basis amongst all shareholders. Such double dipping is very commonplace in the VC business and start-up companies will frequently have to accept these terms and conditions as part of the relative bargaining power in early stage financing. So, for a founder it is simple math: the less capital goes into his or her start-up company and the sooner an exit might take place, the more likely it will be that the excess cash returned over and above the liquidation preference.

So, in the Curetis case, the EUR 20 million Series A financing at a hypothetical 1.5x liquidation preference would have meant paying the first EUR 30 million from any exit proceeds to the Series A investors. Around that time there had been a successful trade sale of mtm Laboratories to Roche Diagnostics for EUR 130 million cash plus an earn out of another EUR 60 million or so (VC Magazin, 2011). So, a group of founders owning say 20% of the company after the Series A would have received some EUR 20 million out of the first EUR 130 million following the standard waterfall exit analysis;

this would surely be a nice sum to incentivize all of them to go along with the early strategy of building the company on a platform prototype and one-trick pony, i.e. a single product application to then flip and sell it to one of the large IVD players. Common metrics used in the molecular diagnostics (MDx) industry for M&A multiples in high growth companies would be a 5x to 6x of revenue (JMP Securities, 2010) – sometimes even forward revenue 12 to 24 months out discounted back at typically 10% to 15% discount rate depending on the stage of product development and commercialization.

8.3 Growing Curetis and strategic options

But when the R&D phase takes longer and as often happens costs more than originally expected, further equity capital financing rounds are needed. After two further closings of the Series A in 2011 with new investors CD Venture, Forbion Capital Partners and the Roche Venture Fund and then a Series B in 2013 with new lead investor HBM Partners joining the syndicate and that round getting expanded in a second closing in Q4-2014 with LSP Health Economics Fund and QIAGEN also coming in as new investors the whole game had changed (BioRegio STERN, 2011, Forbion, 2013, Forbion, 2014).

Now with EUR 63.5 million in equity capital raised over the years and a liquidation preference in place this would have led to a situation where a trade sale or M&A situation would have left very little for the founders and management. The incentives in such situations can become rather skewed between a trade sale and an IPO. So, there was little surprise that when actually some of the VC investors suggested an IPO might be the best possible route for the company to go in terms of corporate development and future funding, there was every incentive to go along with that idea and pursue it aggressively from the company's executive team and founders.

But why did the company along the way change its path and strategic corporate development plans? Looking at other successful trade sales in the molecular diagnostics industry there seemed to be a few key ingredients to such successful transactions. Having solid top line revenue and strong revenue growth being one of them. Also, having de-risked the products and portfolio from a clinical as well as regulatory standpoint, especially in the all-important US market also appeared to be of major importance.

Following a phase of typical teething problems with a brand new and innovative platform, its hardware and software as well as all content and consumables being brand new, it had become clear that an FDA clearance would not become available before sometime in 2017 at the earliest. Also, the distributor model in all markets except for the German speaking DACH region proved to be slower and much less controllable than desired. When partnering discussions on distribution in several key European markets fell through, the management and board of Curetis were faced with either much slower commercial development or significantly higher costs for building these operations up internally. The latter was the path eventually chosen. In spring of 2015 the company decided to expand its direct sales footprint in Europe to also include the UK, France and BeNeLux markets and potentially Scandinavian markets as well in addition to the DACH region.

For the USA, the publicly declared strategy had always been one of "finding the ideal commercial channel partner" (cf. Curetis corporate presentation at JP Morgan conference Jan 2014), which many capital markets stakeholders might well have interpreted to be paraphrase for putting the company up for sale. Once the decision was made to go for an IPO the immediate strategic consequence was also to opt for a direct marketing and sales route and channel in the US. Proceeds from the IPO would be used i.a. to build a US commercial organization owned and controlled by Curetis. It is hard to determine cause and effect here – in order to have a compelling story for an IPO one needs a use-of-proceeds story that is logical and once you have the capital raised you need to deploy it. So, did we create strategic options in order to be able to IPO the company or was it the IPO that opened up these doors? In the end a bit of both is probably the most realistic assessment.

8.4   Change of heart, change of mind

In this section let's examine the various stakeholder groups with a vested interest in the ultimate IPO decision. First and foremost, the owners of the company, i.e. at this stage the VCs and private equity firms that owned close to 80% of the company. As stated at an industry conference by Arthur Franken, partner at Gilde, a Dutch VC firm (and not an investor here at Curetis) put it very succinctly: "In our portfolio the companies that have missed their timelines and milestones and the ones we could not sell to big pharma are the ones we end up doing an IPO with as a refinancing, since this is not an exit for us as a VC this is always the second-best option only" (statement made at a SACHS Forum Panel Discussion, Zurich, Switzerland March 2016).

That said, the VCs also need stories of companies in their portfolio that mature and are able to go public and successfully do an IPO. In their own fundraising efforts, the IPOs are also a key factor as down the road the public capital market access of course allows placing secondary tranches of shares, do block trades and / or a gradual trickling out of shares by the funds. So, whilst probably not their dream scenario, typically an IPO is celebrated as a success by the VC community also. So, when indeed some of the earlier stage investors triggered the debate about an IPO rather than continuing as a private company with a goal of a trade sale as a private company, the above considerations certainly played a role. Also, as a VC you always need to keep some reserves for future financings of your portfolio companies and usually as long as a company is privately held the then current VCs will always be asked and looked towards for a pro rata investment in future rounds. When funds near the end of their life-cycle and have rather limited reserves left for any given portfolio company it may make more sense for them to take it all into one final transaction and invest it into the IPO, knowing that from then on out as insiders they will not be the ones carrying future capital raises.

A wrinkle in that whole set-up is that the fund managers from various VCs typically sit on the supervisory boards of their portfolio companies and of course by virtue of their legal mandate as non-executive supervisory board directors are obliged to act in the best interest of the company also. So, in these types of situations it is not always clear whether you are actually talking to your board or your shareholders or both of them at the same time. It is therefore important to look out for any potential conflicts of interest (Curetis, 2015) and take those into account very clearly in the whole decision making process and leading up to an IPO itself.

Other non-executive board members may be independent from the VC funds but may still have vested personal interests, be it as company founders or beneficiaries of certain equity linked incentive programs such as carve-out agreements between shareholders (Curetis, 2015).

Then of course management and founders will have their own potential conflicts of interest. Typically, in an exit situation and IPO long-term equity linked plans such as Phantom Stock Options may vest, even on an accelerated basis, and their value will get crystallized immediately. So again, the fiduciary duty towards the company and its shareholders may conflict from time to time with personal economic interests and the opportunity for large lump-sum gains (Curetis, 2015).

As executive board of the company one also has to look at stakeholder such as the early phase private angel investors who do not have a say in the IPO decision itself, but are all needed to make sure that any relevant shareholder meeting resolution in preparation of the IPO gets passed unanimously and in a timely fashion. Creating buy-in and spending the time early on to get them comfortable with all of the complex legal issues that will be brought up over the course of the IPO project itself is time well spent.

Also, the employees of the company who collectively do not have a say in the decision making on whether or not to go for an IPO but of course all have vested interests in the well-being of the company on the one hand and are often all beneficiaries of equity based incentive programs with accelerated vesting in case of an IPO obviously also have clear incentives to help support the IPO in any way they can. At this stage, it is probably wise to start telling your staff that the company is about to change dramatically and that from now on out you will stop openly communicating about all major corporate developments and shift towards a "no comment" routine and go radio-silent on your teams. But if and when it matters you will need their unequivocal support and their willingness to sign far reaching powers of attorney, so it is imperative that a strong level of trust is established between the executive team and the entire organization right from the outset.

And of course, the parties needed in an IPO such as bankers, lawyers, auditors, corporate communications advisors etc. are typically all in favor of doing an IPO as it means big ticket projects with nice upside for all of them. So again, buyer-beware and take any advice with regards to the IPO-readiness and the need to immediately prepare for an IPO with a grain of salt – there are inherent conflicts of interest between those who stand to financially benefit from a(ny) transaction and the company itself.

One final word of advice – if and when a decision has been taken to head for an IPO and prepare the company for that life-changing event, there is no turning back and no second-guessing one's own decision. From here on out it needs to be an "all hands on deck" mentality and mindset. We brought all our staff together and told them about the project and swore them to secrecy and told them we would be heading into a tunnel but that at the end of that tunnel would be light in the form of an IPO and much needed double digit million funds available to further grow the company.

9 Pre-kick-off preparations

Curetis came out of almost two full years of constant battle with the technical and clinical trial challenges of completing our product development and getting the quality of our hardware instrument systems, our software and our consumable cartridges right. Each year had required another round of private equity financing that we put together with several new institutional investors. In the fourth quarter of 2014 we found ourselves at a point where in December 2014 we had literally just closed a EUR 14.5 million expansion to our series B financing with another corporate investor and another new VC fund with all other institutional shareholders participating as well.

On the back of that one of our board members, representing one of the major VCs at the table put on the table the notion that we should not let any more time go by but really should go immediately for an IPO preparation process.

This led to a whole series of roadshows and IR activities talking to investment banks, research analysts, institutional investors and the media in both the USA and across Europe. In parallel our finance team worked day and night with Pricewaterhouse Coopers (PwC) our auditors to convert from German HGB accounting to IFRS for the 2012 to 2014 periods and 2015 H1 financials. Knowing that preparation is key and all elements need to be in place for a successful IPO project it is worth noting that there is no getting back the time lost due to having postponed certain preparation such as IFRS conversion of the financials in 2014 when delays in product development and technical challenges cast many things into doubt and maximizing cash reach and reducing cash burn were the flavor of the month.

All said and done at a board meeting in June 2015 we were faced with a choice: go to NASDAQ and accept the fact that US healthcare specialist investors would require us to do yet another private mezzanine or crossover round prior to an IPO (really to get into the stock rather cheaply and get a guaranteed IPO allocation) or look at Europe as a listing venue. Another angle of the US investor feedback was that they would have rather postponed any IPO until after Curetis was expected to have its FDA trial data in the US. This would have squarely pushed any IPO into the fall of 2016 and nobody knew how long the IPO window would remain open for biotech and life science companies this time – in a sector that had been red hot for well over two years and counting. Therefore, the decision was to not delay the IPO and rather select what many might have viewed as second best option after a US NASDAQ IPO – a listing on Euronext Amsterdam (and eventually also Brussels) emerging as top choices.

This chapter will look at key work packages and strands of pre-IPO preparation. From the IFRS conversion, valuation and audit side, via pre-IPO non-deal roadshows to get a sense for the market sentiment and IPO readiness of the equity story to banking syndicate selection and negotiations as well as choices to be made for all sorts of additional advisors.

9.1   IFRS conversion and audits

Prerequisites for an IPO process – why it is not just the company and the investment banks who are key

In order to IPO a company a prospectus including at least two or even three years of audited financials are required. Depending on the listing location, either US GAAP statements or IFRS statements are needed. Given the fact that Curetis was looking at both options, a US NASDAQ IPO as well as possibly a European listing on Euronext or even Frankfurt, choosing IFRS as accounting standard for Curetis made most sense since it maximized flexibility. Despite the fact that only two years of audited financials would have been required in the US, most European listings would require three years' worth and the incremental effort for the additional year was not big enough to warrant taking a shortcut here. This is a subject that is certainly worth discussing in quite some detail between your auditors, bankers and lawyers so as to understand what is (i) legally required, (ii) market standard in your industry and segment, (iii) demanded by the banks just because they have always done it that way and (iv) reasonably doable for the company in the time allotted to the exercise (PwC, CMS, Curetis, 2016).

In this context looking at simplification options such as presenting 3 years' worth of financials in a single statement side by side rather than doing two separate sets with 2013 numbers (including 2012 prior year comparisons) and 2014 numbers with 2013 comparisons may help streamline things quite a bit in terms of notes, explanations and sheer work load.

No matter what cut-off date is chosen for starting the conversion, i.e. the date of first time adoption of IFRSs also requires one to have the corresponding starting balances as of 1st January that year correct. In the case of Curetis we chose to have 2012 – 2013 – 2014 annual financial statements all in one report audited and needed to convert to IFRS with first time adoption as of 1st January 2012.

Now when converting from German GAAP (HGB) into IFRS there are a few obvious items to watch out for potential accounting differences such as "revenue recognition", "leasing", the accounting for "share based payments" etc.. However, the biggest ticket item proved to be the fact that like any other venture capital backed start-up company Curetis had various classes of preferred shares as well as shareholder agreements between all shareholders that laid out clear criteria for liquidation preferences and indeed the notion that in certain (rather unlikely) situations even common shareholders might require liquidation of the company. The consequence of these agreements that obviously had been put in place as part of the various Series A and Series B financing rounds and closings, was that our auditors deemed it necessary to have an independent valuation analysis done on these various classes of shares. The IFRS accounting reality was that none of these shares would end up in equity but would be accounted for as a long term financial liability in the IFRS statements (Curetis, 2015a, Curetis 2015b). Seeing your balance sheet go from strong equity to more than EUR 100 million in long term liabilities and virtually no equity in a matter of simply converting to another accounting standard is certainly not for the faint hearted.

Also, once determined that indeed the various classes of shares would be dealt with as liabilities the immediate next question was that of valuation. And here it was really down to the expertise and specialist teams of Duff & Phelps to conduct an independent valuation analysis. Looking at business plans as close as possible to the year-end and period end dates of 2012, 2013, 2014 and half-year 2015, respectively they ran various discounted cash flow models. Furthermore, the fact that shareholder agreements clearly differentiated between an M&A deal or trade sale on the one hand and an IPO on the other hand begged the question as of each relevant valuation date what the relative likelihood of one type of exit versus the other and on what timelines might have been. Using as little post-hoc rationalization as possible and digging deep into the corporate archives and corporate memory of founders, investors and executives alike, we indeed managed to figure out the values of IFRS accounting based long term financial liabilities over the relevant period. So, in close collaboration of PwC's IFRS conversion team and Duff & Phelps over the course of less than 6 months we managed to implement the complete IFRS conversion including getting the 3 years of historic financials duly audited by another PwC team. Having to establish Chinese walls between the various teams on the part of the auditors clearly does not help keeping the processes simple, lean and cheap… so of the roughly EUR 900 thousand that PwC received in total remuneration for services in 2015 (Curetis, 2015c), approximately one third had gone into the IFRS conversion and audits of 2012 to 2014 IFRS statements, respectively.

9.2   Non-deal roadshow, pilot fishing and test the waters

Whilst a board and management may think it is time for a company to go public, the ultimate arbiter of whether or not the company is actually ready will be the capital markets. Every bank interested in the story and potentially in becoming part of a banking syndicate will need to carefully weigh the upside of a transaction fee versus the risk of a failed one and having tied massive resources over prolonged periods of time without any pay-out.

So, when we started talking to banks about possibly doing and IPO and looking for syndicate members we were faced with a healthy dose of skepticism on their part. The company might be considered "too early stage", it may not have the right "revenue profile for a med tech or diagnostics company", investors may want to see "FDA trial data and approvals" and so on and so forth. For every reason to ever look at an IPO there are probably a dozen or more not to do it.

In our case the banks requested that we share investor feedback and some banks actually took us on extensive non-deal roadshows that were sort of early test the waters meetings or pilot fishing exercises. Getting in front of some 45 to 50 top-tier institutional investors, mostly in the US, was certainly a very helpful exercise. If you are really interested in getting rather unfiltered or unplugged feedback, it is well worth spending some extra time and money and have your own IR firm set these up alongside some investment banks. The banks will often get you in front of their best fund manager contacts and you may or may not actually hear the full picture feedback. However, we managed to put together three non-deal roadshows in April and May of 2015, meeting with almost 50 accounts in the US and Europe. About half of these meetings had been organized by banks and the other half by our IR firm and even in the bank organized ones we ended up taking our IR advisors who subsequently collected and interpreted the feedback.

The unequivocal feedback from this exercise was that the particular space (i.e. infectious disease diagnostics in hospitals), the company and our technology would be a great story. However, the push from US investors went clearly in the direction of not launching an IPO transaction right away but rather to do a mezzanine or cross over round with a small number of top tier US institutions, each probably putting in at least US$ 10 million and then complete the US FDA trial first before considering an IPO on NASDAQ.

The banks were clearly looking at whether or not this whole exercise would yield a few possible lead investors. Some banks even proposed a debt financing structure rather than an IPO or equity based construct. However, looking at an uncertain and largely untested cash flow pattern in the future, levering up the balance sheet with significant amount of debt capital was too risky in our minds and the board clearly preferred an IPO.

Comparing and contrasting the 2015 Curetis pre-IPO roadshow activities with my only other data point from the 2004 IPO of epigenomics, it is fair to say that investor education and confidential pre-deal or non-deal roadshows have become a major part of the whole process under the US JOBS Act (The Wallstreet Journal, 2015) – to the extent where really as part of any biotech IPO these days you have to plan and allow for virtually three full roadshows – the pre-IPO one described above (c. 45 meetings in 9 days), the official "test the waters" roadshow during the IPO process (another 40+ meetings in 10 days) and then finally the IPO transaction roadshow proper (56 meetings in 10 days). This is only feasible in a set up where a small company has assembled a capable team of executives and management who can spare their CEO and CFO for several weeks at end and are still able to run the day to day operations of the company.

In addition to the feedback from investors, all banks that were seriously interested put us in front of their respective research analysts. And in a day and age where research analysts can no longer be cross funded from investment banking fees, the key consideration coming from research is not only going to be one of whether a transaction is likely going to be consummated and a corresponding fee hence earned but much more one of whether future trading volumes and patterns will justify spending the time and resources to initiate and maintain coverage on a small-cap and likely initially rather illiquid stock. While there no longer is any written contractual commitment by the banks in the IPO engagement letters that their analysts will in fact cover the stock post-IPO, there is an implicit understanding that the research analysts will prepare a major IPO research study and will most likely maintain some level of coverage post-IPO, too.

Thus, in a stock where insiders were to commit a sizeable chunk of the IPO, would be and remain subject to a 12-month lock-up post-IPO, and where a few major investors were most likely going to carry the IPO transaction itself, i.e. in a stock that would most likely be rather illiquid in the immediate aftermath of the IPO, the type of feedback from many analysts was a tell-tale sign of whether they would likely commit to the story and stock in the medium term. It is therefore fair to say that research analysts, their specific knowledge of a sub-sector or segment, their rankings in such sector, and their true commitment vis à vis management and a company are material selection criteria in putting together the ultimate syndicate.

9.3   Syndicate selection symphony

Practical considerations of how banking syndicates can be put together – roles and responsibilities – a company perspective

However, without a banking syndicate there is no IPO… and of course the minute we decided to go for a European IPO rather than a NASDAQ listing the US banks dropped out of the process. The bulge bracket banks told us that whilst they were set up to do these types of smaller sized biotech IPOs in the US, their European teams were not. So, it was all about bringing together a coalition of the willing and the hungry.

By July we had selected Royal Bank of Canada (RBC) as our lead bank. Their head of healthcare banking had recently joined from Citi and previously had been at UBS in the 2000s – that is how long we have known each other and there was an important element of trust on both sides here. The selection was also based on the commitment by RBC to recruit one of the most highly ranked research analysts in London with deep sector and specific molecular diagnostics industry knowledge and expertise – yet at the time of signing the engagement letter that hire had not yet been made and the kick-off meeting would take place without even knowing who that analyst was going to be – such was the level of trust on both sides of the table to make this happen (Relationship Science, 2015).

We also quickly settled on a boutique German bank ICF – a team of former DZ Bank and Close Brothers Seydler bankers whom I had worked with on a number of transactions during my epigenomics years. Again, a deep sector and diagnostics segment know-how helped. However, the fact that ICF did not have their own research analyst team as a boutique bank meant that both parties would jointly need to select an independent re-search firm to become part of the process and again the pick was made based on specific coverage universe and expertise by Independent Research, a firm covering some of our larger peers (Independent Research, 2015).

But hey, we wanted to IPO on Euronext Amsterdam and Brussels and without a BeNe-Lux bank that would be close to an impossibility. Challenge here was that a syndicate of the top 3 banks in the region had just taken one of our key competitors public in spring of 2015 (Biocartis, 2015). Given the potential conflict of interest and competitive tension between Biocartis and Curetis it took a lot of convincing also using our two Dutch VC funds and their relationships to convince Petercam to become our second lead bank and joint bookrunner with RBC. A further complication was that we knew going into the transaction that Petercam had agreed to a merger with Bank Degroof which was scheduled to close in October which would be right in the middle of our IPO transaction – a bet on the fact that indeed the Petercam life sciences and investment banking team would prevail in such a merger of (sort of) equals (Investment Europe, 2015).

Engagement letters were circulated and following the usual haggling about fixed gross spread fee and incentives and above all, how to divvy up a fee yet to be earned amongst the three banks eventually, were signed in late July with a kick off meeting to be held on 29th July 2015 at our HQ in Holzgerlingen.

Small piece of advice that I have learned the hard way: getting in the middle of the haggling between the syndicate banks when it comes to agreeing on fee split is not the most fun part of things as everyone is either whispering sweet promises or shouting verbal abuse down the phone at each other and trying to convince you that "unless they get 22.5% of the fee instead of 20% they are not going to become part of this deal" etc.. Most of it is likely exaggerated and blown way out of proportion but as the one who will need to manage relationships, herd cattle and fleas, nudge everyone along and having to keep everyone reasonably motivated and engaged throughout, it is in your very best interest to take a very active stance and set your own clear expectations on who gets what and why – in the end they will all work with each other as they almost always do and typically in a successful IPO there will be enough gross fee spread handed out at the end to pay for bonuses and bankers' salaries.

From an entrepreneur's perspective and the management board of a start-up company's the actual fee pool size and gross spread is of secondary importance. Benchmarks are readily available from other peer companies' IPO prospectuses and there are well established precedents for a typical European versus typical US banking syndicate. While in the US the typical gross spread for a four bank IPO syndicate in the small-cap biotech industry is likely around 7% of gross IPO proceeds, in Europe that figure is more likely in the 5% range. However, whilst in the US the banks will pay their respective underwriters' legal counsel from their gross spread, in Europe these legal fees are typically billed on top of the banking fee to the company. Therefore, the real difference in fees is almost negligible. Also, one should not forget that the banks are indeed the only player in the IPO process who simply will not get paid anything in case of a failed transaction or a postponed or pulled IPO, whereas all other advisors, counsels and service providers are likely going to be paid either in full or at least most of the fee subject to customary "broken deal" discounts.

Once the decision had ultimately been made to IPO on Euronext Amsterdam and Brussels it also became clear that none of the syndicate banks were ideally set up to be or be-come our listing agent and therefore yet another bank would have to be selected. ABN Amro as largest player in Amsterdam as well as a few other shortlisted banks provided their bids and for a rather moderate additional fixed fee ABN Amro agreed to provide the required services such as actually listing the shares with Euronext and Euroclear and distributing the shares to individual shareholders post settlement as well as wiring proceeds to the company.

9.4   Advisors and more

In addition to investment banks and auditors – who else is needed for a successful IPO project?

The honest answer is that while banks are certainly important in an IPO, the real heavy lifting is typically done by the lawyers and auditors. The latter will have been de facto selected based on the need for IFRS conversion and audited 2 or 3 years of financials.

Now when it comes to selecting legal counsels, I can only recommend that as entrepreneurs and management teams you spend just as much time, energy and diligence in selecting those than you will have done picking your banks. But let's look at some of the key team building elements one by one:

Selection of issuer counsel

Most importantly for you as the issuer and management wanting to IPO your company is the choice of issuer legal counsel. From my own painful experience, do not let your board or VC investors take this decision for you. Every so often someone will owe someone else a favor and VCs of course know that the company will be picking up the bill but a lot of the legal footwork will immediately benefit and impact upon the VC funds. In our 2004 IPO we had been pressured by some of our VC board directors to change corporate counsel literally less than a week prior to the kick-off for the IPO. Not that Latham & Watkins whom we ended up taking back then was a bad choice, but the inefficiencies created by bringing in a new set of lawyers from the outside who have no knowledge of the company, have never advised management before, have zero historical reference points and never conducted due diligence on the IPO candidate as part of a VC financing round, these inefficiencies are material and will add to the pain and workload level for the company management team. It will also likely lead to more (potentially avoidable) hours being clocked and billed – or frustration once the hours underlying the fee cap have been reached or exceeded and the IPO is nowhere near completion yet.

So, this time round we actually heard three pitches from reputable law firms. The cheapest fee capped offer actually coming from a firm that had never worked with us before and in all likelihood was trying to get a foot in the door, take a hit on fees in the IPO itself and book some of that as acquisition cost for a new client… but surely that will come back to haunt you post IPO in terms of higher legal fees on post IPO work where every minute will be charged at premium prices.

So, in the end at Curetis we took the middle ground. Chose the mid-level offer with a hard fee cap, a modest broken deal discount but went with CMS Hasche Sigle as our corporate counsel of many years. They had worked with Curetis' VCs as well as the company since 2009 in all private financing rounds and AGMs. So, theirs was truly a detailed knowledge of the history, the intricacies of the various shareholder agreements, the peculiarities and idiosyncrasies of our shareholder base. Arguably they knew what they were getting themselves into. However, adding the corporate restructuring, redomiciliation to the Netherlands, and the US part of the IPO with a rule 144a tranche (International Financial Law Review, 2016) which required CMS adding as part of their comprehensive offer a US firm in McDermott Will & Emery, also made it really hard to stay within agreed upon budget caps when all was said and done. But there was not a single day throughout the IPO process where we as issuer ever regretted having chosen our counsel of many years and suffice it to say that while 6 months post-IPO at epignomics in 2005 we had actually terminated working with our then post-IPO corporate counsel we continue to be a happy and loyal client of CMS' various European offices since the IPO.

Selection of underwriter counsel

Just as much as one should make sure that issuer counsel is really the best possible fit one should also ensure that underwriters' counsel is a good fit to the selected issuer counsel. It will be the two sets of lawyers at the interface of the transaction between the company and the banks as well as all other advisors. Any friction or inefficiency at this critical interface will be a thorn in the side throughout the entire IPO process – far too many months, weeks, days and nights and long weekends to not care about this being as smooth as reasonably possible. Now I am not talking about the natural tension and opposing viewpoints when it comes to arguing the substantive matters of risks and liability, indemnifications, reps and warranties etc. I am talking about egos, personalities, styles, the urge to demonstrate to everyone else who is smarter, tougher, can pull more all-nighters and doing so at the expense of the company and its management team trying desperately not to see the project delayed or derailed at any moment.

Therefore, with all that I have seen and learned as well as overheard from many colleagues in the industry, I would never-again not get myself directly involved in the selection process for underwriters counsel. Let's face it – the company will always pick up the bill anyway so one might as well influence the selection process as best as possible. In our case we agreed with the lead bank on 3 firms that were allowed to submit bids for underwriters' counsel and in the end decided to go with Linklaters based on a very reasonable fee quote, solid past experience with the firm and the fact that the lead partner there used to be a colleague of the head of ECM at RBC our lead bank. Thus, we at least knew we would have a personal back door channel if things ever got tough. Never once in the IPO process did we regret this decision. The team they put to it was lean and very experienced and the senior associate working the long hours was stellar – and here is another lesson… like with any party to an IPO, it is the senior partners pitching and selling but it is the more junior and mid-level guys doing all of the heavy lifting. So, it is absolutely key to get to know them as early as possible in the process and to ensure that the pitch includes and involves the folks you will be dealing with throughout the project – make sure your buying decision is based on WYSIWYG principles.

IP counsel

In the life sciences industry there is probably no company and no IPO project that does not also involve IP due diligence and IP opinions at one point or another. Often enough the banks and issuer as well as underwriter counsel will carve IP topics out from the scope of their fee quotes and opinions. So invariably we did bring up the topic of a patent opinion very early on in the process. That, however, did not help alleviate the pain that ensued at the 11th hour. While early on the banks and all sets of counsels assured us that IP was a minimal issue at best and no major IP opinion and FTO search would be required, when push came to shove as usually does during negotiations of the underwriting agreement and wording of counsels' opinions, all of a sudden the need of a patent opinion arose. Which at that point our patent attorneys who had been doing all of our patent filing and prosecution work but had not been involved in the IPO process early on, did become the one item on the due diligence list that almost became a show stopper. Not that there were any material IP issues nor was a thorough due diligence really possible given the extremely aggressive timelines, but the wording of the ultimate IP opinion was contentious until the last second. Shuttle diplomacy, countless telcos, bringing our Director R&D who is also responsible for IP at Curetis into the IPO project for that specific matter, did not get our IP counsel to budge. Despite repeated and ever more heated conversations of passing blame in either direction and us making clear that we really needed an IP counsel and firm going forward that would be able and willing to provide customary IP opinions also for IPOs and public capital market transactions, ended up being rather counter-productive. Did it get resolved somehow in the end? Yes it did... do I know how? Not really... do I want to know? Nope... that neither. But the lesson learned from this issue is that no matter if you would rather want to save the several tens of thousands Euros in additional cost by involving your IP counsel very early on, this is no place to skimp and be too frugal. The nerves lost and pain inflicted, were higher than some incremental expense that ultimately would come out of the total transaction cost budget.

US legal counsel

For a European IPO with a US 144a tranche, i.e. a private placement to QIBs (qualified institutional buyers) you have one of two choices. Either go with one of the large US / global law firms that cover the world and will bring any and all offices they can get involved to the table. Or alternatively you pick a European law firm that at the back end brings into the fold a US firm that is hired and expected to exclusively deal with the US specific legal, regulatory and tax issues.

With CMS' offer to include McDermott Will & Emery we got exactly that and it panned out really well. Again, having worked with the senior partner at MWE in another post IPO capital markets transaction at epigenomics before, I knew we were getting a very experienced and very efficient US counsel based in Germany, speaking perfect German as well as bringing all of the US legal perspective and his partners and associates in the US offices in NY and DC to the table when needed. As a client, what we got was truly seamless and one stop shopping experience which is rare enough given the multiple P&Ls at the law firms and their multiple offices.

PR & IR advisory

Every industry has its specialist boutique PR and IR firms, and of course there are the global generalist firms. What you will need as a small company in an IPO process is the undivided attention and focus of your corporate communications people right from day one. This will probably be next to impossible if this is the first time you speak to these firms. In general, an IPO cannot come "out of nowhere" and some prolonged and sustained as well as planned and systematic PR and IR work will need to have taken place in the year(s) prior to the IPO project itself.

Having selected two small firms, one in Europe and one in the US as well as an additional IR team for non-deal roadshows prior to the IPO project itself made sure we received multiple sets of views, opinions, feedback and advice. Unlike banks or legal counsel these firms have much less of a direct financial interest in the IPO transaction itself – whether a deal happens or not they typically get paid on a project fee or retainer basis and are not tied to any particular outcome – which ironically may be some of the best and least biased advice you are likely going to hear from anyone during an IPO project. Even telling you that the story needs much better explaining, the management presentation needs tightening and sharpening of messages and management needs to get training before going on the road. These are your own personal advisors so use them as much and as openly as possible.

Also you will need to make sure that the PR and IR firms know their way around and are accustomed to navigating the tiny wiggle room left after legal counsels have agreed to a communications guideline (aka "gag order") typically right at the start of the transaction. There is always a way to talk to the press about the company, its products, its growth prospects and the opportunity, as long as you stay within the boundaries of past communications practice and stay clear of running afoul any particular IPO related black out issues. This is where having had a long term strategically planned corporate communications policy for years ahead of the IPO will come in extremely handy since you will have amassed plenty of precedence as part of the company's PR and IR efforts of the types of topics and specific guidance you have been using. No harm continuing along the same lines…. Subject of course to every press release and news / media meeting being cleared through a steering committee of lawyers, bankers, PR and IR firms and the company throughout the IPO process itself.

Printers

Printers used to be the proverbial bottleneck in any IPO. In 2004, this was an exercise of the legal and IR team spending 36 hours straight at the printers waiting to push the button on the printing press. There used to be rather few specialist providers for IPO prospectuses and when it was still customary even as a small cap company to print several thousands of the IPO prospectus and having them delivered by courier to thousands of accounts all on the first day of the IPO roadshow globally this could easily run into the six figures in terms of costs. These days with everything digital, outsourcing to India and other low cost places and a much more pragmatic approach by bankers and lawyers alike for small cap companies this was a walk in the park. The fact that I cannot even remember the name of the printing firm that we paid for little more than ten thousand Euros all-inclusive and had no more than 200 hardcopies produced, means it never was an issue. Just make sure your bankers and lawyers know that this can be done on the cheap these days.

Roadshow services

This is an area where having the banks take care of everything really makes everyone's life easier – that said if a small Swabian company used to tight coach class travel budgets and hotels just above the youth hostel level for years all of a sudden tries to fathom chauffeured luxury limos, business class travel and really nice hotels in any major city it can be a culture clash. As a CEO and CFO, I have always run tight ships in terms of fiscal discipline and our travel policy at Curetis until this very day basically consists of four words: "We do what's right". And that is where you can convince your own team that once in a (company's) lifetime it is "all right" to indulge in the few small luxuries of global corporate travel on an IPO roadshow. The incremental cost is small compared to the banks and legal fees and all other items on the IPO price list. But it makes a world of difference in terms of how well you sleep, how rested you are, how much you actually enjoy doing this – and it will show. So, the only piece of advice: sit back, relax and enjoy the ride that your banks lay out before you and don't worry (too much) about the budget for these last 2 weeks of an IPO.

So when all is said and done – what does it cost?

Adding to banking fees and legal counsel as well as audit fees and insurance expenses, the aforementioned costs for roadshows, PR & IR advisors, IP counsel for patent due diligence, listing fees for Euronext stock exchange, the listing agent (4th bank in the mix with ABN Amro) and you have yourself a grand total of EUR 4.3 million quite swiftly... add the greenshoe and once determined that the banks had actually done a great job in very difficult times indeed and a pro-rated portion of the incentive fee had also been agreed upon and paid by the company the grand total of EUR 5 million i.e. 11.3% of IPO gross proceeds had gone into the project. So, if you ever wanted to know what the real cost of capital was... there you have as close an approximation as possible (Curetis, 2015c). Now to be fair, these expenses (except for banking fees) do not change with the size of the offering, so let's hope we get as close as possible to the higher end of the size range for the IPO. Otherwise the cost of capital would be in the teens.

10 Project "Cactus" – memorable milestones

This chapter puts the concepts of Part 1 chapter 2 into the context of an IPO real life study.

10.1 Kick-off meeting

Why getting all stakeholders on the same page on day 1 is absolutely mission critical

Over a pub dinner with a nice real ale reminiscing with an old (and again new) colleague who had been there during the public market times with me at epi and recently joined as our chief commercial officer here at Curetis we shared some of those war stories. Having 52 people at a kick-off meeting where the company's own IPO team consists of 6 or 7 people is quite something. Each bank with at least 3 people, three law firms, auditors, PR & IR advisors and so on and so forth...

The initial project plan had us go out in early November, a mere 99 days after kick off – a target that unfortunately due to the turmoil in the capital markets created by the VW Dieselgate, China's economic slowdown and Hilary Clintons offhand tweet about extortious pricing in the biotech world (CNN Money, 2015) all did not help – but there we were on day 88 of this great endeavor and we had filed our ITF (Intention to Float) with just under a week of delay and were expecting to go live with the IPO transaction upon publishing the prospectus with the Offering Details. Delaying the ITF in October was a fight. The bankers tried to provide us with their best advice but sometimes it is really hard to discern whether they are truly acting in the best interest of their client (us) or protecting themselves from yet more egg on the face of a shaky transaction going south. To be fair with hindsight, this was the absolute right thing to do and waiting that one week might have been a golden opportunity seeing some positive trends and stability come back into the markets.

But first things first. The initial milestone in such a project of humungous relative proportions to the size, resources and capabilities of a small cap biotech company, is to actually get to a kick-off meeting. This means as a company you have succeeded in convincing not only yourself and your team, but also your board, your shareholders, a group of banks and other advisors that it will be in everyone's best (financial) interest to spend the time and energy and deploy the resources required to make this happen. A veritable milestone indeed – and after more than 6 months of meticulous preparation the actual kick off meeting was a blast and truly motivational for the entire troops.

The day-long meeting is really meant to get all parties and stakeholder aligned, assign roles and responsibilities, set deadlines for first work packages and drafts, align schedules for everyone. Sometimes it helps sharing the travel burden equally, so we agreed on having three actual face-to-face prospectus drafting sessions, one in Frankfurt, one in Brussels and one in London. And having your lead bank assign an experienced senior associate to be the keeper of all schedules, minutes and project plans is also a good idea. Make sure you have someone who has done this before and knows how to crack a whip and make people agree on day by day detailed project plans.

From the day of the kick-off meeting things feel quite like being on auto-pilot as well as everyone on the company's team including myself are on remote-control. Given that deliverables are so tightly scheduled there is rather limited time to think and a lot of long days and nights are required to simply function and do stuff.

10.2 Prospectus drafting and the AFM

The reality of external influence of regulatory bodies on IPO projects

One of the very first things is to start drafting the prospectus immediately. Bankers and lawyers will divvy up the chapters and sections and the art with an internal team of a handful of folks is to provide adequate counterparts on your side – a feat almost impossible.

To put this into perspective, an IPO prospectus these days is some 350 odd pages long including the financials (F-Pages). We had that first draft into the AFM (Dutch equivalent of Germany's BaFin) on August 31 i.e. within exactly one month from kick-off… think writing a PhD thesis in 4 weeks is fun ??? Especially when it is not one or two PhD supervisors critiquing but rather dozens of reviewers with very different agendas and interests.

A simple piece of advice: just tell things as they are. Use your words, your language and tell exactly the story you want to tell about your company. Rest assured that others will do their utmost to make the text unrecognizable to yourself. Wordsmithing is what lawyers and bankers are compelled to do and there always seems to be someone who will twist the last comma and hyphen into a warped debate.

To make things even more fun, we were actually going to put our audited IFRS statements into the very first prospectus version – but that was to become a story in and of itself… PwC had audited them, had given them their unconditional audit approval and then withdrew the audit opinion several weeks later when a discussion about our working capital statement in the prospectus highlighted the possibility of not being able to continue as a going concern in case the IPO were to fail… what a surprise, especially when the hours clocked up by PwC since Q1-2015 were by then in excess of half a million EUR and thus a contributing factor to shortening the cash reach of our start-up. But hey, I am not an accountant, no auditor – just a former CFO turned CEO trying to do right by our company and its shareholders.

So, we had a week-end in summer to put together a complete "Plan B scenario" of all the drastic action we would take in case the IPO were to fail. To this date nobody has been able to explain the factual dilemma that in case the IPO had failed, there would have been no shareholder to protect and no prospectus talking about a qualified working capital statement. In any scenario where the IPO did happen, however, the working capital would have been just fine… but as I said, there are surely certain legal and audit compliance rules that out of principle have to put a square peg into a round hole.

A word of praise for the Dutch AFM regulators. They not only keep their word on every timeline, they hosted a very early courtesy meeting with banks, lawyers and the company. They went out of their way to ensure we had absolutely the maximum number of days to draft and revise and they stuck to their promised review cycles and comments were factual, to the point and concise – always with a very constructive attitude trying to help us move things along towards a successful deal… something in my past career I had not always felt to be the case at the German BaFin.

After several iterations, hundreds of sources that had to be quoted correctly, put in the literature list and not to forget needed to be checked for the respective publishers' willingness to actually allow us to use them in the context of an IPO prospectus. This drove our most junior team member to the brink of collapse at one point but she pulled through, handled the lawyers marvelously and prevailed.

Two rounds of comments and bickering about font sizes, CAPS versus small letters, table formatting, wording and other assorted irrelevancies the lawyers and bankers finally all signed off on prospectus draft version number 5. In the morning, the AFM had come back with another set of comments on the previous week's draft submission and all of their edits were worked into the final prospectus. As of 7pm CET on this October night in 2015 that version was submitted for approval to the AFM. The corresponding press re-lease on the price range setting and offering details was drafted overnight and true to the same process here with plenty of egos and eccentrics involved in editing it to death.

On the home front (aka office) there are huge sighs of relief with the submission and our board is in jovial congratulations mood – enjoy it while it lasts. Browsing through the no less than 200 (!!) emails from this single day here I was getting some rest at home before heading out to Amsterdam the next evening. We are also preparing for yet another "Bring-Down Due Diligence Call". Tentatively scheduled for the next evening before the prospectus would get printed and couriered to all major financial centers we once again needed to confirm to the audience of lawyers and bankers that "no, there have not been any material adverse changes"… packaged in a set of about 50+ questions asking the same things over and over again. It is like taking an oath and should not be done lightly given the liability issues associated with any wrong, misleading or incomplete information in an IPO prospectus.

At the end of another day with almost 200 emails flying left right and center between lawyers, bankers, auditors and PR & IR advisors we were on the eve of going live with the IPO the next day. As of this afternoon the AFM had approved and cleared the prospectus and passported it into Belgium and Germany for approval by the respective national authorities (e.g. BaFin in Germany) by next morning. Surprising what some of these bureaucratic behemoths are able to do in just hours when the need arises.

At 8am that morning of 28 October 2015 the price range announcement press release (Curetis, 2015d) crossed the wires in Europe and the prospectus went onto the IPO website behind appropriate filters to ensure only citizens of countries where there was a public offering (i.e. not in the USA etc.) would be able to download it.

Check out http://www.curetis.com/ under /IPO and confirm you are actually based in Germany and then agree to the disclaimer and you'll have the prospectus there along with a bunch of other documents such as the IFRS financials for 2012, 2013 and 2014 as well as H1-2015 IFRS financials, articles of association of Curetis BV/NV, our insider trading policy etc. All cleared by all advisors during the afternoon and evening.

10.3 Due diligence delirium

How to balance the needs of banks and advisors with the company's

From several capital markets transactions, I had learned one key lesson: always be prepared with your data room for the most stringent due diligence. At the kick-off meeting they will play this down and then hit you hard with a list only two sets of law firms can relish in. Endless pages of request lists for any document no matter how benign and immaterial it may be, from more than 8 years of corporate history. Thanks to our COO having done an outstanding job of setting up a data room for the very first private financing round and then each year and upon every new financing round he had systematically grown and completed the data room. So, tell your lawyers how much work this is and that you will need more time to put it all together... smile, relax and then a day after the deadline you send them some DVDs full of everything under the sun. Keeps them busy and off your back for a while.

Once the hordes of lawyers have gone through every aspect of our data room from the company formation, all financings, all contracts, all board meeting minutes, any material document they could think of and from the due diligence questions that at some point will start coming up you will get a pretty good idea who actually looked at the data room docs and who did not.

Sometimes you can just enjoy the live entertainment of lawyers going up against each other on some technicality and comparing egos in lengthy emails belaboring their legal prowess... left me speechless – by the end of more than two months into the project all legal counsels were so far beyond their estimated hours on the project that the flat rates have long since kicked in... cool thought that lawyers used to making EUR 350 and upwards an hour (partners more like 700 to 800 EUR per hour) will get EUR 0.00 per hour of self-procrastination.

The pile of legal documents from CMS Netherlands is ever growing... Code of Conduct, whistleblower policy, Policy on investor contacts, Terms of References for the 3 Supervisory Board Committees, Management Board Rules, Supervisory Board Rules and Compensation Policy for the Supervisory Board. Various Deeds of Transfer, Deed of Conversion, Deed of this, that and the other... at some point you simply no longer have the stomach and bandwidth to really read everything the lawyers put in front of you. At some level, you have to trust them to do their job well on your behalf and just close your eyes and sign, sign and sign some more. Liability and responsibility of course lies with us... but hey you have to have a D&O (Directors & Officers) Insurance for something... and added on top of that an IPO prospectus insurance that costs an arm and a leg but will protect you for over a decade post IPO from anyone coming after you for statements in the prospectus.

PwC figuring out that the Dutch HoldCo (Curetis BV) also needs to be due diligence and audited – mind you that company has a balance sheet of EUR 0.01 (ONE CENT !!!) and no transactions so far. Great ratio of auditor fees to total company assets... I am sure this will take them a few hours – counting the entire balance sheet might take a while.

Also behind the scenes the piles of documents for the final re-domiciliation and share swap are being prepared. That final day when all shareholders will dissolve their shareholder agreements, contribute their shares in Curetis AG into the BV in exchange for BV shares which then become NV shares upon IPO pricing the next day.

On the home stretch of getting the prospectus ready these last 48 hours of the project before going live with the prospectus and ITF are a blur of email blasts with 20+ people doing CYA memos left right and center. In the end, no one but the company actually signs the prospectus – and in addition to that in the Underwriting Agreement with the banks pretty much it is the issuer / company that assumes any and all risk anyway. Accentuated by endless due diligence "bring-down" calls where the same questions about any potential material adverse change get regurgitated and answered in stoic fashion by the team and myself. Oh and of course with no more than 36 hours left the banks finally agree – after some ferocious fights and verbal abuse being shouted in rapid succession telcos between board members, investors threatening to pull the plug on the deal and do a private round instead, management stuck in the middle doing shuttle diplomacy and herding fleas.

A feeding-frenzy of signature collection in full swing with lawyers and auditors competing for most creative signature collection. While on the road at a Boston fund we ask the receptionist to scan and fax a PoA (Power of Attorney) and corporate restructuring documents to our legal counsel. Some of our investors still have not authorized legal counsel to make use of the PoAs and so on… Jan our COO has figured out that we can provide a power of attorney to one of our finance staff, send her to Munich on Monday and stay there until early morning hours and sign round after round of documents on behalf of the managing board members. We will set her up in a really nice hotel and pretend this is exciting and fun… while the rest of the team will huddle in Amsterdam where we have a dinner reception but will also bring a laptop, printer and scanner to get the dozens of signatures executed with all N.V. board directors and the management board in that room.

10.4 Analysts briefing and pre-IPO research 2015 vs. 2004

How analysts build valuation models and how that impacts ultimate IPO pricing and performance (reality-check on chapters 3.2 and 6.4)

Relatively early in the process by the second month you will need to brief the research analysts of all participating syndicate banks. In the 2000s it was customary for bankers and analysts and company to all be in the same room and have a full day of presentations, Q&A etc. Not anymore. In an era post Elliott Spitzer when analysts are no longer paid out of investment banking fees, the rules have been tightened so much that it is virtually impossible to provide any decent guidance and answer questions in a straightforward manner. Every analyst instead had to go off and draft their own research report and come up with a list of questions they wanted to have answered. Questions would go via banks and legal counsel for redacting and clean up and so did our answers. There were two one hour long telcos that were scrutinized and chaperoned and thus it was not too surprising to see analysts come up with a more than 2x diverging set of numbers a few years down the road. Same on valuation ranges.

Each analyst published a c. 50 page research report talking about the company, its products, markets, competitors, business outlook and each one of them built a 10-year financial model on which they based their valuations… ah that sweet moment when some independently thinking analyst tells you what the business you built over the past 8 years in their esteemed eyes is worth… safe to say that they could disagree up to a factor of two… but somewhere between 130 and 250 million might be the answer… and in a bull market one could shoot for the moon… but then prevailing volatility made it extremely hard for any tech company to successfully complete its IPO.

Virtually all IPOs in the US in our industry since September 2015 had priced below the book building range and in Europe of the 7 IPOs that were planned not a single one made it to pricing… they all pulled or postponed…. Against that backdrop – why not have another pint of that real ale?!?

Another key lesson learned. While you may not have more than a say 5-year business plan, make sure you have a wild-assed guesstimate for years 6 through 10 and beyond if you can. What happened in our rather Swabian conservative setting was that analysts took our guidance on product pipeline for the 5-year timeframe where we had visibility and some then simply ran out of ideas and assumed a lackluster terminal growth rate of 2 to 3%. Compare that to competitors that some of the very same analysts had covered in their IPO several months before where the second 5-year period was envisaged as another period of more than doubling top line revenue. And mind you, the vast majority of any DCF valuation model will come from terminal value so it makes a huge difference what those latter years look like. But in the absence of being able to even see the analyst models we had to get blindsided and then had to work with what we got. The analyst models are all publicly available and if anyone is interested they can read up on methodology, risk adjustments, discount rates, terminal growth rates, pipeline expectations etc. (RBC, 2015, DGP, 2015, ICF, 2015).

10.5 Price, place and packaging

Rationale for pricing an IPO based on valuation in a European listing context and how to spin the story

Oh and mind you – in between all these IPO project milestones we also did a "pilot fishing" roadshow… no not the real thing yet, not selling anything – just getting investors familiar with the story and the team and technology etc. What 10+ years ago would have been a couple of days with a handful of true "pilot fishing" discussions has since then turned into a complete shadow roadshow. So, they put us through 10 full days meeting more than 40 investors one on one… in Amsterdam, Brussels, Antwerp, Paris, London, Frankfurt, Zurich, Boston and New York… And now off to do a similar parcours again.

It may have been no more than a symbolic victory, but we did push the price range suggested to us by the bankers ahead of the public announcement and prospectus publication up by 50 cents… from EUR 9 to 9.50 at the lower end… because the low end of the analyst research had EUR 130 million valuation in there of course a healthy discount (expect 20%+ for a high-tech IPO) is needed for the IPO itself… So, EUR 9.50 to 12.00 it was. Issuing somewhere between 3 million and up to 4.8 million new shares, thus planning to raise between EUR 29.3 million and EUR 50 million in gross proceeds.

Why you might ask would anyone come up with EUR 29.3 million as the lower boundary of gross proceeds… quite simple – we needed to get EUR 25 million net cash proceeds from the IPO at least to be able to execute on our basic strategy and business plan. Thus – no rocket scientist needed – the total cost of the endeavor would be around EUR 4.3 million. The banks took 4.5% off the gross proceeds (plus a discretionary incentive fee payable at the sole discretion of the company if they did a great job). They share that amongst the three of them amicably after some bitter infights at the outset. The lawyers – whether it is issuer counsel, or in fact underwriter counsel all get paid by the company – taken together a solid EUR 1 million and a bit – oh and for that you get every sentence twisted and edited 360 degrees before getting back to square one. But to be fair they not only had to write the prospectus but also do a complete corporate re-organization for Curetis. Starting with a German AG, setting up a Dutch BV then doing a share exchange and in the end listing the BV (akin to GmbH) which becomes an NV upon IPO (like the AG). New corporate legal docs needed, new board etc.

And when thinking about perceptions of an IPO which easily morph into reality, think about what a "success" will be. Had we insisted on a EUR 50 million IPO size which arguably would have been a ballpark worth shooting for and had we then ended up with EUR 44.3 million and hence below the target, the IPO transaction would have been viewed as a miserable failure. Contrast that with a base deal size of only EUR 29.3 million that was upsized to EUR 44.3 million including green show eventually, that is a highly successful IPO deal in the eye of the market and its constituents. And when our board was rather unhappy with the headline a German daily newspaper wrote about how that air of modesty (Focus, 2015) had gotten us over the finish line as the only biotech company IPO in Europe in that Q4-2015 and indeed the only German biotech company getting an IPO done in all of 2015. Just remind everyone of that good old German proverb: modesty is an ornament (Bescheidenheit ist eine Zier).

And whatever your expectations are, always structure your deal such that you as the issuer keep back something beyond the closing of the IPO until after the trading pattern and stabilization period have run their course, after you know whether – and if so how much – of the greenshoe got placed. Make sure that your engagement with the banks allows for sole discretion of the company on whether and on how much to pay of such incentive fee. It almost always works, and for good work, solid performance and a greenshoe well placed with solid after market performance you can easily convince your board to allow you to pay out the incentive fee at the appropriate time (likely more than 30 days post IPO though!).

11 Blog from the IPO road show

Now the money is all spent and everything is geared up we will meet with the first institutional investor tomorrow morning here in Oxford. A guru, hedge fund in healthcare, knows the industry like few others in Europe and we will need them to be supportive from the get-go. After that the fun part starts… chauffeur service, dark luxury limos picking you up, a ride in style to London, briefing the equity sales team of RBC and get them revved up about the deal. Equity sales people are modern-day rug traders. They need to be greedy, hungry and must have that sense of invincibility that is so Wall Street (the movie) like. Then one last day in the office… budget time – and all the things that you need to already have thought about and implemented in anticipation of that life changing event for a company of going public.

So, my immediate concern now – apart from getting a few precious hours of sleep – is to get into selling mode. No more worries about the prospectus, the due diligence, all of the legal stuff, the obstacles – now it is all about the OPPORTUNITY. We offer investors a unique opportunity to buy a share (or lots of them actually) in one of the most exciting companies in the diagnostics industry. We have ready and marketed products that we are selling in Europe, Russia and the Middle East today. We raise growth equity capital to build our own US commercial organization, to expand our European sales and marketing team and to accelerate our product development pipeline.

It will be tremendously helpful that the IPO is greatly supported by all existing institutional investors. Nobody is selling, the deal is 100% primary issuance, even if the 15% greenshoe (overallotment option) comes into play. We already have EUR 15 million in the book from our VCs and corporate investors. And then in the past week another corporate player (STRATEC) emerged and put a EUR 1 million order into the book before we even started selling the deal. So that should hopefully get some momentum going… off to Amsterdam, Brussels and Paris first this week and then on to Luxemburg, London, Frankfurt, Zurich, NY and Boston and London again…

And being the optimist that I am we have already planned the party in Amsterdam for the day of pricing and allocation (10th Nov) and the first day of trading (11th Nov). But more to follow on that in due course.

11.1 Start it off in the BeNeLux and France

Early deal dynamics upon launch of the deal – what the first couple of days may mean for an IPO transaction

Sunday 25th October 2015 – Oxford

As I am sitting here at the tiny wooden desk in my faded charm old style British Victoria House Hotel room in Oxford I have begun contemplating how it feels in the eye of the storm. Looking back at the past weeks and months of the IPO preparation project and looking out at the coming weeks of roadshow madness with a dozen cities or so in 10 days across Europe and the US.

Monday 26th October 2015, Oxford & London

After an early morning full English breakfast, we made our way to Woodford Investment Management, one of the largest institutional investor in the healthcare sector in the UK. Knowing this would be a key meeting to kick things off we had brought some real products to show, including the one about to be launched in spring of 2016 as a teaser. Great discussion ensued and what was scheduled as a 60-minute intro meeting turned into a very engaged 90-minute Q&A session – typically a good sign… but maybe that is just us wanting it to be that way. S-class Mercedes with chauffeur to pick us up and take us to London. On the way, we are hectically checking emails and provide instant feedback to those following the nail-biter on the home front.

Despite the deadline at midnight Sunday several powers of attorney only ever got to our lawyers this morning. And then KfW (German Federal Banking institution) informed us that they could not issue the power of attorney since their legal counsel would be unavailable today. This could seriously derail any timeline so carefully crafted. Using some of our VC contacts and political pressure via the BMWi we make it abundantly clear that if KfW were to be the one derailing this tech IPO of a German company we would not be sitting in silence…. Miraculously they found another in-house lawyer who then read the documents for the first time but low and behold issued the PoA at 12 noon. Just in time… so our legal counsel was in a position to sign all of the Lock-Up Agreements (typical in IPOs for all current shareholders and management to enter into such Lock-Up Agreements basically preventing anyone from selling their shares for 365 days post IPO as a strong signal of commitment by existing shareholders to any new investor coming in).

The PoAs also allowed legal counsel to sign the Commitment Letters spelling out the amounts that each of the institutional investors would commit to buying in the IPO. So basically, we have an order book with EUR 16.15 million in it before launching the road-show proper.

We spent the afternoon in London with our lead bank and did the "Hooray Speech" for their sales team. Those guys will be the make or break for this IPO and they will need to pick up the phones after every investor meeting we have and get feedback and convert tacit interest into orders asap. It will be crucial like in any IPO to get out of the blocks fast and hit early and hit hard to generate momentum in the deal. Otherwise investors will keep their cards close to their chest and everyone will wait for everybody else to place their orders first… leading potentially to a failed or pulled deal.

Cheesy as it may sound but today on the Heathrow Express I picked up a penny from the floor of the train and thereby literally raised the first penny in this deal. I put it in my shirt pocket and will carry it around as lucky charm on the IPO roadshow. Last time that happened to me in January 2008 during the global financial meltdown and with just days left on a prospectus and public markets financing I came out of the last meeting of that day with US$ 20 million signed irrevocably from Federated Kaufmann a US$20 billion hedge fund. So, whilst I am not particularly superstitious this has to be a good omen for the coming weeks. And here it is…

Exhibit 14: This Lucky Penny Was First Funds Raised, © Oliver Schacht

Heathrow airport for a quick pint and ploughmans sandwich over which we strategize roadshow tactics and message fine tuning.

Wednesday 28 October, Rotterdam, Amsterdam

The roadshow schedule is taking shape. Flight to Amsterdam the night before was uneventful, a nice Indonesian Rijstaafel dinner in an Amsterdam favorite restaurant and with the certainty of our driver picking us up at 7:45am tomorrow we are going to hit the road.

Overnight the IPO prospectus will get printed (only special financial printing houses allowed) and couriered to all cities where we'll be meeting investors in the coming 10 days. First stop Rotterdam with one of the richest Dutch family offices who passed on the IPO by one of our direct competitors this spring… we'll need to do a better job of convincing them of what we have to offer. Our roadshow team is a great mix of a company founder (our COO and electrical engineer with 20 years in industry at HP, Agilent and Philips before starting Curetis 8 years ago); our Chief Commercial Officer who is a PhD Molecular Biologist and has been in biotech marketing, sales, business development and corporate communications for 15+ years. And myself – I just absolutely love roadshows.

There is no task more noble than selling equity in your "own" company. The shares are an embodiment of the company's spirit, its products, its USPs, its values, its people and so on. Selling biotech shares is a bit like Medieval trade in sin-forgiveness papers (Ablasshandel) by Tetzel in town squares. People did not quite understand how the afterlife might work – but they sure believed him and paid top Dollar for it… so in a way every share in Curetis is the right to participate not only in the economic future of the company and in a way a fair share in the NPV of the future DCF but really the right to participate in our mission of helping to save lives in hospitalized patients suffering from severe infectious diseases such as pneumonia. Every cartridge sold to a hospital and used to test a patient's sample is the opportunity to provide the treating physician with the information needed to select the right antibiotics, reducing length of hospital stays and lowering mortality and in the process saving hospitals money.

So that is why we are truly excited about telling our story and in the process selling our shares…. Up to 4.8 million of them if the maximum deal size is reached and the 15% greenshoe gets exercised – but frankly we'd be happy selling 3 to 3.5 million of those shares in the IPO… the often forgotten fact of what the "I" in "IPO" stands for… "Initial" – not the one and only and not the final offering of shares to the public, but really the INITIAL time one does it. One of the few benefits of being listed (along with many drawbacks) is the ability to come back to the capital markets again and again for more money to finance further growth.

The next press release announcing our new chairman of the board and chairman of audit committee are also ready to go out later this week. Great to know that industry experts such as Bill Rhodes, a 30-year veteran of the diagnostics industry and former executive board director of Becton Dickinson will become chairman. I had the great privilege of selecting and hand picking some of my own bosses as part of this IPO process. In April, our board had formed a sub-committee and let me run it – we retained Coulter Partners as search firm to help us identify, screen and select and then on-board top notch non-executive directors. These guys will have to approve every major strategic and financial decision we take, annual budgets, our own contracts… and yes there is another net benefit of going public.

Compensation as a public company CEO (same for COO, CTO, CCO etc.) is around 25% to 35% higher than as a privately held VC backed company, and bonuses are some 50% higher and equity linked long-term incentives being created…. So, from a financial angle this is not a bad deal – although there are plenty of ESB graduates in banking or other advisory roles making a multiple of what you can make as CEO of a small cap publicly listed biotech company – that said, EUR 240 thousand fixed and EUR 120 thousand bonus plus equity / options that could be worth 7-figure sums are not to be frowned upon. But rest assured – there are easier ways of getting rich than running a small tech start-up! And yes, I do know that from tomorrow onwards our employees and everyone in the world will be able to read up on what we make each year, what bonuses – if any (and there are years when there are none!!) get paid… part of the flip side – whatever you do from now on you do in the eyes of the public. On paper the phantom stock options we were granted 5 years ago are worth the price of a share minus EUR 1 nominal strike price. So even at the low end of the price range this is a healthy multi-million EUR figure total – but unfortunately this does not get paid in cash – it converts into shares a year from the IPO post expiry of the lock up and then of course under good corporate governance it is really hard for any executive to ever sell shares. Every trade must be made public immediately and will invariably be viewed (in case of a share sale) as a negative signal by the markets… so don't count on actually realizing any of those funds any time soon… and who knows what the stock price does in the next 1, 2, 3, 5+ years…. I still hold my epigenomics founders shares – 18 years and counting. Not a particularly rational decision but behavioral finance is not always rational…

Short and sweet – six excellent one-on-one meetings starting with one of the wealthiest family offices in the Netherlands in Rotterdam. Quite something, a private elevator going up to the 29th (top) floor and a rooftop wintergarden with indoor bamboo furniture and lush tropical vegetation. Good meeting with great Q&A and the request to also speak to some of our customers… always a double-edged sword but no way to get around it entirely. Followed by meetings with a major French bank's fund operations and various Dutch funds, some more lackluster, others very engaged. Great start to the roadshow.

Then typical roadshow mania – on the way to the train station in the car a telco with bankers and lawyers… two of our existing institutional shareholders wanting to dissolve a co-voting and pooling agreement… might result in a prospectus amendment and supplement which nobody wants… bankers and lawyers desperately trying to convince themselves and everybody else that in the first instance we should convince the two investors to rethink whether dissolving this agreement is indeed necessary and even if so – determining whether this would be at all material for other shareholders… let's see how this one ends – but just another brick in the wall of legalese-mania. Hail to the flat-rate… let them slug it out at their own expense… average hourly billing rates coming down as more and more hours get clocked…

New Asterix on the Thalys as distraction… cool stuff! Then check in and quick dinner of moules frites and a bottle of Sancerre between the three of us. On the home front, they are dealing with an influx of retail calls – "where can I sign up for shares" or "how do you make sure I get mine allocated…" – but also some really cool ones like the owners of one of our core suppliers – a mid-sized (Mittelstand) plastics injection mouling company. This could be a nice ticket and they would buy themselves into a strategic customer of theirs…

During the day, we also had a few calls with journalists (e.g. dpa) to explain our rationale for the flexible structure in terms of volume of shares and price range as well as listing location in the BeNeLux. More press meetings and calls scheduled for tomorrow – this is one way of leveraging your roadshow and the message by putting it out in various forms via the press in different cities and countries.

Tomorrow promises to be a rather light day – tough grounds in Brussels with our staunch competitor being the darling of the investor community here – but we'll give it our best shot and then intend to beat them in the market… and the best piece of news for the day… another direct competitor from the US today had to announce yet another delay to the launch of their platform and products in Europe – postponed yet again… gives us another 3 to 4 months alone in the market without direct competition … let's use it. In fact, we are raising capital to grow our commercial team – on the train we strategized and may instruct our search firm to boldly approach their entire sales team in Europe and try and steal some of them away who might get frustrated by the third delay in the past 9 months to the launch – we can commiserate and had gone through exactly the same teething problems in 2013 and 14… but it is a cutthroat business out there and no friendships to prevent us from hiring some of their best.

Onwards and upwards and staying in brutal selling mode for the days ahead.

Thursday 29th October Brussels

The hotel was less than stellar but getting the opportunity to sleep in and have breakfast at 9am is a rare oddity on an IPO roadshow. First meeting with a fund manager of a very wealthy Belgium family office. The company had been in the floor tiling business and got sold to a corporate for US$ 1.2 billion and a part of these funds are now being invested in listed equities of different Belgium public companies. So, with our dual Amsterdam and Brussels listing we actually fit the bill. It might help that the fund manager was previously a senior guy at our underwriter DeGroof Petercam. He confessed that this indeed was his own very first buy-side one-on-one meeting in an IPO and that he was nervous… for someone in his mid-fifties rather rare also. Suffice it to say that we ended up having a very open and direct conversation. He apparently liked the frank Germanic style and placed an order in the book that same day. Not too bad.

Last night I had reached out to several of our commercial distribution partners around the globe and in fact the managing director of our new Chinese partner spontaneously put an order for 15 thousand shares (up to EUR 170 thousand) into the order book. Not bad for someone who has never actually met some of our senior team.

A luncheon with the private wealth management team of DeGroof Petercam followed – seated lunch with 7 or 8 attendees on their side – mostly generalists so you had to reduce the rhetoric to blunt rainbow press statements. Our bankers made it no secret that the minimum ticket to play for any of the private wealth management clients would be EUR 100 thousand each.

Today was also the day of the press taking real notice – they had to digest the price range announcement yesterday and our press release we issued this morning about our new board of directors... Belgian as well as Dutch financial press took note and I ended up doing several telephone interviews. My favorite quote of the day actually came from the Belgium press... the journalist upon listening to our pitch and description stated matter of factly: "I cannot help it but have to conclude that your IPO and you going public and raising capital is bad news for Biocartis (Belgian competitor of ours)"... I begged to disagree and tried to be real gracious about it and put this in the context of the two of us going in the same direction and trying to change medical practice in the marketplace.

Dinner in a nice corner bistro at the Tuileries with steak tartare and a nice bottle of red wine. What will tomorrow bring? Paris is a special environment but very open to biotech investing. We will be meeting several funds that we had met in pilot fishing so should make for some solid order conversions also.

Our sales team in the meantime has put together a list of customers... what I would call the list of the "willing and the coerced" who are willing to take calls from some of these funds and go on the record about our platform, products, customer service and how satisfied they are with Unyvero and Curetis.

Finally, the PR and IR team at home is preparing for next Monday where Tagesschau TV has asked for a live shooting and interview with one of our key customers at Charité in Berlin – combining the IPO story with a broader theme on fighting antibiotic resistance... could not have been scripted better but sometimes you just have to get lucky. Let's see how this turns out. Our Director Finance sent a nice email depicting "Olli at work" on the road... with a big "I like" thumbs up. May the orders keep flowing in.

Friday 30th October, Paris

French croissant breakfast and nice brioches... on to meeting with several French funds. Aviva had invested in one of our competitors and made money on that IPO, so a great opportunity to let them know that they can buy into the better company and story at an even more attractive valuation. Lunch meeting at Restaurant Laurent which was a forest hunting castle for one of the French kings a few hundred years ago. Today a private lunch and dining room facility par excellence. Set lunch with printed artsy menus, a starter that optically resembled a modern painting of colorful fruit and veggies and sauce spots draped across a huge plate... Pinot Blanc going with the superbly cooked Cod in orange sauce... if it weren't for the silly aspect that while everyone is enjoying their lunch and wine the management team is presenting the dog & pony show and has to focus on getting the story across between bites. Great dialog and honestly, on a sunny day in Paris in a palace with great food and wine investors may be more prone to put an order in the book.

Exhibit 15: Paris Roadshow in Style Restaurant Menu,
© Oliver Schacht

Afternoon meeting at another major French bank at one of their main corporate locations. Fantastic old building with an atrium like a 19th century cathedral, glass ceiling and the meeting rooms underground in what used to be the gold vaults – metal doors the thickness of a wall and hidden stone doors with marble coverings… what a show. Another great discussion and the notorious Q&A of how the hell we as a small company want to be able to compete effectively against the elephants of the diagnostics industry. There having our chief commercial officer who joined us straight from Siemens this summer helped – he vividly explained how a large corporate simply is not set up to do the development, early launch and innovative commercial roll-out and would rather acquire companies once everything is de-risked.

On the way back to Charles de Gaulle Airport we held the first round of feedback telcos with the syndicate banks. Three days done and seven more to go on the road until 11th November. Several orders from Brussels and Frankfurt already in the books. RBC working behind the scenes to get the first UK accounts nudged along. Amsterdam major funds in process of doing their homework and expected to take decisions next week on order sizes. This morning our COO held a call with some of our private business angels who have supported the company since 2008. A local entrepreneurial family took another entrepreneurial decision and just put another order for EUR 1 million into the books. So, momentum is building and we are off to the races.

ICF in Frankfurt is getting antsy and wants the media and retail blogs and pamphlets targeted to stimulate some buzz around the IPO in the day-trader communities. So, with our PR firm on the phone I find out that one of their buddies who made a small fortune in the New Economy in 1999/2000 and runs a small venture fund now would also like to get into the deal… great stuff… people scrambling to get a foot in the door and start using inside angles to get to management for preferential allocation – boy that sounds eerily familiar and reminds me of the 2000 frenzy and friends and family lists back then. Hopefully the landing will be softer eventually than what happened then.

In the car and at the airport is one of the only opportunities to actually deal with some operational business – gets forgotten quite easily, but we are a company of 57 staff and have a business to run with real customers, real business partners, real day to day operational issues – and our own staff on the home front of course dying for any snippet of info and gossip from the road. Self-organizing system they are they put together a team in marketing that is taking shifts in answering the central phone line. Nothing worse than a small company being called and going incommunicado as management is on the road. Every call is an opportunity to excel and shine and demonstrate to the outside world that we are worthy of being a public company. Some of our core suppliers are calling and asking whether they or their management could buy some shares, so there is even an element of stock selling in this. Telco with insurance broker on the IPO insurance, call with our US clinical trial operations team and talking to the co-founders and our CTO who makes sure our cartridge production plant keeps churning out product.

Now we are headed back to Stuttgart for a week end of sleep, doing nothing, unpacking and re-packing the baggage, getting suits and shirts off to the laundry and mentally preparing for the whirlwind that will be next week: Luxemburg Sunday night with a chauffeur picking us up at home, London, Frankfurt, New York, Boston and back to Germany by Saturday morning for a last short weekend before heading to London, Zurich and back to Amsterdam for pricing, allocation and listing.

On y va !!

Week-end 31 Oct / 1 Nov – at home

Of course, our supervisory board is curious and wants an update which I type vegged out in front of the TV barely following the soccer games in the background. I keep reminding myself that an IPO roadshow is really much more like American Football than soccer. Much less creativity than soccer but much more planned and orchestrated.

In American Football you have 100 yard of field in front of you and you get 4 downs to go 10 yards with each play. As long as with these 4 downs you manage to advance by 10 yards you get another 4 downs… and so on. So absolutely no need to get creative and let alone throw hail-Mary passes early on. The way I look at this is every day on the 10-day roadshow is like a play, like one set of downs. Every investor meeting is a single down. Sometimes you as CEO (quarterback) get sacked behind the line of scrimmage and get pushed back a few yards. Sometimes your COO (running back) gets a few ugly run yards and sometimes you throw a short pass to your tight-end (CCO). Managing the clock and managing each play and never ever deviating from the well-rehearsed and well thought out plays is the art of American Football and IPO roadshows. We have a Q&A document (aka play book) that covers several hundred questions we had heard from investors, analysts, bankers etc. in the previous months. We now regurgitate the same answers in the same way over and over again. Make sure every investor hears the same consistent message – guess what they all talk to each other, too.

In American Football if you have 2 minutes left on the clock and maybe a timeout or two then you have plenty of time and no need to rush it. With that in mind we will just keep pushing ahead, one meeting at a time, one investor at a time, one order of a few hundred thousand Euros or a million at a time. If you are down to 30 seconds and in the red-zone (last 20 yards before the goal line) and you have exhausted your first two downs then indeed as quarterback or CEO you may need to take it upon yourself, take a gutsy decision whether to simply run with the ball yourself or to trust your eyes and arms to throw that one dart-like pass to a receiver who might be partially covered by the defense in the end-zone... that is when teamwork comes to its ultimate display of what a few individuals put together in a tight spot can accomplish.

And the 12th man (that's what the Seattle Seahawks my home team in American Football call their 60,000 fans in the stadium)... they cheer you on. Getting emails from our staff and the IPO team at home wishing us best of luck, cheering us on, delivering messages of small successes, sharing news with the entire staff, keeping everyone focused on what needs to be done: manufacture cartridges, ship Unyvero instrument systems to customers, deliver and invoice products, develop new assays and advance clinical trials. Just this past few days we learned that for the first time ever our manufacturing team made a single lot of 2,600 cartridges in a single week – that is a 500% improvement over 12 months ago – perfect 100% first pass yield on the QC front... and our US FDA clin ops team letting us know that while in the prospectus we talk about Sept 30th 2015 numbers of "more than 400 patient samples enrolled" we are now approaching 600 at the end of October... which puts us on a really solid path to completing this trial and major corporate milestone in Q2-2016 as we guide investors towards. If we continue at that rate we might be done by Q2-2016 which would be earlier than the street expects... let's keep that in our hip pockets for a rainy day of news.

Weekends are also times to contemplate some of the more philosophical aspects of why the hell one is doing this to oneself. But then the memories of those who give you that strength to journey on come flooding in. A brilliant little engineer and fellow scuba diver who had been with the company since day one and took his own life a day after last year's company Christmas Party as he could no longer battle his own health issues; our former Head of Marketing who just weeks after joining the company had received a diagnosis of cancer, resigned her job to get better but did not live another six months; an incredibly strong guy in our manufacturing team who lost the youngest of his kids aged just 10 years in February this year to an infection that progressed so fast that the little boy did not wake up again after they had put him to bed with a fever the night before... glad to have one of our other manufacturing operators back after she had been in a terrible car accident and months of recovery – which she gladly made!

The days when a call comes in of someone who knows the company and our products, desperate as a relative or friend lies in a hospital battling with an infection that doctors cannot properly diagnose and cannot get under control. We literally had one of our scientists come in on Christmas Eve (he had volunteered) to run some patient samples that we had a taxi pick up at a hospital several hundred kilometers away. Our Medical Director, making calls throughout the night to medical staff at a Munich hospital to try and help out with a Unyvero system somewhere else in the region or have a patient sample picked up to be tested in our own labs for an entrepreneur whose family member was fighting for his life. All of these things from a shareholder value perspective may not matter, may not influence share price, may not grow our wealth or bank accounts... but these little things for sure are the moments that I am most proud of the team and spirit and most proud and privileged to be part of running this company. I would not give it up for anything. So that gives me the strength to fight another fight out there in the capital markets for that next single order, the next investor to be convinced that we can help them make more money and a healthy return on their investment, build a bigger and better business and at the same time help make the world a tiny little bit better for someone out there.

Monday 2nd November – Luxemburg

Luxemburg was nothing short of a jam-packed day. Six one-on-ones and a group lunch... but the start was anything but smooth. We were well ahead of time for our 8:20 am early morning meeting outside of the city. Just that the fund manager was not there. We were ushered into a meeting room and then simply left to wait. It turned out that someone had put that meeting onto his schedule while he was on vacation and he simply had forgotten about it. When he finally rushed into the meeting room we had no more than 5 minutes left. We did the high-level elevator pitch and invited him to the group lunch later that day. He was so embarrassed about his own screw up that he not only accepted the lunch invite but also brought along another friendly fund manager. Good that we had sales guys from two of our syndicate banks in town that day such that one was able to walk him through the story in more detail.

Other meetings included the private banking arm of the Rothschild family, the private wealth management arm of a major bank and several other funds. Lunch was in a Michelin star restaurant and the group size had grown to about a dozen or so. Very good discussion and awesome food – just that the rack of lamb arrived as I was presenting key aspects of our business and by the time I finished they had taken my plate virtually untouched.

An evening meeting with a fund that is also limited partner in one of our VC funds. Great team with deep insight into the private equity space. They loved the story, dug into a lot of detail and mentioned they would consider taking a long-term 5 year plus perspective with a EUR 10 to 15 million position. However, they also stated that their approach to investing in public equities would entail just as much thorough due diligence as a private company investment. In an IPO process where everything that is deemed material by definition has to be in the prospectus there is simply no room for sharing any additional data and information. Thus, there is a good chance that they will not be placing a big order into the IPO book but rather continue their diligence and eventually take out some of the larger VC holdings over time.

Off to the airport in Luxemburg and facing fog as dense as chick pea soup we were sitting and contemplating our options and Plan B... what if the Easyjet flight gets cancelled just like many other flights that day...? Wait to take a 6am flight and risk missing your first meeting in London? Try to make it to Brussels and take a train? To Frankfurt and catch a 6 am flight?? Delays piling up and the last Euros stuffed into the chocolate sweets vending machine and finally the flight arrived in Luxemburg and did leave with one hour delay.... To Gatwick.... 100 British Pounds Sterling later we had made it to our Strand Palace (faded palace) hotel and fortunately pub closing hours do not apply to hotel bars... at 1am we enjoyed our shared antipasti and caught some 5 hours of sleep.

Tuesday 3 November 3, 2015 – London

Full English breakfast.... Yeah, "heart attack on a plate ☺ "

Driver with another S-class Mercedes picking us up and taking us to the first meeting with a British hedge fund. Funny meeting with the fund manager leaving midway through and the analyst digging in deeper the remainder of the meeting. Made it back into the car in W1 on time with 30 minutes to return to the offices of RBC for a telco next. Traffic in London totally mad and choc-a-bloc... took us 50 minutes and we were running so late that in the end the three of us literally jumped out of the car in the middle of a Thames bridge and ran to the RBC offices.

Then the fund manager for the telco in Switzerland had left his desk... we finally got a hold of him with a mere 20 minutes left. Fortunately, the guy had prepared very well. The bankers had met with him as had the research analyst. So, he had a few very specific questions about our new Chinese business partnership and certain commercial aspects of our business model. With these answers he sounded pretty impressed and ready to pull the trigger. Another meeting with a blue-chip fund as possible anchor investor but no idea how their process will pan out internally. Their analyst likes the story but needs to build a case to present internally at their fund manager team meeting to get one or more of them to buy into the story and the IPO.

Another conference call with a US hedge fund who asked very savvy questions and might be really interested or just be doing competitive intel on some of our US NASDAQ listed comps... And a final one on one with an old set of allies at a UK venture fund running a public investment fund also. They had been the largest single shareholder in my previous company post IPO – not an easy backdrop. But in the end a very funny, sarcasm driven and black humor prone debate with their buy-side analyst and it turns out that they are major shareholders in some anti-infective companies – one of which they have made an absolute killing on... and we happen to have been involved with that company in their phase III pivotal trial and helped them succeed by using our Unyvero system... quote: "Oh well that will make our due diligence rather simple – I will just give the Cempra Pharmaceuticals CEO a call and see what she has to say about your company and technology..." – strike! Let him... those guys were totally happy with the data that we delivered.

Back to Heathrow and a Ploughman's sandwich, fish and chips and a round of real Ale... typing these lines in the pub at Heathrow. About to board our flight to Frankfurt where we take the IPO roadshow to our home turf. A night in a grandiose (sarcasm off) EUR 80 a night hotel near Frankfurt Hauptbahnhof... the name "Savoy" sounds epic but believe me this is a place just one notch above the street level around the corner there....

11.2 From London via Frankfurt to the USA

Covering different markets, different investor types and styles and the issue of "home field advantage"

Wednesday 4th November & Thursday 5th November – Frankfurt

Nothing like being "at home" with your equity story. Despite the Dutch NV holding we are definitely seen as a "German" company... and doing our pitch in German – or rather Swabian (COO), Rhineland dialect (CCO) and Hessisch (CEO) – made for a welcome distraction. German hedge funds, private banks such as Metzler, generalist small and mid-caps funds and the German office of some US family offices made for a greatly diverse set of meetings. Everything from highly sophisticated scientific deep dive due diligence questions, via balance sheet driven metrics to the more personality and story based approaches.

At the end of day one in Frankfurt we were rather pleased with the outcomes... a first order from the day's first meeting already in the book by close of business and we headed for Zenzakan, a stylish and hipster Asian fusion and high end sushi place... surprise 7 course menu and an accompanying bottle.

Next morning started with a downer – we head for one of Germany's largest investment fund managers... their healthcare fund had already determined in pilot fishing weeks ago that unless we were to raise 200 million or more we would simply be too small for them... but the private wealth management arm that caters to the 1,000 richest German families was interested... just that the fund manager called our chaperone broker no more than 15 minutes before the meeting that he had to cancel as he was taking his daughter to hospital for an emergency... not shy and rather creative we played lounge lizards in the lobby and the equity sales guy of ICF started making one call after the other... one of the fund managers colleagues – home office... another one on vacation... others tied up... so in the end we scrapped the first meeting but determined to offer the fund manager a telco first thing next morning from New York... said and done... we scheduled the telco an hour later for 5:30 am Eastern time on Friday... hoping to see a fund manager with a bad conscience and wanting to make up for it with a nice order... and ICF truly excelled and made the very best of this with another 4 funds in that telco from all over Europe – cities we simply could not touch during the roadshow for logistical reasons... so in the end this might have been a blessing in disguise.

Later that Thursday we met with guys from our past at epigenomics... not easy on a day where epi was cut in half due to the ad hoc the night before of FDA delaying approval for a third time and requiring yet another study... but that also made for great talking points as I convinced several funds that this might be an excellent buying opportunity and telling them I will be staying long in the stock... they were all very willing to listen to the contrast we put up for show why Curetis is a very different story and much lower risk profile than epigenomics. Sometimes the bad news of one company can be turned into an opportunity to highlight some of the more subtle points of regulatory risk (510k for Unyvero vs. PMA for epi proColon), commercial focus (750 hospitals vs. 60,000 GPs), reimbursement (well established DRG Fallpauschale for our ICU products vs. separate CPT coding needed for colon cancer blood test) etc. Again, this resonated quite well and hopefully people will no longer associate Achim and myself with today's epignomics after the 5 years that we have been gone...

Flight to New York was rather uneventful and business class seats actually make for some comfy sleeping sofa... only biz class fare tickets ever bought at Curetis in 8 years but I sneaked those past our COO and told him to see the opportunity of a meeting after a good sleep compared to being totally knackered.

Hotel in NY happened to be directly across from a massive road construction that went on all night though.... So rather little sleep there...

New York & Boston 6th November

Three meetings in the US are rather few given the fact that we had done 3 entire roadshows to the US during pilot fishing and had seen some 40+ funds. But since the biotech industry was put in a tailspin after Hillary Clinton's tweet in August (CNN Money, 2015) the interest of US funds to look at any IPO – let alone a European one – has dwindled. I have been cursing all the extra work in the prospectus for the US 144a part of the deal (private placement to QIBs = Qualified Institutional Buyers), the extra auditor comfort letters needed under SAS72, the hassle of IR in the US and roadshows etc. ... but after all the three meetings were top notch. Hopefully one or two translate into an order into the book.

Mid-day on our way to JFK for our flight from NY to Boston we dialed into the banking update telco on the status of the order book... rather disappointing in terms of firm orders... we are still marginally short of the 29.3 million base deal size and hence in no position to shout out the "book covered" message to the street quite yet...

Knowing that we will have only 36 hours left from Monday morning I start some shuttle diplomacy with our existing investors... if only there was a way to coax out some incremental order size and volume from them such that we bridge that gap to the 29.3 million as early on Monday as possible... spoke to 2 of my board members and VCs at the air-port and one of them verbally offered another million.... If we can get a few of those from the insider round we might just get there Monday... but some of them would rather consider down-sizing the IPO – technically probably doable with a prospectus supplement and extending the book building period by 48 hours... but a signal of weakness in my mind with a very real risk of seeing the share price go into a tailspin post IPO and not easily recovering from it.

Strange situation, many very good meetings but so far 27 out of the 42 investors we met in 1-1s are still keeping back their decision and are sitting on the fence. Some large names have declined due to lack of size, expected limited liquidity post IPO, time to break even etc. Not too surprising but many others are still doing their due diligence. But without the "book covered" message it will become a games theory play... all funds holding back their orders until the very last minute... so my pitch to the insider VCs is simple – give us some additional volume orders into the book over the week end, we will leverage that Monday if book is covered and will simply not allocate to these insider orders on Tues-day... a bit of a risky gamble but in my book the better option compared to downsizing the IPO deal.

Boston airport offers some excellent seafood (Clam chowder and a seafood platter) with a Sam Adams to wash down the order book situation. Cannot picture a situation where we have our board, staff, guests, business partners etc. all flown into Amsterdam on Tuesday 10th and no good deal to show for it. So, it will turn into a dog fight over the weekend and early next week – one order at a time.

Over the phone everyone is pointing at everyone else – pointless blame game. But here is where the banks either earn their keep and fees or screw it up. With an order book such as this they know that there is little chance of getting much of the discretionary incentive fee and they may instead optimize their workload for the gross spread.

My flight will land in Munich at 10 am and I will only be at home in the early afternoon hours. Truly sucks since my 5-year-old son has learned to swim these past few weeks and he was so much looking forward to show it off to his daddy on Saturday –

but I will miss that by a couple of hours…. Have the video my wife shot from last swim lesson on WhatsApp and that keeps me sane – seeing the little fella so joyful and proudly climbing out of the pool after swimming all by himself really warms your heart – and you ask yourself if it is all worth it – plenty of key moments in the life of a little kiddo missed while being on the road somewhere, doing business all around the globe and not being at home… I hope one day he will understand and not blame me for not being there one too many times.

Another hour before the flight leaves Boston and the lounge is filling up with more and more business types… changed into jeans and t-shirt and will just stretch out as soon as I hit that sleep position button on my business class seat… trying to rest my mind and body… it is about time this is over!

Weekend 7th & 8th November

Landed in Munich and took the train to Stuttgart – trying to kick start the shuttle diplomacy with our existing investors. Last ditch effort – we need to close that EUR gap between where the book stands and the "books covered" message somehow by Monday. After calls with LSP and Forbion who have always been some of the staunchest shareholder supporters I know we can get another couple of million from them – but it will not be sufficient all by itself. The other condition they put out there is that they require the management and founders to also put into the order book some hundreds of thousands EUR which coincides with the net after tax amount due to be paid out post IPO to those in the team who in 2007 to 2009 had waived certain salary pay-outs. Getting on the phone somehow from the ICE train with our COO and co-founder Jan Bacher. He has to make the calls to his founder colleagues and within an hour we have verbal hard commitments from all of them. I have decided I will also put in my fair share to get us to the full amount. Turns out that most of them do not have any significant liquidity sitting around in their bank accounts…. The company cannot provide a loan as in our bring down due diligence calls we have to confirm that there are none – otherwise would have to have been disclosed in the prospectus. Ok here is my pragmatic solution – since we are buying a house and have an approved bank loan I have some cash sitting around at 1% interest rate – walking into the door at home I simply tell my wife that we have to wire the few hundred thousand EUR immediately first thing Monday morning to one of the founders who will actually place the order into the book … let me put it this way, I was not Mr. Popular at home that day… The small risk that the money might get "lost" to me was never an issue but unless you are in the midst of such a transaction it is hard to understand the dynamics of things that simply have to happen no matter what.

We head back to London Sunday evening and have a telco with our existing VC investors at 9pm. Banks are on the call as well and the good news is that every one of them has scraped together another few hundred thousand EUR for a grand total of several million plus the funds from management. The gap just narrowed to a couple of millions. So, our work is cut out for us for the last two days on the road.

11.3 The finish line in sight in London and Switzerland

Dealing with adversity and book building sluggishness on the home stretch of a deal

Monday 9th November, London

So, we know this is the home stretch and now every meeting really counts… First one with Aviva was a great meeting – Mark Denham the fund manager at the time (now with Carmignac) seemed to really like the story and at the end shared some personal suffering of his little son who is repeatedly suffering from infections and every time he takes him to hospital it takes several days until they get an answer from classical microbiology culture diagnostics. On the way out he goes through the deal structure with 29.3 million base deal size and more than 15 million committed from existing investors the remaining 14 million could be taken up in their entirety by Aviva… we reiterate our flexibility and ability to upsize the deal above the 29.3 million.

Further meetings throughout the day give us some level of confidence that there should be some incremental orders. But despite multiple calls from the equity sales guys of two of the syndicate banks to Aviva there is no order in the book yet from them. In an update call that we simply could not even dial into due to roadshow commitments there was some live actions with orders flowing in. One order from a Finnish fund that we had not actually met but just done two conference calls in pilot fishing and during the IPO roadshow came in while the team was on the call. Another order from Frankfurt and an up-sized private wealth management order via DeGroof Petercam gets us really close to the finish line. By the end of the day we still a few hundred thousand EUR short – Petercam will confirm another private wealth management order tomorrow morning first thing. But unfortunately, we simply cannot get to the "books covered" message for the sales teams out tonight. Off to Switzerland for Achim and myself and Johannes flies out to Munich for the legal marathon of corporate re-structuring tomorrow.

11.4 Roller coaster and the last 24 hours – build your own book

How deal dynamics can be changed within minutes and what is practically possible in a single day

Tuesday 10th November, Zurich

Early morning breakfast in the hotel. The team is anxiously awaiting the confirmation by DeGroof Petercam whether the small incremental order can be confirmed. That would put us exactly at the EUR 29.3 million base deal size and we would finally have the book covered. Our lead banker joins us at breakfast and everyone is kind of sitting on the edge and nervous. This deal still looks rather shaky and in the absence of a "books covered" message we simply cannot give the green light to all of the sales guys at the syndicate banks for the final day push.

My appetite is barely there, sipping some tea and aimlessly chewing on a piece of toast I watch the banker check his smartphone every minute or two. All of a sudden, he breaks a huge smile and grinning he shoves his phone over to me... an order from Aviva has just come through.... For EUR 12.5 million... yes TWELVE POINT FIVE million Euros...at EUR 10.- per share... incredible, we stare at this screen, at each other and then there are some high fives. This is the break we have all been working towards, the anchor order that totally and dramatically changes deal dynamics in a split second. We look at each other and get on our phones, spreading the news to all banks and all sales guys in a matter of minutes. Now we are off to the races. Meetings in Zurich all of a sudden start with a bold message: "The book is covered, including 15% greenshoe, nicely oversubscribed and pricing will be within the range"... we discuss tactics and basically agree that we ought to tread carefully and would still want to allocate at EUR 9.50 per share to be on the safe side.

The following meetings run into a blur... as the day goes on every investor knows this deal will close and will print! One of Germany's largest fund operations who have been meeting with us since April again and again are on a call. Their order comes within 30 minutes... several million additional demand in the book. Other funds now keep throwing orders into the book, either at EUR 10 or at strike... We meet with some of our existing shareholders such as HBM and aeris (the respective public trading funds sides). Strong support from them also.

We board the flight to Amsterdam... the body shuts down and we doze off for 60 minutes... driver picking us up at the airport and taking us straight to the "5 Flies" famous Amsterdam restaurant where the IPO team and some 40+ guests are waiting. Some bubbly stuff in a glass, smiles, high fives, embraces, and shouts of relief... The board members have all flown in, from Italy, from the US (our new chairman) ... speeches by outgoing chairman, new chairman, our lead banker and myself... telling each other how well we have worked together. It is a moment of triumph for sure, but I cannot help but tell everyone that the proudest moment for me at Curetis were the silent ones... when we stood together in 2014 in the face of adversity, waiving bonuses, freezing salaries and hires, keeping the team together and resisting the pressure from our board to start reducing headcount when we faced technical challenges in the product development 18 months ago... when we supported those of our staff that needed it most in the face of personal and health crises, folks going the extra mile for patients and family members of relatives... those were the real signs that we were on to something truly special.

As the dinner gets served our COO and CTO are busy at the CMS Amsterdam offices signing pile after pile of paper... tired, pale, eyes shot red and knackered they eventually come over at 11 pm... just before getting another call that some further documents have to get signed and delivered before midnight... this marathon of documentation ends at 2:30 am... well 23:59 pm somewhere in the world I am sure.

11.5 Deal is done, let's deal with it

Considerations in final IPO pricing, allocation and greenshoe

At 4 pm on the last day of the roadshow on 10th November we do another bring down due diligence call – going through the motions at the airport... confirming that nothing has changed, no material adverse events have occurred etc. Through airport security we get on the pricing and allocation call with our board and VC shareholders and all banks... what a finish... the book stands at EUR 53 million in demand... this is a full 25 million more than a few days ago and we almost doubled the demand side in the last 24 hours of the roadshow. And we simply cannot believe the advice from our syndicate banks... they collectively advise us as a sign of strength to price the deal at EUR 10.00 per share. This is where the largest orders came in unprompted with no negotiations. We also agree to allocate a base deal size of EUR 40 million, which is an upsizing of 36.5% over our base deal size.

Curetis is the first European biotech or life science IPO since early September that actually gets it done... 7 others had tried and failed, pulled, postponed... of the last 10 US IPOs in our industry in recent months 9 had to price below the bottom end of the range and most traded down from there... We are pricing in the range on an upsized deal with the ability to cut funds back – some of them by 50%, others by 25% or 15%... leaving room for after market demand and performance.

Wednesday 11th November, Amsterdam

After a short few hours of sleep we all head over to the stock exchange at Beursplein no. 5... the oldest continuing stock exchange in the world – since 1609.

The marketing team had done an awesome job at decorating everything, balloons in corporate colors, cacti (for the IPO project's codename had been "Cactus") all over the place, videos running, pyramids of the grow your own cactus giveaways... welcome speech by the CEO of Euronext Amsterdam... the gong ceremony with a 10 second count down and then the gong opening the day's trading, the electronic banner in the trading floor welcoming Curetis. The stock opens at EUR 10.00 and starts trading up a little bit with the day's high at 10.45 and the low at 10.04 where it closes – but nicely above the issue price, never below EUR 10.00 – also thanks to the banks stabilizing this.

Some of the company founders and former board members are obviously emotionally captured by the moment. We get presented with a statue of the God of Trade, Mercury in a room that normally is used by the royal family... We present our cactus arrangement as a present to the CEO of Euronext and all agree that this will be something he will remember for a very very long time... these plants are resilient and live looooong lives on very little water...

Media frenzy starts, interviews, photo shootings, a video statement that I have to give... at 10:40 we all head down to the trading floor for a group photo from the balcony. Our very own photographer is busily capturing every precious moment.

Is it different now for the second time? Yes for sure, a bit less emotional, a bit more matter of factly, but nowhere near routine. This is something that as an entrepreneur you typically do not experience too many times in your life... so having two of them done sure feels exceptionally privileged.

A boat tour with lunch being served with our guests follows and then the first board meeting as a public company with our new chairman. Back to business, preparing the first budget discussions and 2016 planning meeting to be held with the board on 2nd December. And one last flight back to Stuttgart... with some last-minute airport food and a non-alcoholic beer.

Thursday 12th & Friday 13th – Closing and Settlement

First day back in the office – more paperwork to be signed, another bring down due diligence call – chasing all of the items required for closing as condition precedents... IP attorney opinions are nail biter right to the end. We are starting to prepare for the IR function build up. Website needs to be revamped with an IR section, a database of investor contacts established, the friends & family distribution list augmented and so on. Stock still barely trading since settlement will not occur until Friday.

ABN Amro acting as listing and settlement agent subscribed to the 4 million shares at EUR 0.01 per share i.e. EUR 40 thousand Friday morning. We signed the deed of issue for the new shares and those get transferred from ABN Amro to RBC and the syndicate for settlement against cash with the IPO investors. First wire from the 7 existing investor committed shares hits our account mid-day... EUR 18.3 million ... the final settlement amount of another EUR 19.2 million expected later this afternoon – net of legal fees for underwriter counsel, the 4.5% banking fee and some assorted expenses – not too bad – less than we had expected on the travel and assorted line items. We have, however, kept the carrot out there.... Our decision on whether or not to pay some or all (or none) of the up to 1.5% gross spread incentive fee to banks will be kept open until 30 days post IPO by which time we will know whether – and if so how much – the greenshoe will be exercised and up to additional EUR 6 million will flow to the company (minus fees of course…). After market performance is also a criterion for the incentive fee… and then we get a call from one of our largest shareholders about their intention to significantly increase their stake and they start hunting for sellers… great position to be in…

An all hands meeting with the entire Curetis staff takes place mid-day – I get to do a final motivational speech, share some anecdotes with everyone, highlight that everything we do from here on out will have to be viewed in light of its accretiveness to shareholder value creation… also mentally prepare folks for the change in tone, internal communication and restrictive sharing of material information as part of our insider trading rules. A Mexican buffet with cacti in the room wraps up the celebration… and some very happy faces.

We will only realize just how much of a stunt it was that we pulled off in the coming weeks and months. The European biotech community was looking at us in awe and the 100 or so congratulatory emails keep asking the same question in many different ways… what was the secret sauce in this deal? Well, if only I knew… one large part of it was the team – their motivation, the spirit, the endless energy that everyone put into it, their hearts and souls behind the product, the platform and the company. The banks leaving their egos at the entrance and a syndicate of eclectic less than stellar names but with everyone rooting for the deal and it matters to all of them – what better place to be… the share trading up some 10% above issue price at the end of the first week of trading… means we got the initial pricing and allocation reasonably right… onwards and upwards as a public company.

12 IPO aftermath and "being public" lessons learned

12.1 First day(s) of trading

Why they are so important and what messages they send to the markets on your order book and investor base

When that announcement of the IPO pricing has gone out (Curetis, 2015e) and the opening bell on the day of first listing rings – or in the case of Euronext Amsterdam when that gong is sounded, then everyone holds their breath. What is the first price and will we see an uptick? We had issued the 4 million shares at EUR 10.00 and indeed that was the first price. The stock then traded up by about 11% within the first week – typically a good sign. The signal this sent to the markets is that the allocations were made in a measured and cautious way. Most investors were healthcare specialists and known long-only investors. However, there are always a few hedge funds involved and one can never be 100% sure. We had tried to mitigate this on the night of pricing and allocation by cutting back some of them down to less than 50% of their demand in the order book. This of course is only possible if one has an order book that is nicely over-subscribed and covered multiple times.

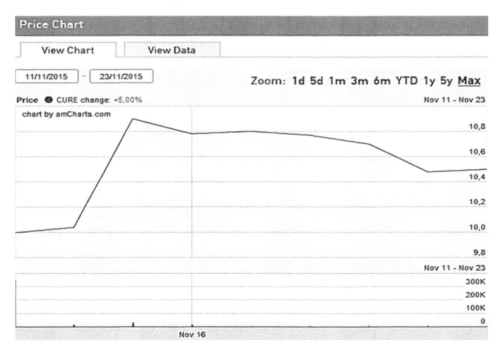

Exhibit 16: Curetis Post IPO Stock Price
Source: Enternext, 2017

On a scale of 1 to 10 we probably had a 5 to 6 middle of the range order book. Nicely covered a couple of times including greenshoe but not exuberant x-times over. We also knew that some of the funds would expect pretty sizeable allocations and really wanted a chunk of the stock that would make it a significant position in their portfolios. The risk of cutting any investor back too far is that a position stops being meaningful and that in and of itself may create a situation where the fund might sell the share pretty quickly in those days where liquidity is typically good.

The lead book runners will then also act as stabilization managers and will be actively looking at buying and selling stock in the immediate aftermath of an IPO. Indeed, in the first couple of weeks we learned that our lead bank had used only a small proportion of the greenshoe to buy back a few shares and only in the first 2 to 3 trading days. After that the share had stabilized in the market and every holding seemed to be in safe and stable hands.

These first few days are also a good opportunity to get some rest, reduce the adrenaline level to sort of normal, sleep, work reasonable hours at the office, start talking to the people in your company again who for the most part had not seen a lot of you in the past three to four months. Making sure that the IPO gets celebrated in those early days when the optimism is boundless and the aftermath of compliance and other unplannable capital markets events have not yet had any negative impact on the stock may also be a good idea.

In 2004 that phase had been cut pretty short as the epigenomics stock never even reached its IPO price again and started trading down almost immediately following the IPO – and that does put a damper on things fairly quickly although it also behooves everyone well to not take things too personally as there are things in life that are simply out of one's control.

Also, these first days post IPO will be the days when journalists from across the world will try to get a time slot from management to discuss the IPO experience, whether the company is happy with its IPO or not, what the plans are etc. Especially in a small company this typically will squarely fall on the shoulders of the CEO and / or CFO. Thus, I ended up doing something like a dozen telephone interviews in the first two days post IPO plus a few journalist one-on-ones that had been pre-scheduled with our PR firms right at the listing ceremony and afterwards. Beware that you cannot say anything that you had not stated in the IPO process and that you must not deviate from the equity story told in the IPO. And rest assured a good journalist will try to pull out some unique tidbits of information that no one else has picked up on. Do not fall into the trap of commenting on analyst research for example. The IPO research from all syndicate banks is out there and financial journalists will have it. They will also try to get a sense of how long the cash reach will now be, what future financing plans might be etc. – just feel comfortable sticking to the often underestimated and under-appreciated "no comment".

Again, a hard lesson learned from our 2004 IPO with epigenomics where our CEO after a night of post IPO party that had ended the next morning at 8 am in Berlin had answered his cell phone just hours later and responded to a Spiegel journalist to the question on how he felt with an epic "it felt like running a brothel" (Der Spiegel, 2004b). Not the type of thing you want to read many years or even a decade later? Then just don't say things – a PR advisor once taught me that "there ain't no off the record – if you don't want to see it in print, don't say it!". A lesson that some politicians also learned the very hard way after hours at hotel bars with rainbow press journalists. This can easily cost you your career and journalists savor nothing like a scoop of dirt and a juicy headline…

So, with that in mind we were actually reasonably pleased with the IPO coverage. Especially the BeNeLux press treated us very nicely, was in a congratulatory and celebratory mood and helped round off the overall positive experience of the Euronext listing with some nice lines that I am sure everyone will still feel comfortable reading years from now (Going Public, 2015, Labiotech, 2015, Euronext TV, 2015).

12.2 The quiet period

The do's and don'ts once public – time to build some of the required post IPO infrastructure

Over the first four to six weeks the Curetis stock after trading up for a while and then getting hit at the four-week mark for a day or two then eventually closed the year at the IPO level. Not great but looking at global capital markets in that period nice enough.

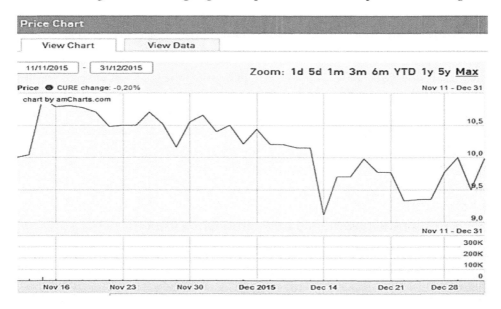

Exhibit 17: Curetis Post IPO Stock Price
Source: Enternext, 2017

During the initial 30-day period, the so-called "quiet period" the company is typically not allowed to make any announcements or statements of any material importance or including anything material that had not been included in the IPO prospectus itself already. So, best thing is to avoid having any news flow in the immediate period following the IPO and save up the good news for thereafter.

This also gives the company some time to prepare its corporate communications infrastructure, website, compliance processes and documents, map out how exactly going for-ward press releases will be drafted, reviewed, edited, who should be involved and who should not, sign off procedures, distribution across all required platforms: from the company's very own friends & family news distribution list, the PR and IR firms' target lists, the legally required AFM and FSMA pathways, as well as a global newswire system that ensures full legal compliance with all capital markets requirements such as NASDAQ Globe Newswire or the likes.

Within a couple of weeks, we received word from the underwriters and lead bank that stabilization would no longer be necessary and that the greenshoe allocation in large part was also successfully done. So, we agreed with them to put out the announcement of the successful over-allotment option exercise (Curetis, 2015f) on 3rd December 2015 already. Adding another 431,033 shares to the offering and thus increasing the gross amount raised in the IPO from EUR 40 million to EUR 44.3 million.

At that point, it is also a good idea to be talking to your board about the discretionary incentive fee. For us the success of the IPO itself in combination with solid aftermarket trading and greenshoe exercise and a high quality group of 30+ institutional investors who came in as new shareholders at the IPO is a good enough outcome to warrant most – if not all – of the discretionary incentive fee. It is also a signal to the markets and the world at large that this indeed was not a transaction on shaky grounds.

Contrast this with the 2004 IPO of epigenomics where the book was covered only just and immediate post IPO trading had the stock under water and no greenshoe ever got exercised since the banks needed all of it to stabilize the share price in the weeks post IPO… and yes in such a case it is also fine to determine that any incentive fee is not really warranted. After all, the fee spread for the banking syndicate should in large part be driven by the selling commission and not just the project management and underwriting fees.

12.3 Corporate governance and compliance mania

Small company perspective on how to deal with the legal and regulatory requirements

From that day onwards nothing will ever be the same. We have hired another experienced finance and accounting person, an HR person, an in-house legal counsel who will also dub as compliance manager, and so on.

And we will need an IR person – that is where our ESB European School of Business Reutlingen recruit of the class of 2013 comes in. Elena Billig had done her 2nd internship in our marketing team in 2012. She wrote her bachelor thesis and Master thesis (St Andrews) with and about certain aspects of Curetis. We hired her as management trainee in early 2015 and she was a full-time member and integral part of the IPO project from day one. No safety net, no chaperone – Elena was the one responsible for the Industry chapter and Business chapter in our prospectus; she was the one digging up the hundreds of sources and references needed to back up every number and claim in the prospectus. She co-authored the analyst presentation and presented to the assembled research analyst teams of our banking syndicate on the market potential analysis for Europe, the US and Asia. And she has then post IPO taken over the responsibility as IR Manager to build our own in-house IR function from scratch. In that role, she has had to run the annual report project at the interface of corporate communications, finance and accounting, the boards, auditors, audit committee and the creative guys in design, layout, photography and storytelling.

Our IR website post IPO and after expiry of the quiet period needed to be built and evolved. Incorporating key information on corporate governance, insider trading policy, whistleblower policy, rules of procedure for all board committees, rules of contact with outside parties, a corporate code of conduct and so on.

In theory, of course all rules and procedures must be in place right from day one as a public company. The reality as a small company with rather limited resources and a very lean overhead organization you will have no choice but to build it one step at a time. Make sure that your lawyers as part of the IPO process provide you with the essential documents from a compliance standpoint. In our situation, we had our Dutch corporate legal counsel as issuer provide us with the basic tool kit and set of documents that we then needed to upload and go live with immediately once we announced our intention to float.

Once we had our in-house general legal counsel on board in February 2016 we organized for an orderly hand-over from our HR manager who had acted as compliance manager in the interim to him. It greatly helps to hire someone into such a corporate function who has had to deal with these issues before. Bernd Bleile our compliance manager and general counsel had spent several years at a Mercedes subsidiary MB Tec being responsible for compliance management – definitely a perfect fit for the role.

It will, however, not be until you actually draft the first press releases and especially some news that would reasonably be deemed to be material and stock price sensitive information. Releasing such information needs to run just like clockwork. Having your PR and IR firms set up the news distribution and also using reputable providers such as NASDAQ Globe Newswire. Then of course your analysts will want to be informed through the appropriate wall-crossing mechanisms and channels the night before after market closes to give them a few extra hours to digest the news, write up their early morning notes and get out in front of the message right from the start. Also they will not appreciate the issuing of news in the late morning hours or even in the afternoon. Analysts will prefer news to go out well before market opens. We then set ourselves the goal of having every news teed up by 7 am CET on any given day and go live before 7:30 am. This enables a process whereby analysts can pick up the phone and actually talk to management on the news before putting out their flash notes and before markets open for trading. But make sure you have the mandatory emails and infos uploaded to regulators such as AFM or FSMA well before.

Also from my own painful experience it does not help as a small company to argue that on a Friday night after 9 pm nobody was in the office anymore to issue an ad hoc relevant release. As a member of the executive Management Board but also Supervisory Board people will quickly appreciate the potential personal liability and although D&O insurance protection may offer some relief, it is one painful experience nobody really needs if the relevant regulatory oversight bodies issue a fine. So, as a piece of advice: never listen to anyone, not a board member, not a major shareholder not anyone telling you to stretch the rules of compliance, e.g. to delay an announcement such that it may have a bigger impact on your stock price (on good news of course) at the beginning of the next week rather than a Friday evening. Same holds true for bad news. On 16th December 2006 at epigenomics we had received notice of Roche's decision to terminate the multi-year and EUR 100 million plus collaboration in its entirety for no apparent reason (other than management change and strategy shifts). That release went out within hours and hit the markets well before they opened in Frankfurt the next morning... (Reuters, 2007) lucky that we were all on the US West Coast that day and had the evening Pacific Time to get this written and lined up for release. There will be many moral hazards and opportunities for doing the right thing versus maximizing your own and anybody else's shareholder value in the short term. But in the long run, the ability to deal with bad news, the way you act and react to adversity and the way you openly and honestly communicate such news to investors and shareholders will build or destroy your credibility and will allow you or prevent you from going back to such investors years later to raise capital once again.

Your auditors will likely also weigh in on the annual report sections on corporate governance and compliance. Again, no matter how small your company may be, the rules are the same for everyone. Just also realize that most corporate governance codices will stipulate for a "comply or explain" approach. Thus, we ended up disclosing quite a number of deviations from the Best Practice provision under the Dutch Corporate Governance Codex. Some of these were simply due to the fact that as a small company you will not have an internal auditor who is independent – and your Finance Director will by definition not be deemed independent. Also, you will work very closely with your board members. Some of them may even have provided a few extra days of consulting advice under a small and simple service or consulting agreement. But that in turn will render them "non-independent" for the next years. Disclosing everything from management board contract and remuneration details, conflicts of interest (yes as a founder or executive in a small company you will have significant shareholdings or stock options and thus may have interests that align with all shareholders but may not be viewed as completely independent in a purist's view.

Corporate risk management is another area where post IPO compliance will be mandatory. Having had standard operating procedures under our ISO 13485 certified quality management system as a diagnostics company greatly helped. Simply applying such best practice tools and metrics to the corporate level is a good way of getting everyone in the company on board as they will be intimately familiar with the approach and tools used. Still, getting this all documented and put together will take a few months as a small company. In the respective annual report you will also find great examples of dozens of pages of small print on any and all fathomable risk versus other companies taking a rather pragmatic key risks approach in a tabular format on a few pages. But again, the fact that as a small company even seemingly minor events may have a material impact on one's stock price sets the bar and threshold for materiality rather low.

Apart from endless checklists, memos from lawyers, auditors etc., using common sense and the policy we had written into our corporate code of conduct years ago as one of "we do what's right" actually really helps. Deep down if you do not feel comfortable with a situation or decision it is probably wise to check it against compliance demands and determine the best course of action.

Above all compliance is a mindset that needs to be instilled in every employee of the company. It is up to the leadership to lead by way of good example. Cutting corners as management will lose you all credibility with your teams and staff if you then force them to adhere to different standards that you are willing to abide by yourself. In a recent book the authors have laid out the topic of compliance in a very broad sense making clear that simple adherence to the law will likely be insufficient (Niewiarra & Segschneider, 2016).

12.4 Starting the IR song and dance

How to ensure there is continuity from the IPO to the being public

Apart from the compliance stuff there will be ample opportunities to get back into a modus operandi where you can get out there, tell your story, deliver messages and provide some context (aka spin) on issues. In fact, a disproportionate amount of any CEO's or CFO's time in any small public company will be spent on corporate communications post IPO. For some it is what they enjoy and love doing, for others it is viewed as a distraction from running the business and building a company. This is often also a point where people in the C-suite of start-up companies need to be honest with themselves: is this still what they like doing? are they good at it? is this the time to consider bringing in additions to the management team and board?

Your IR firms and advisors and your own IR folks will tell you what they expect. The annual financial calendar gets established way ahead of time with dates for quarterly earnings releases, shareholder meetings etc. being set. In any given industry there are key conferences that are a "must-go-to" event. For us in biotech it is the annual January trek to San Francisco for the JP Morgan conference where thousands of biotech executives, bankers, analysts, investors and press meet for a start to the IR year. It sets the tone for the capital market mood of the biotech industry in any given year. Quarterly roadshows albeit non-deal roadshows will be staple food – recurring trips to New York, Boston, London, Amsterdam, Brussels, Zurich, Frankfurt and other places to meet with then current shareholders but also to drum up interest and excess demand from new institutional investors, family offices etc.

Of course, one should get the banks that took you public to also invite their IPO candidates to their regular industry specific conferences and investor days. Angling invites from additional banks immediately following an IPO may not be the easiest feat. Likelihood has it that some of those banks were simply not chosen in your IPO syndicate. Also, now that the company is well funded and the need to raise additional capital may not be imminent, the selling aspect for any new bank may be less obvious. Still, in the interest of long-term relationships it is always good to stay in close contact with banking teams. There will invariably be a future transaction of some sort where they may have another shot at bidding for the business.

Short of getting invited by all the coveted major banks, there will likely be boutiques and middle market banks who also have high quality conferences worth going to. And then there are industry specific investor conferences that are paid for by the participating companies. Shows such as BioEquity, BIO Investor, BIO CEO & Investor Meeting, BioCapital, Rodman & Renshaw and others…. Is it worth spending the EUR 5 thousand or more per conference? Not always, but consider it as an option – a real one at that – to meet that one incremental buying investor who may move your stock price just a little bit and create some liquidity. You will need such demand should you ever wish to place blocks or need to do a follow-on raise.

How much should one spend on IR and PR? Just like the old adage with marketing expenses: I am pretty sure that 50% of any IR spend is in vain – I simply have no way of knowing which 50%. So, then it boils down to working with your board and getting some benchmarks in. Having a minimal in house IR infrastructure (usually 1 person dedicated in a small company) is key. Paying PR and IR firms is an open ended proposition. Even for small cap biotech companies this will quickly add up to a six-figure amount p.a. One way of thinking about this is: what concrete and measurable input and value do I get every month? Personally, I have always been a fan of a flat monthly retainer fee. This ensures that as a company you will always have access to your IR firm's teams. You do not need to think about extra billing every time you pick up the phone or ask them to provide you with input and drafts. It is fair both ways. You can clearly define what is included in the retainer and what type of project would be outside its scope. For the often small boutique PR and IR firms it also provides planning security and a way of balancing peak months around earnings with quieter summer months and still have the same amount come in from any client every month.

Selecting someone to be market maker in your stock which as a small cap company with a heavily concentrated shareholder base even post IPO will be rather illiquid might make good sense. We eventually contracted Degroof Petercam as our Liquidity Provider (4-traders, 2016). This ensures that every trading day by 9:15 am latest there will be both buy and sell orders in the book and the spread between bid and ask will be limited. Otherwise in illiquid stocks you sometime see a single trade of 10 shares effecting wild swings in stock price. Adding other brokers and getting them to take you out on non-deal road-shows to get in front of new investors is always a key priority. Some will do it as part of their business development free of charge, others will ask you pay a moderate fee – either per day or per meeting. The latter would be my advice to any small company such that you are guaranteed to only pay if the bank can fill your schedule on any given day with high quality meetings.

On the message side, it always helps to refer back to whatever your equity story was in the IPO. You will have set out clear use of proceeds expectations and will have communicated upcoming milestones and will have given some form of guidance on earnings or other key metrics. This is the point in time when you wish you had set them out more carefully in the IPO. Anything that was done without thinking it through, without looking at the risks of delays, not meeting them etc. may come back to bite you. At Curetis we had laid out three main areas for use of proceeds:

[1] Expanding our EU commercial organization to more markets
[2] Building our own direct sales and marketing organization in the USA
[3] Expanding and accelerating our product development pipeline.

Every press release, every earnings call, every roadshow meeting is then an opportunity to refer back to what you laid out at the time of the IPO and make sure you get across the fact that (by and large) you are hitting milestones, meet expectations (ideally exceed some). While you will be telling your own story hundreds of times and may get bored by it eventually, it is worth remembering that the person or fund you are sitting across from will only have heard it a few times and the last time may be months ago and things will have evolved and they will not have had the time to really follow your small company terribly closely. So, it is always good to set the baseline back at "here is what I told you at the time of the IPO and here is what we have delivered and here are the upcoming milestones". Investors and analysts hate few things more than surprises…especially bad ones.

Use your corporate presentation as another IR tool to evolve your story telling. At Curetis we quickly got into the rhythm of updating the corporate "dog and pony show" slide deck at least once per month. Internally that requires that your IR person will solicit inputs from all areas of the company, edit the slide deck accordingly and tries to keep things fresh. After a while you may realize that the deck gets ever longer, more detailed…never a bad time to have someone from the outside take a totally fresh look – it is extremely difficult if not impossible for any person to really reinvent themselves. But if you are willing to embrace the messages and formats that others put in front of you, then having literally start with a blank sheet of paper and writing your company's equity story brand new after a few quarters or a year in the public markets may not be a bad idea. The good thing is that whilst in the midst of an IPO process, lawyers and bankers will make sure every detail is source referenced and laid out in excruciating level of detail – but now as a public company you are once again in control of what messages, what priorities and what tweak you would like to put on it. So use that latitude while you can – the next capital markets transaction will surely reign you in again… but anything that you have established as regular corporate communications practice will likely also be allowed during the next regulated capital raise. Deviating from past practice simply because it is now opportune when raising capital will most likely not work.

12.5 Outlook (2016 and beyond), lock-up expiry and growth

How different shareholder groups view the "end game" of a public company – what if an IPO is not an exit for anyone?

Very often an IPO for any VC backed company is not an exit but rather a growth financing event with the opportunity of maybe in the future selling some blocks of shares or trickling out holdings into the market over time. About a third of the EUR 44.3 million in the Curetis IPO had come from its previous VC and private equity as well as corporate backers. Conversely two thirds had come from the 30-odd new institutional investors in the IPO – not too bad for a high risk small cap biotech. By 2016 when IPO activity in the biotech space has significantly dwindled, transactions that do get launched at the time of launch will likely have insider commitments at or exceeding 80% of the target amounts.

Also, the underwriters in the IPO will require all pre-IPO shareholders to enter into so-called lock-up agreements. Typically something like 6 to 12 months (sometimes even longer) where no shares can be sold. However, VCs will often make sure that any shares they actually buy in the IPO itself like any other new IPO investors' s will not be subject to such lock-up provision. As the company's CEO and CFO you will be facing a situation where upon expiry of such lock-up period and agreement all of a sudden millions of old shares might come onto the market. And every new investor out there knows exactly what will invariably happen at one point. Some funds will be nearing the end of their fund's lifetime, may have to liquidate some or all of their holdings in your stock So if you were a new investor, why would you buy shares in the open market, risking that you start buying up the share price in an illiquid stock even with rather small volumes? Why not simply wait for the offers on potential block trades becoming available? It is therefore highly desirable to be able to put the expiry of any lock-up into a period of time where potential for good fundamental news flow exists and on good news you may actually achieve some gradual evolution in your shareholder base.

We went so far as to make the careful management of the expiry of the lock-up, share price development around it and excess demand creation a specific goal for the management as part of their bonus plans. Again this helps align interests in a period that may very quickly turn into one of stock price decline and significant pressure on the stock even upon good news.

To the extent that you cannot actually provide for a realistic ultimate exit for your long-term VC and private equity shareholders the pressure will likely rise and build up to a point where ultimately more drastic measures, be they management change, board change, strategic M&A processes etc. get triggered. Surely advisable to remain in front of such issues and ideally running a very orderly and well defined process.

Looking at the chart several months post IPO may not be a pretty sight even if you have delivered on all promises, hit all milestones, had nothing but positive news flow. Competitors getting thumped in the capital markets, pressure on small cap biotech stocks in general, molecular diagnostics falling out of favor for the month all may play a role. But ultimately it may just be that threat of an overhang of millions and millions of shares that VCs eventually want to sell – couple that with a financial profile where most biotechs – including Curetis – are still loss making and cash burning at the time of their IPOs, relatively binary events such as clinical trial results and FDA approvals still some months or quarters into the future may lead to a chart such as the one we are facing – on very few shares being traded.

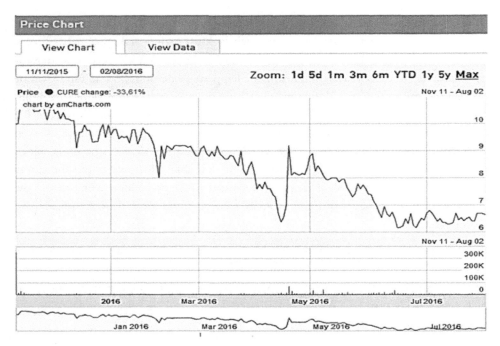

Exhibit 18: Curetis post IPO stock price
Source: Enternext, 2017

Another tool in the IR arsenal is often also the timing and shape or form of insider buying of shares. Now, it is never easy to find a period where management or board are not insiders to some potential deal or clinical data or other even that might prevent them from buying – but equally well it is always possible with some planning ahead to get this set up such that right after certain announcements, financials etc. members of your team and board can start buying. And compliance forces everyone to declare each and every purchase (or sale) of insiders without any delay. Thus having members of the team buy in close succession over a period of several days or even weeks with constant notifications hitting the market about insiders buying shares may also trigger others to buy into the stock based on such signs of confidence and commitment from insiders. Never easy though for people who have their jobs, their time limited contracts and most of their personal net worth as founders in equity of their own company. Unless and until you have actually sold any share and realized whatever gain, this is all paper and virtual money. And the streets are littered with folks who might have been millionaires on paper in the boom cycles and went bust without ever having had any chance to sell anything. In that spirit… there will always be another opportunity, another company and maybe even yet another IPO in the future… onwards and upwards.

Despite all of the hassle and burden post IPO, there are undoubtedly a number of strategic moves that would not have been possible at all in the absence of an IPO. In September 2016 Curetis acquired the sole global rights to what some believe to be the world's largest database, based on next generation sequencing for antibiotic resistance biomarkers (GEAR) (healthcare-in-europe.com, 2016). These GEAR assets will broaden our product pipeline, keep it differentiated from competitors' product offerings and is expected to boost future growth of non-dilutive funding through public grants as well as R&D collaborations and licensing arrangements.

Then, in December of 2016 we were able to make a truly strategic double-move. On the one hand we acquired the Gyronimo Platform assets from Carpegen and Systec (Nasdaq Globe Newswire, 2016) and on the other hand we were able to raise up to EUR 25 million in non-dilutive debt financing (Reuters, 2016). The European Investment Bank (EIB), one of the world's largest infrastructure financiers, had gone through an in-depth due diligence process and at the end of that were able to offer a highly competitive and flexible debt financing instrument which bolsters Curetis' financing cushion and allowed the company to complete its asset acquisition. The EIB deal of senior unsecured debt with a 24-month flexible draw down period (in tranches of at least EUR 5 million) each and then for each debt tranche a 5-year interest-only period with more than half of the interest actually deferred into the re-payment of the principal at maturity makes the cash flow pattern of such debt very conducive towards R&D growth funding at a time the company is still cash flow negative and loss-making.

Finally, on 27 April 2017 the announcement that a Chinese-led investor syndicate is attempting to acquire all shares of epigenomics AG at EUR 7.52 per share hit the news wires (Seeking Alpha, 2017).

Time will tell whether the epigenomics trade sale to China and the Curetis acquisitions in combination with the incremental debt financing will deliver the longer-term value generation, but without a trace of doubt – if the IPO had not happened then none of these deals would ever have been possible in the hands of private VCs.

Bibliography

Part 1

Altman, E. I., 1968. Financial Ratios, Discriminant Analysis and the Prediction of Corporate Bankruptcy. *Journal of Finance,* September, 23(4), pp. 589-609.

Ballwieser, W., 2011. Unternehmensbewertung – Prozeß, Methoden und Probleme. Stuttgart: Schäffer-Poeschel Verlag.

Ballwieser, W., Beyer, S. & Zelger, H., 2005. Unternehmenskauf nach IFRS und US-GAAP. In: *Impairment-Test nach IFRS und US-GAAP.* Stuttgart: Ballwieser, Wolfgang; Beyer, Sven; Zelger, Hansjörg, pp. 191-223.

Black, F. & Scholes, M., 1972. The Pricing of Options and Corporate Liabilities. *Journal of Political Economy,* May – June, 81(3), pp. 637-654.

Bloomberg (2017). Global Capital Markets League Tables FY2016. Retrieved from: https://data. bloomberglp.com/professional/sites/4/Bloomberg-2016-Glb-CAPM-FINAL. pdf

Box, G., 2013. Time Series Analysis, Forecasting and Control. In: *A Very British Affair.* Houndmills(Basingstoke): Palgrave Macmillan UK, pp. 161-215.

Brealey, R., Myers, S. & Allen, F., 2016. Principles of Corporate Finance. International Edition ed. New York: McGraw-Hill.

Burgstahler, D. & Dichev, I., 1997. Earnings Management to avoid Earnings Decreases and Losses. *Journal of Accounting and Economics,* 24(1), pp. 99-126.

Campbell, J. Y. & Viceira, L. M., 2005. The Term Structure of the Risk-Return Trade-Off. *Financial Analysts Journal,* January/February, 61(1), pp. 34-44.

Copeland, T., Koller, T. & Murrin, J., 2002. Unternehmenswert: Methoden und Strategien für eine wertorientierte Unternehmensführung. Frankfurt/Main: Campus Verlag.

Damodaran, A., 2012. Investment Valuation: Tools and Techniques for Determining the Value of any Asset. 3 ed. Hoboken(New Jersey): John Wiley & Sons.

Damodaran, A., 2006. Damodaran on Valuation: Security Analisis for Investment and Corporate Finance. Hoboken(New Jersey): John Wiley & Sons.

Deutsche Welle (March 6, 2017). The rise and fall of the Schlecker empire. Retrieved from: http://www.dw.com/en/the-rise-and-fall-of-the-schlecker-empire/a-37824141

Ernst, D., Schneider, S. & Thielen, B., 2012. Unternehmensbewertungen erstellen und verstehen: *Ein Praxisleitfaden.* Müchen: Vahlen.

EY (2016). EY Global IPO Trends 2016 4Q. Retrieved from: www.ey.com/Publication/ vwLUAssets/ey-4q-2016-global-ipo-trends-report/$FILE/ey-4q-2016-global-ipo-trends-report.pdf

EY (2016). Anzahl der weltweiten Börsengänge in den Jahren von 2001 bis 2016. Retrieved from: https://de.statista.com/statistik/daten/studie/198574/umfrage/anzahl-der-boersen gaenge-weltweit-seit-1996/

EY (2014). EY Global IPO Trends 2014 Q4. Retrieved from: http://www.ey.com/ Publication/vwLUAssets/ey-q4-14-global-ipo-trends-report/$FILE/ey-q4-14-global-ipo-trends-report.pdf

EY Transaction Advisory Services (2016). In: *Valuation & Business Modeling.* Stuttgart: Ernst & Young, pp. 99, 158 & 249.

Fama, E. F. & French, K. R., 2004. The Capital Asset Pricing Model: Theory and Evidence. *Journal of Economic Perspectives,* Summer, 18(3), pp. 25-46.

Fama, E. F., 1968. Risk, Return and Equilibrium: Some Clarifying Comments. *Journal of Finance,* 23(1), pp. 29-40.

Financial Times (April 4, 2017). Convertible bonds catch a ride on equity rally. Retrieved from: https://www.ft.com/content/ee51a030-1893-11e7-9c35-0dd2cb31823a

Forbes (May 5, 2004). IPO Dutch Auctions vs. Traditional Allocation. Retrieved from: https://www.forbes.com/2004/05/10/cx_aw_0510mondaymatchup.html

Foster, G., 1977. Quarterly Accounting Data: Time-Series Properties and Predictive-Ability Results. *The Accounting Review,* January, 52(1), pp. 1-21.

Gordon, M. J., 1962. The Investment, Financing, and Valuation of the Corporation. 1 ed. Homewood: Richard D. Irwin.

Graham, J. R. & Harvey, C. R., 2001. The Theory and Practice of Corporate Finance: Evidence from the Field. *Journal of Financial Economics,* Volume 60, pp. 187-243.

Graham, J. R. & Mills, L. F., 2008. Using Tax Return Data to Simulate Corporate Marginal Tax Rates. *Journal of Accounting & Economics,* December, 46(2), pp. 366-388.

Graham, J. R., 1996. Proxies for the Corporate Marginal Tax Rate. *Journal of Financial Economics,* February, 42(2), pp. 187-221.

International Valuation Standards Council, 2016. *IVS 105: Valuation Approaches and Methods,* London: IVSC.

Investopedia (October 31, 2016). Violin Memory Now Trades on OTC Markets (VMEM). Retrieved from: http://www.investopedia.com/news/violin-memory-now-trades-otc-markets-vmem/

Koller, T., Goedhart, M. H. & Wessels, D., 2010. Measuring and managing the value of companies. Hoboken, N.J.: John Wiley & Sons.

Little, I. M., 1962. Higgledy Piggledy Growth. *Oxford Bulletin of Economics and Statistics,* November, 24(4), pp. 387-412.

Lloyd's (2017). Corporate History. Retrieved from: https://www.lloyds.com/lloyds/about-us/history/corporate-history

Mercer, Z. C. & Harms, T. W., 2008. Business Valuation: An Integrated Theory. Noboken(New Jersey): Wiley.

Nasdaq (2017). Offering History. Retrieved from: http://www.nasdaq.com/markets/ipos/offering-history.aspx?expert=self-underwritten

Nasdaq Globe Newswire (June 25, 2015). Molycorp Common Stock to Move to OTC Trading, Retrieved from: https://globenewswire.com/news-release/2015/06/25/747615/0/en/ Moly corp-Common-Stock-to-Move-to-OTC-Trading.html

New York Times (February 14, 2013). Berkshire and 3G Capital in a $23 Billion Deal for Heinz. Retrieved from: https://dealbook.nytimes.com/2013/02/14/berkshire-and-3g-capital-to-buy-heinz-for-23-billion/?_r=0

New York Times (October 29, 1987). US Underwriters Face Losses on B.P. Offering. Retrieved from: http://www.nytimes.com/1987/10/29/business/us-underwriters-face-losses-on-bp-offering.html

Nwankwo, O. & Osho, S. G., 2010. An Empirical Analysis of Corporate Survival and Growth: Evidence from Efficient Working Capital Management. *International Journal of Scholary Academic Intellectual Diversity,* 12(1), p. 8 & 12.

PriceWaterhouseCoopers (2009). IPO Watch Europe – Review of the year 2009. Retrieved from: https://www.pwc.pl/pl/ipo-watch-europe/2009_summary.pdf

PWC (2011). Capital markets in 2025 – The future of equity capital markets. Retrieved from: https://www.pwc.com/gx/en/audit-services/publications/assets/capital_markets-the_future_of_equity_mrkts.pdf

Rosenbaum, J. & Pearl, J., 2013. Investment Banking: Valuation, Leveraged Buyouts, and Mergers & Acquisitions. 2 ed. Hoboken(New Jersey): Wiley.

Schira, J., 2012. Statistische Methoden der VWL und BWL: Theorie und Praxis. München: Pearson.

Sharpe, W. F., 1964. Capital Asset Prices: A Theory of Market Equilibrium under Conditions of Risk. *Journal of Finance,* September, Volume 19, pp. 425-442.

Stuart, T. E., 2000. Interorganizational Alliances and the Performance of Firms: A Study of Growth and Innovation Rates in a High-Technology Industry. *Strategic Management Journal,* 21(1), pp. 791-811.

Wöhe, G., Bilstein, J., Ernst, D. & Häcker, J., 2013. Grundzüge der Unternehmensfinanzierung. München: Vahlen.

Part 2

Bain & Company (2016) Global Private Equity Report 2016. Retrieved from: http://www.bain.com/bainweb/PDFs/Bain_and_Company_Global_Private_Equity_Report_2016.pdf   (last visited 1 August 2016)

Brealey, R./Myers, S. (2000) Principles of Corporate Finance (Sixth Edition), Irwin/McGraw-Hill

Euromoney (2011) How do you fix the IPO market? Retrieved from: http://www.euromoney.com/Article/2877089/How-do-you-fix-the-IPO-market.html?p=1 (last visited on 4 August 2016)

Facebook, Inc. (2012) Prospectus for the public offering of 421,233,615 shares Class A common stock. Retrieved from: https://investor.fb.com/financials/sec-filings-details/default.aspx?Filing Id=8629552 (last visited on 14 June 2016)

IAS Plus, IAS 34 – Interim Financial Reporting. Retrieved from: http://www.iasplus.com/en/standards /ias/ias34 (last visited on 28 June 2016)

J.P. Morgan (2014) Knocking on the door – Shareholder activism in Europe: Five things you need to know. Retrieved from: https://www.jpmorgan.com/jpmpdf/1320656894344.pdf (last visited 29 July 2016)

McKinsey Global Institute (2016) Diminishing Returns: Why Investors May Need to Lower Their Expectations. Retrieved from: http://www.mckinsey.com/industries/private-equity-and-prin cipal-investors/our-insights/why-investors-may-need-to-lower-their-sights (last visited on 25 July 2016)

McKinsey & Company (2014) Preparing for bigger, bolder shareholder activists. Retrieved from: http://www.mckinsey.com/business-functions/strategy-and-corporate-finance/our-insights /preparing-for-bigger-bolder-shareholder-activists (last visited on 26 July 2016)

MSCI (2016) Index Fact Sheet: MSCI AWCI IMI. Retrieved from: https://www.msci.com/resources/factsheets /index_fact_sheet/msci-acwi-imi.pdf (last visited on 25 July 2016)

Practical Law (2016). Emerging Growth Company (EGC). Retrieved from: http://us.practicallaw.com/3-518-8137 (last visited on 21 July 2016)

PricewaterhouseCoopers (2016). Q2 2016 Equity Capital Markets Briefing. Retrieved from: https://www.pwc.de/de/newsletter/kapitalmarkt/assets/pwc-briefing-equity-capital-markets-q2-2016.pdf (last visited on 4 August 2016)

PricewaterhouseCoopers (2015). Considering an IPO? An insight into the costs post JOBS-Act. Retrieved from: https://www.pwc.com/us/en/deals/assets/ipo-costs-considerations-pwc-de als.pdf (last visited on 19 April 2016)

PricewaterhouseCoopers (2014). An overview of Russian IPOs: 2005 to 2014. Retrieved from: http://www.pwc.ru/en/capital-markets/publications/assets/a4_brochure_ipos_eng_print.pdf (last visited on 4 August 2016)

Rocket Internet AG (2014). Prospectus for the public offering of 32,941,177 new ordinary bearer shares with no par value. Retrieved from: https://www.rocket-internet.com/themes/rocket3/download/ipo-history/Rocket%20Internet%20Prospectus.PDF (last visited on 6 June 2016)

Spiegel Online (2016). Ex-Chef Breuer zahlt 3,2 Millionen Euro an Deutsche Bank. Retrieved from: http://www.spiegel.de/wirtschaft/unternehmen/kirch-pleite-rolf-breuer-zahlt-3-2-mill ionen-euro-an-deutsche-bank-a-1084788.html (last visited on 19 July 2016)

Wall Street Journal (2012). Citi to Settle Suit for $590 Million. Retrieved from: http://www.wsj.com/articles/SB10000872396390444914904577619410325528148 (last visited on 25 July 2016)

Weil (2015). A Look At Sponsor-Backed Going Private Transactions. Retrieved from: http://peblog.wpengine.com/wp-content/uploads/2015/08/150482_Going_Private_Sur vey_2015_v21-Final. pdf (last visited on 1 August 2016).

Part 3

4-traders (February 18, 2016). Curetis N.V: Appoints Bank Degroof Petercam SA as Liquidity rovider to Facililtate Trading on Euronext Brussels and Euronext Amsterdam. Retrieved from: http://www.4-traders.com/CURETIS-N-V-24872715/news/Curetis-N-V-Appoints-BankDegroof-Petercam-SA-as-Liquidity-Provider-to-Facilitate-Trading-on-Euron-21872373/

Alex Wilmerding, Term Sheets & Valuations, Aspatore Inc. 2003

APA-OTS (January 11, 2011). EANS-News: Epigenomics Appoints Thomas Taapken as New CFO, Effective April 1, 2011. Retrieved from: http://www.ots.at/presseaussendung/OTE_2 0110111_OTE0002/eans-news-epigenomics-appoints-thomas-taapken-as-new-cfo-effective-april-1-2011

Biocartis (April 24, 2015). Biocartis raises EUR 100 million in successful Initial Public Offering. Retrieved from: https://media.biocartis.com/biocartis-investors/documents/Biocartis_PR_I PO%20RESULT_20150424_ENG.pdf

Bionity (July 14, 2010). Curetis vervollständigt Aufsichtsrat und ernennt neuen CFO. Retrieved from: http://www.bionity.com/de/news/120022/curetis-vervollstaendigt-aufsichtsrat-und-ernennt-neuen-cfo.html

BioRegio STERN (October 28, 2011). Curetis AG gewinnt Forbion und Roche als neue Investoren. Retrieved from: http://www.bioregio-stern.de/de/aktuelles/aktuelles/curetis-ag-gewinn t-forbion-und-roche-als-neue-investoren

BioSpace (December 7, 2009). Life Sciences Partners leads € 18.5 million Series A Financing Round of Curetis. Retrieved from: http://www.biospace.com/News/life-sciences-partners-leads-18-5-million-series-a/164829

Biospace (August 18, 2006). http://www.biospace.com/News/epigenomics-ag-announces-change-in-the-executive/27841

CNN Money (September 22, 2015). Hillary Clinton tweet crushes biotech stocks. Retrieved from: http://money.cnn.com/2015/09/21/investing/hillary-clinton-biotech-price-gouging/

Curetis (October 28, 2015). Curetis N.V. IPO Prospectus. Retrieved from: http://www.curetis.com/fileadmin/Dokumente/Downloads/Investors/Financial_Reports/Prospectus_Curetis_Printer.pdf

Curetis (2015). Financial Reports – IFRS 2012-2014. Retrieved from: http://www.curetis.com/fileadmin/Dokumente/Downloads/Investors/Financial_Reports/IFRS_2012-2014_Notes_20151022_FINAL.pdf Cited as: Curetis, 2015a

Curetis (2015). Financial Reports – IFRS 2015-06. Retrieved from: http://www.curetis.com/file admin/Dokumente/Downloads/Investors/Financial_Reports /IFRS_2015-06_ Notes_2 0151022_FINAL.pdf Cited as: Curetis, 2015b

Curetis (2015). Annual Report. Retrieved from: http://www.curetis.com/fileadmin/Dokumente/Investors/Annual_Report_2015_Approve d.pdf Cited as: Curetis, 2015c

Curetis (November 10, 2015). Curetis IPO priced at EUR 10.00 per Share; raises EUR 40 million. Retrieved from: http://www.curetis.com/uploads/tx_news/Curetis_Pricing_PR_EN _10.11. 15_10pm_clean_01.pdf Cited as: Curetis, 2015e

Curetis (October 28, 2015). Curetis Announces its Initial Public Offering on Euronext in Amsterdam and Euronext in Brussels. Retrieved from: http://www.curetis.com/uploads /tx_news/IPO_Launch_Press_Release_Announcement_FINAL_English_27-10-15_01 .pdf Cited as: Curetis, 2015d

Die Welt (July 15, 2004). Ausgezeichneter Unternehmer. Retrieved from: https://www.welt.de/print-welt/article327599/Ausgezeichneter-Unternehmer.html

Der Spiegel (August 5, 2004). „Man kommt sich vor wie der Betreiber eines Bordells". Retrieved from: http://www.spiegel.de/wirtschaft/interview-mit-epigenomics-gruender-olek-man-kom mt-sich-vor-wie-der-betreiber-eines-bordells-a-311583.html Cited as: Der Spiegel, 2004b

Der Spiegel (February 4, 2004). Deutschlands beste Arbeitgeber. Retrieved from: http://www.spiegel.de/wirtschaft/capital-ranking-deutschlands-beste-arbeitgeber-a-284907. html Cited as: Der Spiegel, 2004a

DGP (October 14, 2015). IPO Research Initiation Note DGP – Roderick Verhelst

Epigenomics (March 30, 2010). http://www.epigenomics.com/wp-content/uploads/2016/03/ 20100510_3-Months_Report_2010_02.pdf

Epigenomics (2008). 3-Monatsbericht 2008 – Q1-2008. Retrieved from: http://www.epigenomics.com/news-investors/financial-reports/

Epigenomics (September 12, 2001). Epigenomics CEO Alex Olek ist Deutschlands Entrepreneur des Jahres 2001. Retrieved from: http://www.epigenomics.com/news-investors/news-media/pressemitteilungen/archiv/article/epigenomics-ceo-alex-olek-ist-deutschlands-entrepren eur-des-jahres-2001.html

Enternext (2017). Curetis Price Chart. Retrieved from: https://www.enternext.biz/

Euronext TV (November 11, 2015). *Curetis celebrates dual listing on Euronext Amsterdam and Euronext Brussels.* Retrieved from: https://www.youtube.com/watch?v=lriaeClJIiA

Finanznachrichten (2017). Epigenomics Chart. Retrieved from: http://www.finanznachrichten.de/chart-tool/aktie/epigenomics-ag.htm

Focus (November 10, 2015). Biotech-Firma Curetis schafft dank Bescheidenheit Börsengang. Retrieved from: http://www.focus.de/finanzen/news/wirtschaftsticker/ipo-biotech-firma-curetis-schafft-dank-bescheidenheit-boersengang_id_5077524.html

Forbion (November 24, 2014). Curetis Closes EUR 14.5 Million Extension to Series B Financing. Retrieved from: https://forbion.com/en/news/curetis_closes_eur_14_5_million_extension_to_series_b_financing

Forbion (April 23, 2013). Curetis raises EUR 12.5 million in Series B round. Retrieved from: https://forbion.com/en/news/curetis_raises_eur_12_5_million_in_series_b_round?page=5

genomeweb (December 18, 2006). Roche's Termination of Epigenomics Alliance Topped Most-Read GenomeWeb News Stories Last Week. Retrieved from: https://www.genomeweb.com/ archive/roches-termination-epigenomics-alliance-topped-most-read-genomeweb-news-storie s-

Globenewswire (December 3, 2015). Retrieved from: http://inpublic.globenewswire.com/releaseDetails.faces?rId=1971191

going public.de (November 12, 2015). Curetis feiert IPO in Amsterdam. Retrieved from: http://www.goingpublic.de/curetis-ag-feiert-gelungen-ipo-amsterdam

going public.de (March 24, 2004). IPO-Fehlstart, Teil II. Retrieved from: http://www.goingpublic.de/ipo-fehlstart-teil-ii_Cited as: Going Public, 2004b

going public.de (March 17, 2004). Fehlstart in ein hoffnungsfrohes IPO-Jahr. Retrieved from: http://www.goingpublic.de/fehlstart-in-ein-hoffnungsfrohes-deutsches-ipo-jahr Cited as: Going Public, 2004a.

going public.de (February 23, 2004). IPO-Zitrone 2004... . Retrieved from: http://www.going public.de/ipo-zitrone-2004 Cited as: Going Public, 2004c

healthcare-in-europe.com (August 9, 2016). Curetis Acquires Rights to GEAR Database. Retrieved from: http://www.healthcare-in-europe.com/en/article/17059-curetis-acquires-rights-to-gear-database.html

ICF (October 14, 2015). Investment Research Curetis NV, IPO Research Initiation Note ICF – Stefan Röhle

Independent Research (2015). Retrieved from: http://www.irffm.de/

International Financial Law Review (2016). Frequently asked questions about Rule 144A. Retrieved from: http://www.iflr.com/pdfs/faqrule144a.pdf

Investment Europe (October 1, 2015). Bank Degroof and Petercam complete merger. Retrieved from: http://www.investmenteurope.net/regions/benelux/bank-degroof-and-petercam-com plete-merger/

JMP Securities (2010). Charles Duncan, Molecular Diagnostics – Wall Street Perspective, Q3-2010. Retrieved from: https://quebecinternational.ca/media/280482/mdx%20presentation % 20october%202010.pdf

Labiotech (November 13, 2015). Curetis Molecular Diagnostics IPO Exceeds Expectations. Retrieved from: http://labiotech.eu/curetis-molecular-diagnostics-ipo-euronext-closed/

Manager Magazin (July 8, 2004). "Sie müssen den Preis senken". Retrieved from: http://www.manager-magazin.de/finanzen/artikel/a-307843.html.

Morgan Stanley, Dan Mahony, IPO Research initiation on ECX, July 2004

Nasdaq Globe Newswire (December 13, 2016). Curetis Acquires Real-Time qPCR Platform from Carpegen and Systec. Retrieved from: https://globenewswire.com/news-release/2016/12/13/897061/0/en/Curetis-Acquires-Real-Time-qPCR-Platform-from-Carpegen-and-Systec.html

Niewiarra, K. and Segschneider, D., Balanceakt Compliance, Juli 2016, Frankfurter Allgemeine Buch

PR Newswire (December 18, 2000). Epigenomics Completes Its Merger with Orca Biosciences Creating the Industry's Leading Force in DNA Methylation Analysis Technologies. Retrieved from: http://www.prnewswire.com/news-releases/epigenomics-completes-its-merger-with-orca-biosciences-creating-the-industrys-leading-force-in-dna-methylation-analysis-technologies-76235697.html

PwC, CMS, Curetis (March 3, 2016). Presentation at the Bio Deutschland CFO Gipfel, Eine Europäische Erfolgsstory – Curetis' IPO an der Euronext

RBC (October 14, 2015). Curetis N.V. – Made to Measure, IPO Research Initiation Note RBC – Nick Keher

Relationship Science (2015). Nick Kehrer. Retrieved from: https://relationshipscience.com/nick-keher-p5021660

Reuters (January 20, 2007). Roche drops deal with biotech firm Epigenomics. Retrieved from: http://www.reuters.com/article/us-roche-epigenomics-idUSL1582576820061215

Seeking Alpha (April 27, 2017). Epigenomics Goes Private. Retrieved from: https://seekingalpha.com/article/4065970-epigenomics-goes-private

The Wall Street Journal (July 27, 2015). Secret IPO Filings Feed Deal Frenzy. Retrieved from: https://www.wsj.com/articles/secret-ipo-filings-feed-deal-frenzy-1438039559

VC Magazin (July 19, 2011). Trade Sale – Bis zu 190 Mio. EUR für mtm laboratories. Retrieved from: http://www.vc-magazin.de/news/bis-zu-190-mio-eur-fuer-mtm-laboratories/